REMEMBERING
THE
DRAGON LADY

Memories of the Men Who Shaped History In Support of the U-2 Spy Plane

Linda Rios Bromley

By

Brig. Gen. Gerald E. McIlmoyle, (Ret.)
And
Linda Rios Bromley

Cover photo by Maureen McIlmoyle Stephan

11129 Pleasant Ridge Road, Utica, KY 42376
1-270-275-4075   1-800-285-4075
sammcpub@aol.com

Sam McDowell, owner of McDowell Publications,
was assigned to the 4080th SRW and later the 100th SRW
from 1957 to 1965. He was assigned to the jet
engine shop, quality control and PMEL.

REMEMBERING THE DRAGON LADY

Table of Contents

FOREWORD

Just a word or two about what this book is and what it isn't. It is a compilation of contributed memories by some of those who lived through and participated in the Dragon Lady U-2 Program. Some of the memories here are recorded for posterity by those who have taken their "last flight." Many times there are conflicts between the memories in this book and the various histories written by the historians of the CIA, Air Force, Strategic Air Command and others.

We all remember the disparity demonstrated in the kindergarten game when something is whispered into the ear of a person and they whisper the same to the next person and so on until the last person who speaks the phrase aloud. The first person tells everyone the original phrase and we all laughed at how different the phrases were.

As with that kindergarten game, you will find some of these memories in conflict with one another. The idea that caused this book to be compiled was to record for our children and grandchildren the memories of our participation in this historic program initiated by President Eisenhower during the height of the Cold War. Whenever we who lived it get together, we and our spouses regale each other with our memories of those early days of the U-2 Program and frequently is heard the phrase, "I can't believe we did that!"

The Dragon Lady Program was super secret in its early years. Once when my dad asked me what I was flying at the time, I only replied, "The U-2." He gave me a look only a dad can give and stated emphatically, "You are not going to tell me, are you?" So, you will find humor, comradeship, love, anguish and apprehension all seasoned with a little bit of fear.

Happy reading to you because this program was and is all American, for America, and as such, you were part of it even if you didn't know about it.

Jerry

ACKNOWLEDGMENTS

Throughout this project, we have had the cooperation and support of all the men who told their stories. The stories have been funny, serious and some, downright scary. We wish to thank Glenn Chapman, Bob Ingram, Tony Bevacqua, and Buddy Brown for contributing significantly their time and knowledge of the Dragon Lady's complexities and features. Thanks, guys, for your encouragement and your memories of the old days.

We would also like to thank Nancy Ryan Keeling for her continuing support and editing assistance, Alice Calderone, Gordon Rottman, and Stan Marshall for their valuable critiques.

We are grateful to all those who felt as we did, that it was time to tell the story from the perspective of those who lived it.

And thanks to Patty McIlmoyle and Bill Bromley for supporting us each day.

Jerry and Linda

FROM IDEA
TO
REALITY

Man's mind once stretched by a new idea, regains
its original dimensions.

Oliver Wendell Holmes

A TEMPORARY UNIT WAS BORN
4080th Strategic Reconnaissance Wing

The 4080th Strategic Reconnaissance Wing was organized May 1, 1956 at Turner AFB, Georgia, and assigned to the 40th Air Division of the Strategic Air Command. Operational squadrons assigned to the Wing when it was organized were the 4025th, 4028th and 4029th Strategic Reconnaissance Squadrons (SRS). On April 1, 1957, the Wing was reassigned directly to Second Air Force and relocated to Laughlin AFB, Texas. The 4029th SRS and the 4025th SRS were discontinued on January 1, 1960 and June 15, 1960, respectively. The Wing was re-designated as the 4080th Strategic Reconnaissance Wing and relocated to Davis Monthan AFB, Arizona, on July 1, 1963, and subsequently reassigned to the 12th Strategic Aerospace Division. The 4080th Strategic Wing was discontinued on June 25, 1966, 10 years and one month after it was organized.

A NEW DIMENSION: DEVELOPMENT OF THE U-2 PROGRAM

The U-2 project was initiated in the early 1950s with President Eisenhower's request for more accurate espionage information on the Soviet Union. In 1951 modified bombers began overflights of the Soviet Union, but existing aircraft were vulnerable to anti-aircraft fire and a number of border flights were shot down. At that time the planners imagined a high altitude aircraft hard to detect and impossible to shoot down.

The Lockheed Corporation was given the contract with an unlimited budget and a short deadline. The CL-282 AQUATONE was designed as the development name, but the official title took a bit more consideration. The new plane could not be identified with a "B" for bomber nor an "F" for fighter; its purpose did not fit either of those categories. The Air Force decided to call it a utility plane and the distinctive name was the U-2.

Lockheed received approval for their design on December 9, 1954. Lockheed's Skunk Works, headed by Clarence "Kelly" Johnson, began a grueling pace to meet the deadline. Under a heavy veil of secrecy, Kelly and only 81 people, including 25 engineers, began work on the approved design. The project was so secret that the government's first check was made out to Kelly personally and sent to his home address.

Pratt and Whitney produced an engine that would perform at an altitude of 70,000 feet and higher. The cockpit was somewhat pressurized to enable pilots to fly for up to 10 hours without full pressure suits. Pilots were issued partial pressure suits to protect them in the event of aircraft pressure loss.

One of the most radical parts of the aircraft's design was a bicycle gear system. Outriggers, named pogos, held the wings level for takeoff and landing. When the U-2 was on takeoff roll, the pogos fell onto the runway from their sockets in the wing. The pogos would be reinstalled after the aircraft landed. The final design was a masterful blend of innovative technology—the successful matching of airframe, sensors adapted for high altitudes, pilot physiological support equipment, and a finely tuned engine.

Test Pilot Tony LeVier flew the first flight on August 1, 1955 after eight months of production. It was a record-breaking result from contract award to rollout of a new project. Another remarkable aspect of the project was that Lockheed refunded $2 million to the government making the total cost of each aircraft only $1 million.

An amazing group of dedicated and innovative contractors came together to support the project, such as the David Clark Company of Worcester, Massachusetts, designers and manufacturers of the partial pressure suits worn by U-2 pilots and future astronauts. The Hycon Company developed the camera for the U-2 making it legendary for the quality of photography produced.

Flying the aircraft was not for the faint of heart; in fact, it was considered one of the most challenging aircraft in the inventory to fly and required a high degree of skill and ability from its pilots. The difficulty experienced by seasoned pilots who flew the U-2 resulted in it being nicknamed "Dragon Lady" meaning the aircraft was extremely unforgiving.

In addition to its uses for military purposes the U-2 has provided earth resource monitoring, drug trafficking surveillance and national disaster monitoring. NASA routinely performs atmospheric moisture mapping to aid in weather systems modeling. Missions have been flown to both poles from Sweden and New Zealand to measure ozone depletion.

More recently the U-2 has been tasked to perform in peacetime. On September 1, 2005 the Dragon Lady departed Beale AFB, California, to collect imagery of Hurricane Katrina's destruction of the Gulf Coast for Federal Emergency Management Agency disaster relief efforts. The Optical Bar Camera, or film-based imagery equipment that performed so well during the Cuban Missile Crisis, was considered ideal for photographing large areas with very high resolution. The six-hour flight collected imagery over a 90,000 square mile area.

A TRIBUTE TO OUR LEADER

You do not lead by hitting people over the head--
that's assault, not leadership.

Dwight D. Eisenhower

IN MEMORY OF OUR LEADER

BRIGADIER GENERAL JOHN A. DESPORTES
(Deceased January 14, 2001)

Widow - Peggy

Throughout this book, many of the stories have made references to the memorable commander of the 4080th Strategic Reconnaissance Wing, Brigadier General John A. DesPortes. When first assigned to the 4080th SRW, he was a Colonel; but before his tour was up, he was promoted to Brigadier General. No matter the rank, he was a great leader and respected by officers and enlisted men alike for his professionalism. General DesPortes knew many of the 4080th SRW support staff by name and never failed to acknowledge them when he visited the flight line. Personal visits by General DesPortes to the homes of 4080th SRW pilots signaled a critical situation about to unfold. During the Cuban Missile Crisis, DesPortes maintained a vigilant watch as his pilots were

sent over hostile territory and all but one returned. General DesPortes took a personal interest in his troops' welfare and they returned the kindness with their respect and dedication.

8

THE CHOSEN FEW

We live in freedom because every generation has produced patriots willing to serve a cause greater than themselves.

--George W. Bush

THE CHOSEN FEW
Dragon Lady Pilots

The 4080th Strategic Reconnaissance Wing and subsequently the 9th Strategic Reconnaissance Wing "Dragon Lady" pilots played a major role in the overall security of this nation and the free world. They accumulated a record unequalled by any records or previous organizations. Dragon Lady pilots were the first to fly and cruise above 70,000 feet; they were the first to fly with a pressure suit; and they were the first to gather intelligence information in many of the world's hot spots. President John F. Kennedy's appraisal of the 4080th SRW's participation in the 1962 Cuban Missile Crisis recognized the Wing "contributed as much to the security of the United States as any unit in our history and any group of men in our country." President Kennedy's remarks were directed to all the men and women of the 4080th. Each played his or her role well, and each had "A Bag of Tools".

Isn't it strange that princes and kings,

And clowns that caper in sawdust rings,

And common people like you and me

Are builders for eternity?

Each is given a bag of tools,

A shapeless mass, a book of rules;

And each must make, as life is flown,

A stumbling block or a stepping stone.

By R. L. Sharpe

I WANT TO BE A PILOT

When I grow up, I want to be a pilot because it's a fun job and easy to do. That's why there are so many pilots flying around these days. Pilots don't need much school, they just have to learn to read numbers so that they can read instruments. I guess they should be able to read road maps too, so they can find their way home if they get lost.

Pilots should be brave so they won't get scared if it's foggy and they can't see, or if a wing or motor falls off, they should stay calm so they'll know what to do. Pilots have to have good eyes to see through clouds and they can't be afraid of lightning or thunder because they are much closer to them than we are.

The salary pilots make is another thing I like. They make more money than they know what to do with. This is because most people think that plane flying is dangerous except pilots don't because they know how easy it is. I hope I don't get airsick because I get carsick and if I get airsick, I couldn't be a pilot and then I would have to go to work.

Authored by an 11-year old

U-2 PILOTS

1955

Tony Levier
Bob Matey
Bob Sieker
J. Ray Goudey
Bob Schumacher
Pete Everst
Lewis Garvin
Hank Meirdierck
Robert Mullin
Lewis Setter
Bill Yancey

1956

Howard Carey
Glendon Dunnaway
Martin Knutson
Jacob Kratt
Carl Overstreet
Wilber Rose
Hervie Stockman
Jim Allison
Tom Birkhead
Jim Cherbonneaux
Buster Edens
Bill Hall
Dan McMurry
Frank Powers
Sam Snyder
Frank Strickland
Barry Baker
Jim Barnes

Tom Crull
Bob Ericson
Frank Grace
Russ Kemp
Albert Rand
Lyle Rudd
Al Smiley
Carmine Vito
E. K. Jones
John Shinn
Jim Abramson
Jack D. Nole
Joe M. Jackson
Floyd Herbert
Richard K. Nevett
Howard E. Cody

1957

Richard A. Atkins Jr.
Warren J. Boyd
Raymond L. Haupt
Joe R. King
Richard S. Heyser
Michael E. Styer
Lloyd R. Leavitt Jr.
Benedict A. Lacombe
William L. Alison
Anthony P. Bevacqua
Jack M. Graves
Edwin G. Emerling
Richard E. McGraw
John A. Campbell
Kenneth W. Alderman
Leo E. Smith
Ford E. Lowcock

Linus L. Lee
Alfred V. Chapin Jr.
James D. Sala
Scott G. Smith
James A. Qualls
Roger L. Cooper
Patrick J. Halloran
Frank L. Stuart
James A. Black
Edward C. Perdue
Roger H. Herman
Bobbie G. Gardiner
Marvin W. Doering
Nathan J. Adams
Hayden C. Curry
Forrest W. Wilson
Roy L. St. Martin
James R. Bedford Jr.
Rudolph Anderson Jr.
John T. McElveen
Edward B. Dixon
Harry Cordes
Robert D. Pine
Earl S. Lewis
Wesley E. McFadden
Cozier S. Kline

1958

Donald R. James
Austin J. Russell
Adrian W. Acebedo
John W. MacArthur, RAF
David E. Dowling, RAF
Michael G. Bradley, RAF
Christopher H. Walker, RAF

Robert T. Robinson, RAF
William T. Rodenbach
Robert M. Wood
Robert A. Ginther
Paul L. Haughland
Kenneth R. Van Zandt
Horace B. Reeves
Richard J. Callahan
Buddy L. Brown
John B. Boynton
Andrew J. Bratton Jr.

1959

Ronald E. Hendrick
Harold E. Melbratten
Gerald E. McIlmoyle
William R. Stickman
Richard W. Rauch
Floyd B. Kifer
Shih Chu (Gimo) Yang, ROCAF
Huai Sheng Chen, ROCAF
Chung Kuei Hsu, ROCAF
Tai Yu (Tiger) Wang, ROCAF
Chih Yao Hua, ROCAF
Hsi Chun Hua, ROCAF
T. J. Jackson, Jr.
Charles B. Stratton
Robert J. Schueler
Robert M. Powell
Robert E. Hall
Kenneth R. McCaslin
Jack Carr
Elsworth A. Powell
Junior B. Reed
Raleigh B. Myers

1960

Robert F. Wilke
Robert C. Spencer
Donald A. Crowe
Rex R. Knaak
Anthony Martinez
Henry McManus
David B. Gammons
William W. Wilcox
Leo J. Stewart Jr.
Robert L. Primrose
Edward H. Hill
Joe G. Hyde Jr.
David L. Ray
Clifford H. Beeler

1961

Charles W. Maultsby
Ivan B. Webster, RAF
Charles Taylor, RAF
Charles W. Kern
William E. Lawson III
George M. Bull
Donald N. Webster
Eddie E. Dunagan
John A. DesPortes
Daniel W. Schmarr
John W. Wall
Richard M. Bouchard

1962

Arthur K. Leatherwood
James K. Rogers
Donald R. McClain

Clair A. McCombs
Edmund P. Smart

1963

Victor L. Milam
Ward G. Graham
Chang-di Yeh, ROCAF
Lee Nan (Terry) Ping, ROCAF
Julius H. Baughn
Ronald D. Stromberg
Teh Pei Liang, ROCAF
Shi Chuen (Johnny) Wang, ROCAF
Kenneth F. Somers
Eugene J. O'Sullivan Jr.

1964

Li Yi (Jack) Chang, ROCAF
Hui Chia Yang, ROCAF
Martin E. Bee, RAF
Basil W. Dodd, RAF
Chen Wen (Pete) Wang, ROCAF
Shih Hi (Steve) Sheng, ROCAF
Tse Shi (Charlie) Wu, ROCAF
Theodore J. Paader
John W. Fenimore

1965

Liu Jet (Terry) Chuang, ROCAF
Yu Ching (Mickey) Chang, ROCAF
Jen Liang (Spike) Chuang, ROCAF
Thomas C. McMurtry
Kenneth C. Diehl
Jerry M. Davis
George H. Worley

Arnold L. Strasheim
William B. Copeman
Keith H. Spaulding
Earle K. Smith Jr.
Leslie A. Powell
John D. Amundson
Edward L. Rose
Donald R. Wright

1966

Bob Birkett
Bob Hickman
Harold Swanson
Andy Fan Hug Ti, ROCAF
Billy Chang Hseih, ROCAF
Jim Hoover
Lonnie Liss
Marion C. Mixon
Jim Whitehead
Dave Patton
Yang Erh Ping, ROCAF
Sam Swart
Don Aitro
Les White
Richard Woodhull

1967

Tom Hwang Ling Pei, ROCAF
Richard Cloke, RAF
Harry Drew, RAF
Jerry Chipman
Karl A. Larue
Franklin D. Ott
Roy D. Burcham

Bill Park
Art Peterson
Dale L. Kellam
John Shen Chung Li, ROCAF
Tom Wang Tao, ROCAF

1968

Frederick M. Bankis
George V. Freeze
James J. Phielix
Curtis L. Behrend
Gardner D. Krumrey
Ronald R. Williams
Kenneth L. Chisholm
Raphael S. Samay
Jerry R. Wagnon
Stanley A. Lawrence
David Laee Peo Wei, ROCAF
Denny Huang, ROCAF
Mory Tsai, ROCAF

ANTHONY P. (TONY) BEVACQUA
Yuba City, California

Wife: Marilyn

THE RANCH

After graduating from Aviation Cadets at James Connally AFB, Waco, Texas, I attended F-84 fighter training in 1954 at Laughlin AFB, Texas and Luke AFB, Arizona. I reported to the 508th Strategic Fighter Wing (SFW) and the 468th Strategic Fighter Squadron (SFS) at Turner AFB, Georgia. At the time I came into the squadron, the 508th SFW was transitioning from the Republic F-84G (straight wing) to the Republic F-84F (swept wing) aircraft.

A year later, three other lieutenants, Francis Gary (Frank) Powers, Victor Milam and Wes Upchurch, and I rented a house together in the town of Albany, Georgia just outside the main gate of Turner AFB. I was new to the Air Force, quite naïve and truly "wet behind the ears." Not long after my joining the group my roomy, Frank Powers, disappeared; I mean he just vanished with no explanation, no forwarding address, no phone number, no message to the three of us. I learned later he had resigned from the Air Force. The next time I heard anything about Frank was when I arrived at the training site for the mystery airplane.

Back in those days, TOP SECRET meant just that, TOP SECRET. No one leaked anything to the press or news media. I was completely unaware that Kelly Johnson of the Lockheed Aircraft Company had received the "go ahead" to build the TOP SECRET U-2 spy plane. I had never even heard of Kelly Johnson. The U-2 made its maiden flight only 18 months later on August 1, 1955, just a few weeks before I was promoted to First Lieutenant.

When the Strategic Air Command decided in 1956 to close down its fighter operations, we were all wondering where that left us, where we were going to be assigned and what we were going to fly. Without knowing how or why, I was offered this unique opportunity to fly a mystery airplane. Even mission and the base were part of the big mystery. To this day, I cannot believe some of us signed up for this "pig in a poke." I believe we signed up because this mystery program was more attractive than the prospect of going to bombers or other multi-engine planes or possibly even a Tactical Air Command base that no one liked. As I saw it, the choices then were bombers or this weird program—I chose weird! Maybe that said something about my personality.

Once I agreed and signed on to the program, I was administered an oath that required everything I heard or saw to be treated as TOP SECRET. That meant I couldn't talk about my work to my compatriots in the squadron, my wife or any of my family. Those of us who accepted the challenge looked at each other and at least thought, "I don't know anything to tell!"

Almost overnight we became a small cadre within the Wing that had this mysterious assignment. We were then sent to New Haven, Connecticut, to the Berger Brothers Company, manufacturer of brassieres and corsets. At that time, the Bergers and David Clark Company of Worcester, Massachusetts were making pressure suits. In the basement of a cavernous building, each of us was fitted with two high altitude pressure suits. We carried our new pressure suits in hand, and went to Wright Patterson AFB, Ohio and Carswell AFB, Texas where we tested the suits in the high altitude pressure chambers. At the Wright Patterson and Carswell pressure chambers, we were informed that we had to pre-breathe 100 percent oxygen to prevent the bends in the event the cockpit lost pressure. I can tell you two hours is a very long time of just sitting and breathing.

Now we knew three things: One, it was TOP SECRET; two, a pressure suit was required as the airplane would be flying over 50,000 feet altitude; and three, we had to pre-breathe 100 percent oxygen prior to flight.

As 1956 neared its end, we volunteers were being informed of various aspects of the U-2 program in miniscule bits and pieces. We now knew we were going to be stationed at Laughlin AFB, Del Rio, Texas. No one knew much about Del Rio except that it was 155 miles west of San Antonio and located on our country's border with Mexico. I had been there for T-33 gunnery training in 1954. Housing at Laughlin and Del Rio was almost non-existent and what was available was sub-standard.

On February 21, 1957 orders released me from duty at Turner AFB and assigned me to Laughlin AFB. The orders read "Aprx 75 days TDY e/r at Los Angeles Area, Calif CIPCP purpose to estb an opr cadre in connection with a clas proj." I was further ordered to report to March AFB, Riverside, California on March 18, 1957 and to report to Laughlin, June 1, 1957.

I was told from officers at March AFB I would get further instructions on the training phase in the airplane I would be flying. I still didn't know the name of the airplane or even what it looked like. Since my assignment to March AFB was temporary duty (TDY), I was not authorized by the Air Force to move household goods or family there. My wife went to live with her parents in Phoenix, Arizona.

When I arrived at March AFB, I learned I would be undergoing flight training out in the desert somewhere. Now how much more mysterious could it get? Our schedule for the training entailed being flown in a C-47 from March AFB about noon on Mondays to the training site and returned to March AFB early afternoon on Fridays. I was happy with the arrangement because it meant I could commute to Phoenix and be with my wife on weekends. Another trainee, Mike Styer, and I teamed up to make that commute. In the mid-1950s, the Interstate Highway system was still a dream. What we traveled on was mostly a two-lane asphalt road through the mountains and desert to Phoenix.

In late February 1957, I went TDY to March AFB/Groom Lake. After we departed March AFB, we got our first glimpse of Groom Lake, commonly known to the trainees as "The Ranch". On the ground at The Ranch my impression was that it was desolate country, truly cut off from civilization. There were no nearby towns, no roads. There was only a large multi-purpose building where we took our meals, played pool and cards and watched movies. We slept in a crowded Airstream trailer next to the flight line. Ground school lasted seven to ten working days prior to the first flight and was held in a trailer or Quonset hut. Everything on that field was new since it was strictly a dry lake prior to it becoming a training base.

My first U-2 flight was on March 14, 1957. The first couple of flights were low altitude sans pressure suit; in fact, many of us wore Levis and street shoes while flying. The pressure suit came later. On the third flight, after several touch and go landings on the lake bed, I made landings on the 6,000 foot paved runway. On my first paved runway landing after a nice two-point landing, the left wing tip immediately hit the runway and the bird turned 45 degrees left even though I had full right rudder. The Mobile Control Officer was God at the time, and even though I added power, wings leveled off, aircraft pointed down the runway, I was told to shut down the engine. I did as I was told and the bird veered to the left again and went off the runway, crossed a tiny creek, and ripped the landing gear off. After the investigation of this incident I learned that particular bird had a history of this problem but no pilot did more than <u>verbally</u> mention the problem. It was verified, I was vindicated and I lost no time in training. I heard the Mobile Control Supervisor was hit with an error due to faulty judgment - better him than me.

I flamed out three times on my first flight. We flew over desolate areas with almost no emergency fields within gliding distance, so I stayed on course, glided down as fast as parameters allowed, restarted, climbed back up to altitude and continued the mission. Two more times, the same thing occurred. I returned to The Ranch two minutes early. The problem was traced to the Cobra fuel control and it was soon replaced on all the engines with a modified unit.

New ideas were always popping up during training. One of those brilliant ideas was that if we would cover our face piece with red plastic while we were pre-breathing and in the cockpit, we could see more clearly. For some reason, this idea didn't last beyond The Ranch because most of our high altitude flights were made at night.

I flew the U-2 from March 14, 1957 until my last flight in June 1965. I was reassigned to Air Command and Staff College at Maxwell AFB, Alabama. My first reaction after learning of the reassignment was to try to remain in the U-2 cockpit, but the upper level brass held their ground and off I went to school. Soon after arriving at Maxwell, I felt relief. I really enjoyed the school and being at home with my family without worry of TDYs. It almost felt like a vacation after those eight action-filled years in the cockpit.

Major General Montgomery awarding Distinguished Flying Cross to Anthony Bevacqua, May 23, 1958.

Anthony Bevacqua, July 1965

Pat Halloran and Tony Bevacqua at Eielson AFB, Alaska for Operation Toy Soldier

Tony and Marilyn Bevacqua, 2002

HARRY N. CORDES
(Deceased May 10, 2004)

Harry prepared the following document prior to his death and it is submitted here by his widow, Rogene.

THE RANCH

In 1948 General Curtis LeMay was disturbed about the lack of bombing accuracy using radar. At this time we had the first generation atomic bombs with 20 kilotons of explosive force. Two evaluation missions were flown with Dayton, Ohio as the simulated target. The results confirmed both navigation and bombing accuracy problems, enlarged and accentuated by 150 to 200 knot jet stream winds at the bombing altitudes of 25,000 to 30,000 feet. General LeMay called a meeting of lead navigators and radar observers at SAC Headquarters to address the problems. I was assigned to rewrite the Radar Bombing Manual for the APQ 13 Radar System of the B-29 aircraft.

Colonel Edward Perry, an experienced lead navigator who was known personally by General LeMay, was selected in 1948 to head a study group of radar observers from the 509th Bomb Wing. Colonel Perry was directed to work with the Air Force Intelligence Staff at the Pentagon in the analysis of maps and charts of potential targets in the Soviet Union. The analysis provided the best estimates of the results that could be expected from coordinated radar bombing. As a member of that team, I became well acquainted with Colonel Perry. I had been the radar observer on the B-29 crew that won the SAC and Radar Bombing Competition in 1948 and from that success, Colonel Perry became aware of my capabilities.

In 1951 Colonel Perry was Commander of a SAC Strategic Evaluation Squadron (SES) that had tested lead crews throughout the Command. By now Colonel Perry and I had become pilots and our crew went through with flying colors even though we were relatively new to the B-50D aircraft. Enroute to my new assignment at McCoy AFB, Florida in 1954 I visited Colonel Perry at his home in Tampa where he was still Commander of SES. From 1954 to 1956 I flew the B-47 as aircraft commander and flight commander. I amassed almost 1,000 hours of B-47 flight time including deployments to Africa and England. As a Major, I would have been in line for early promotion to Lieutenant Colonel.

At this time the United States was faced with the growing threat from the Soviet Union and its closed society. The Lockheed Aviation Company approached the CIA with a proposal for a new aircraft that could fly at 70,000 feet for 4,000 miles while taking pictures. The proposed aircraft would be safe from all known defenses. The U-2 project, known as AQUATONE, was established with the CIA in charge despite a bitter battle for control between General LeMay and SAC. CIA won the battle and Richard Bissell was put in charge of the project. General LeMay won the right to name the staff and military personnel who would run the flying part of AQUATONE. There would be a SAC training wing with Colonel Yancy in command at March AFB, California, but with duty at Groom Dry Lake in Nevada, later known as Watertown Strip and still later as Area 51. The mission pilots would be screened and selected by CIA from SAC F-84 fighter pilots with long-range navigation experience. The flying units would be organized into three squadrons known as Detachments A, B and C.

General LeMay selected Colonel McCoy to lead Detachment A, Colonel Perry to lead Detachment B and Colonel Stan Beerli for Detachment C. Each detachment commander was authorized to select their military staffs for operations, flight planning, physiological support and engineering officers. Colonel Perry selected several from his staff at SES plus others he had personally known. I received orders to report to the 1007th Air Intelligence Service Group in Washington, D.C. Colonel Perry called me personally telling me a few details of my new assignment.

In February 1956 I swapped our boat for a 1950 Studebaker and got Rogene and the girls settled in Pine Castle, Florida. It was the first home we owned. I had no clue about where I was ultimately going, how long I would be gone, what sort of job I would have or what airplane I would be flying.

WASHINGTON, DC
AND WATERTOWN, NEVADA - 1956

When I arrived in Washington, DC, I signed in at Bolling AFB and was given a room in the BOQ. I found the 1007th Air Intelligence Service Group in an old WWII building near Fort McNair. It was then that I learned that I was now a member of the CIA.

Despite my Top Secret Q clearances from Nuclear Weapons training, CIA insisted I attend orientation classes, physiological tests and interviews and the infamous lie detector exam. I passed all the tests and was admitted to Project AQUATONE. The headquarters for the project was in a super secure area of the Matomic Building at 1717 H Street in downtown Washington, DC. I met the CIA members of the project who were Director Richard Bissell, Executive Officer James Cunningham and the people who would be in my squadron, Detachment B. Colonel Perry had brought his wife and had rented an apartment. Chet Bohart, Cy Perkins, Don Curtis and I rented apartments at 1600 – 16th Street near the Russian Embassy and next door to the Cairo Hotel. We were within walking distance to the Matomic Building.

We studied the U-2 manuals and project documents that had been made up in loose-leaf form. I learned we would be the second U-2 squadron known as Detachment B and following training at Watertown, Nevada we would move to Incirlik Air Base, Adana, Turkey. I would be able to check out and fly the U-2 but only in friendly or neutral air space. The planned overflight missions were operated by ex-Air Force pilots who had resigned their commissions with the promise of future reinstatement depending on conditions at the time. I retained my rank as a Major and was paid by the Air Force. The contract pilots were paid about four times my pay; when deployed, Air Force people were paid $7 per day.

In preparation for the flying checkout, Perry, Bohart, Perkins and I met with Dave Clark of the Clark Clothing Company in Worcester, Massachusetts. The company measured each of us for our custom made partial pressure suits. In CIA spy fashion, we met Mr. Clark in a nondescript hotel in Washington.

To qualify for the U-2 training, we were also required to pass the comprehensive physical examination at Lovelace Clinic in Albuquerque, New Mexico. This was the same physical that astronauts were given and featured in the film, "The Right Stuff."

I studied the flight manual for the T-33 aircraft, required as part of the U-2 training. While waiting for the training to begin, I made two trips in a C-47 to Watertown. We had unlimited access to requisition office and flight planning materials we needed in Turkey. We were not fully occupied at that time. I used the break to drive to Pine Castle to visit with Rogene and our daughters.

Finally we were getting down to business. We were transferred to Watertown (later known as The Ranch) on April 15, 1956. Our mailing address and emergency contact was a post office box in North Hollywood, California. The schedule for military and civilians there was Monday through Friday at The Ranch. We flew either to Burbank, California, or March Field for the weekend. Occasionally we stayed at The Ranch for the weekend when there was required training scheduled. We returned to The Ranch on Monday morning at 8:00 a.m.

The SAC training unit provided excellent ground school and cockpit checkouts. I checked out quickly and easily in the T-33. The Ranch had a 6,000 foot macadam landing strip and continued for about five miles out over the dry Groom Lake. The runway continuation was marked on the dry lake with Los Angeles and Pasadena traffic markers.

We met our contract ex-F-84 pilots who were now assigned to Detachment B. At that time Lockheed pilots were still testing the U-2. The birds we used for training were the first five or so handmade by Lockheed; maintenance and support were also provided by the company.

Colonel Perry offered his resignation following his physical disqualification from flying the U-2. He felt strongly that the commander should fly the unit's aircraft. In the SAC tradition he felt an obligation to those of us he had brought into this project. So Colonel Perry stayed and was authorized to fly the T-33.

The T-33 was used in the U-2 training program to simulate the floating tendencies of the U-2 during landing. I flew the T-33 down the landing area, set 55% power, half flaps and tried to keep the aircraft at just a foot or less over the dry lake runway. This was remarkably close to the actual feel of landing the U-2. After passing the T-33 and ground school training phases,

32

I put on my pressure suit for my first U-2 flight. Although the first flight was only to 20,000 feet altitude, we still went through the pre-breathing 100% oxygen procedure. I felt like a celebrity pre-breathing with Lockheed's ace test pilots, Tony Lavier and Ray Goudey. My first flight was thrilling, because of the short takeoff roll of 500 to 1000 feet, the great power in the engine and the almost straight up climb to altitude. I had no problems with landing because the U-2 gear was so similar to the B-47 landing gear. On my next flight I went to 70,000 feet and learned about the small margin between low-speed stall and high-speed buffet--the so-called "coffin corner."

My final U-2 checkout flight at The Ranch was a unit simulated overflight mission complete with cameras and designated targets. Takeoff was at night and I was one of the first to use the sextant to measure my rough latitude with Polaris. This mission went west to California, north to Montana, east to the Dakotas, south through Colorado and west back to The Ranch. Total flight time was eight and a half hours. When I landed, I was certified, fully qualified to fly the U-2 and I was the first qualified military pilot in Detachment B. Colonel Perry looked to me as his "alter ego." I was the most direct interface with the contract pilots, one of whom was Francis Gary Powers.

INCIRLIK AIR BASE, ADANA, TURKEY

Our training at The Ranch was completed in August 1956. We then deployed to Incirlik Air Base, Turkey in a C-124. What a long flight that was. We also set up shop while we awaited the arrival of our U-2s via C-124 also. The U-2s were then reassembled by our Lockheed and Pratt & Whitney technicians and readied for flying. Because of my performance at The Ranch, Colonel Perry selected me to perform the first test flight rather than one of the contract pilots. I took the bird to 70,000 feet altitude, shut down the engine and restarted it at 35,000 feet. This became a standard test procedure that I performed on all future test flights and I continued to be the Squadron Test Pilot.

At about the time we arrived in Turkey the Suez Canal crisis resulted in open warfare between Israel and Egypt. Detachment A in Germany flew a few missions over the Mediterranean area to determine what the British and French were doing. Detachment B received its first mission task from AQUATONE Headquarters in Washington on September 11, 1956. Since the mission was over neutral territory, Colonel Perry selected me as the pilot. The targets were British and French fleets and bases and units in the Mediterranean. It was a six-hour mission and I flew it as briefed until I passed Cyprus on the way home. I was flying at 70,000 feet on autopilot when the engine flamed out. My suit pressurized and I descended to 35,000 feet, restarted the engine and proceeded to Incirlik. A short time later Detachment B was tasked to fly almost daily missions over the battle and sea areas of the ongoing Israeli-Egyptian war. Our pilots could actually observe fighting between tanks, units and aircraft through the U-2 driftsight.

For the remainder of 1956 and into the spring of 1957 our detachment had only a minimum of mission tasking, a few Soviet penetrations, a number of peripheral intelligence gathering missions and proficiency flying. I flew a four-hour test mission over Turkey with weather sensing package aboard. The whole operation at Incirlik became incredibly boring with only periodic breaks to go to Adana. At times that was off limits. Recreation on base was limited; however, the CIA furnished a boat, motor and water skis for us to use at the nearby reservoir.

34

Colonel Perry thought we were over staffed. He decided to send Bohart, Perkins and Don Curtis home. To pass the time, the remaining pilots did a bit of drinking and playing poker.

In anticipation of future tasks and to relieve some of the boredom Colonel Perry ordered the unit to undergo a simulated deployment exercise in which we packed and cataloged all supplies and equipment we would need at a bare base operations. His foresight was remarkable. In May 1957 we were tasked to move a mobile unit to LaHore, Pakistan, and fly penetrations into the Soviet Union. The preferred base was Peshawar, Pakistan but the runway there was undergoing repairs. Colonel Perry and I moved to a Pakistani air base with weather, maintenance, communications, flight planners and CIA security. We traveled mostly by C-54 through Karachi, but we ferried the U-2 aircraft and a T-33. I used the T-33 to familiarize myself with potential emergency landing sites.

Our Pakistani Air Force hosts were helpful and cooperative. Detachment B personnel lived in a LaHore hotel that had excellent food and service. The menu offered a choice of English or Pakistani selections, the latter being spicier with curry.

Frank Powers piloted one of the U-2 ferry flights; his engine flamed out and he made a dead stick landing on a 6,000-foot runway at LaHore. All of the U-2 pilots had made many simulated flameout landings. Powers landed with no damage to his aircraft, further demonstration of his flying skill.

One of our assignments tasked us to fly out of LaHore. Another covered Tyura Tam Soviet Space and Missile Test Center and recovered to Incirlik. Once we were tasked to fly three missions but we only had two U-2 aircraft. I did the flight plans for all three missions and gave Project Headquarters the option of selection.

In August 1957 the Chairman of the Joint Chiefs of Staff, U.S. Air Force General Twining and a contingent of high-ranking officers, including General William Blanchard, came to Incirlik. Colonel Perry and I were acquainted with General Blanchard. General Twining had been personally involved in the fight with CIA for control of the U-2 program. When I returned to Incirlik, I received permission from Project Headquarters to provide a detailed briefing on our operations. General Blanchard remembered me from the 509th Bomb Wing and he and General Twining were complimentary of my briefing.

Colonel Perry returned to Incirlik and resumed his arguments with Richard Bissell over a number of issues: staffing and lack of meaningful activity, CIA reluctance to turn over photography of Soviet targets to SAC, future project plans and dead ends for military personnel careers. Colonel Perry left Incirlik and the U-2 project in August 1957. I subsequently assumed command when he departed. Richard Bissell didn't trust a Major to command Detachment B. and he sent another Major, a Headquarters officer, Major Joe Richmond, to "assist" me. In November 1957, Colonel Stan Beerli arrived from Detachment C in Japan to take over Detachment B. I requested Bissell to return me to the Air Force.

I met in Washington, DC with Richard Bissell in December 1957. I raised all the objections Colonel Perry had brought up plus an additional one about the project organization. His response was the three squadrons would be "permanently" based and adequate quarters provided for families on or near the bases. Bissell and I went to Adana with a lot of money to locate, lease and refurbish houses for our families. I saw the potential for international incidents with automobiles and wives. I tried to caution him about the danger of project compromise and I suggested a concept of operations similar to SAC's 4080th SRW such as permanent basing at a U.S. Air Force base with detachments sent out on temporary duty. Bissell refused to accept my advice or anyone else's. He thought he knew it all.

I left Washington in December 1957 with orders for the Air University. I served on the Air Weapons Staff at Maxwell AFB from January to August 1958 when I joined the Command and Staff School.

STRATEGIC AIR COMMAND HEADQUARTERS
1959 – 1965

When I completed Command and Staff School, I was assigned as an Intelligence Staff Officer to SAC Headquarters, Offutt AFB, Nebraska. As a member of the Intelligence Staff, I was cleared for all sources of intelligence including photography taken by the U-2 and controlled by a compartmented system known as TALENT. Spy satellites were just coming into existence. I had access to the SAC U-2 program through the 4080th SRW and my experience of the CIA program. My official assignment was joint duty with the Joint Strategic Target Planning Staff. I maintained my flight proficiency piloting the T-33. I was selected as one of the first Instructor Pilots (IP) for the T-39 Saberliner. As a T-39 IP, I was required to fly any SAC General Officer scheduled on any trip. My General Officer mentor was Major General Robert N. Smith, DCS (Deputy Chief of Staff) Intelligence at SAC Headquarters. I later held that same job as a Brigadier General. General Smith and I made many trips together and it was a pleasure to fly for him.

On May 1, 1960 I received all intelligence reports from CIA, National Security Agency and Defense Intelligence Agency pertaining to the shoot down and capture of Francis Gary Powers. I defended Powers and his conduct based on my past experience with him at

Incirlik and LaHore. My immediate boss at SAC was Colonel Keegan who was well known in the intelligence community for his hawkish positions on intelligence issues. Colonel Keegan considered Powers a traitor for talking to the Soviets, for not destroying the U-2 with the detonator switches and for not taking his own life with the lethal needle concealed in a coin. I maintained a file on all intelligence and open source material on Powers including his imprisonment and trial. Later, these files came in handy when Powers was returned to US custody.

An event occurred in 1961 that had little bearing on my duty at CIA but confirmed my judgment of Richard Bissell. He had by then been elevated to the position of Deputy Director Plans and Programs for CIA. Bissell was the main force responsible for the ill-conceived and poorly-executed invasion of Cuba by former Cuban nationals and mercenaries trained and armed by the CIA. This was another example of the arrogance and disregard for the national policy and objectives formed and grown in the CIA under Allen Dulles and his Secretary of State John Foster Dulles. The Cuban invasion as well as Powers' May Day mission were both undoubtedly compromised and doomed to failure from the start. In both cases details were withheld from the military, other intelligence agencies and national command authorities, including Presidents Eisenhower and Kennedy. The SAC role in this fiasco was an increased alert status, intelligence gathering against Cuba and development of contingency war plans.

It was my understanding that both Allen Dulles and Richard Bissell were fired with Dulles replaced by industrial leader, John McCone whose overall role at CIA was reduced. It was hard to believe that one government agency could have become so out of control. Part of the CIA arrogance stemmed from some "successes" they had in Central America in the 1950s, including claims of overthrowing and establishing governments in that area.

The Soviet Union determined in February 1962 that Frank Powers was no longer a military, intelligence or propaganda asset. The Soviets were open to swap Powers for Soviet spy Rudolph Abel who was being held in New York on charges of spying in the US. The exchange was conducted on a bridge spanning East and West Germany with CIA Agent Joe Murphy on hand to positively identify Powers. Murphy had been a CIA Security Officer at Detachment B in Incirlik and he knew Powers personally. The CIA flew Powers directly back to Washington, DC where he was reunited with his wife, Barbara. They were put up in the Hunting Towers in Alexandria adjacent to the Woodrow Wilson Bridge.

Because of the intense media attention, the CIA relocated Powers and his wife in the dark of night to Letterkenny Army Depot near Chambersburg, Pennsylvania where they were set up in a safe house.

CIA still "owned" Powers and they established the interrogation ground rules. The Defense Department was allocated two spaces for the interrogation. John Hughes, an experienced Intelligence Officer, was selected by the Defense Intelligence Agency. The other slot was allocated to the Commander in Chief, Strategic Air Command. General Powers selected me upon the recommendation of Major General Smith and Colonel Keegan.

I flew a T-33 immediately to Washington, DC, and reported to the CIA Project Headquarters. The next morning John Hughes and I, the CIA team, State Department representatives, and White House staff members traveled by unmarked cars to Chambersburg. We spent two nights and three days interrogating Powers.

Frank Powers' reaction to seeing me as part of the team could only be described as joyful. He felt he had someone who would believe in him. We listened to Powers' version of his shoot down, his escape from the U-2, his capture, imprisonment, trial, treatment and the surprise release. I discussed with Frank the discrepancies in his story raised by the NSA analysts and his version correlated with what would have occurred to a U-2 in a near miss with a surface-to-air missile. We returned to Washington on Friday and John and I met on Saturday with DIA. We briefed the Director, DIA on Powers' interrogation and then we went to the Pentagon E Ring. First, we briefed General Lyman Lemnitzer and the Joint Chiefs, then the Director of Defense Research and Engineering, Dr. Harold Brown. When we briefed Secretary of Defense, Robert McNamara, he expressed anger that Powers continued his mission, despite the auto pilot problems. I tried to explain to him the dedication of Air Force pilots to mission completion. McNamara made a scathing reference to "reckless young fighter pilots" and criticized Powers' decision to continue the mission.

I flew back to SAC Headquarters to brief my bosses and General Powers. I returned to Washington to work with John Hughes on the question of what to do about Frank Powers' desire to return to the Air Force and to write a report about Powers.

The Inspector General of the Air Force was the same General Blanchard I had known in the 509th Bomb Wing and the same General I briefed in 1957 at Incirlik. It was his responsibility to decide what to do with Frank Powers. Major Joe Peartree of Air Force Intelligence was assigned to work with me to make a recommendation to General Blanchard. Joe and I examined all the intelligence, press reports and Soviet statements and compared them with Powers' interrogation statements. We reported our findings to General Blanchard at his quarters on Bolling AFB.

Meanwhile, John McCone, the new Director of the CIA, was not happy with the reports he received from the CIA U-2 Staff. He asked retired Federal Judge E. Barrett Prettyman to establish a Board of Inquiry to determine if Powers had acted in accordance with his CIA contract and would be entitled to his back pay. The hearings were informal. Participants were invited to comment and question witnesses. I sat in on the hearings in a dual capacity as a member of the interrogation team and as a representative of General Blanchard and the Air Force.

Dr. Louis Tordello, Deputy Director of National Security Agency and several NSA analysts presented "evidence" that Powers' shoot down story was fabrication. Their recovered intelligence of Soviet tracking led to a scenario of Powers' oxygen problems and descent below 30,000 feet when Soviets shot him down. I had knowledge of the same information but I believed Frank Powers. When I interrogated him, Powers was the same naïve, country boy I had known so well at The Ranch and at Incirlik.

I asked to speak at the hearing and pointed out several differences with the NSA analysts' findings. The Soviet Air Defense System tended to project target tracks based on predicted tracks. I pointed out a prime example in the Soviet shoot down of an RB-47 in the Barents Sea where the recovered tracking showed the plane circled for 30 to 45 minutes before it hit the water. I also showed them similar incidents during other shoot downs. After my presentation, Judge Prettyman asked Dr. Tordello if he knew about this information. Tordello said he would research it and return the next day.

The NSA team returned and Dr. Tordello acknowledged that NSA's scenario could be wrong and Powers' version correct. Judge Prettyman noted in his report that there was conflicting evidence with Powers' version of the events. Although that version was

41

inconclusive, the preponderance of evidence favored Powers. Prettyman's conclusion was that Powers had fulfilled the terms of his contract and was entitled to his full back pay. This was not the first nor was it the last time I differed with NSA.

Because I had been on the Powers' interrogation team and had participated in the hearings, CIA asked me to accompany CIA Director John McCone and senior CIA officials to brief the appropriate congressional committees. Lockheed provided me with a model of the U-2 so I could break it down to show the series of events described by Powers. In closed sessions, we briefed the House and Senate Armed Services and Foreign Affairs Committees as well as the Senate Select Intelligence Committee. Senator Fulbright and his Foreign Affairs Committee were especially critical of the CIA for taking as their own the role of foreign policy. With a non-intelligence background, McCone had to take all the heat generated by Allen Dulles and Richard Bissell.

While I was in Washington, I had one more task to perform. I reported my recommendations on the disposition of Powers to General Blanchard. I reluctantly recommended Powers not be reinstated as a Captain in the Air Force because of the extensive publicity and zealous media interest. I felt his fame and notoriety would seriously detract from his career with any unit he joined. I also recommended that CIA still "owned" him and should use him at their Edwards AFB Test and Training Unit. Lastly, I recommended that Powers receive any future medals and decorations awarded to U-2 pilots and that he be recognized as a prisoner of war.

When I returned to SAC Headquarters, I thought my U-2 days were over. However, when Castro allowed the Soviets to install their missiles in Cuba, I again became involved with the U-2 program. I made several T-39 flights to Laughlin AFB and McCoy AFB to brief the

SAC U-2 pilots on what to look for--most especially the SA-2 missile launch site. I personally briefed Rudolph Anderson and Steve Heyser who found the Soviet missile sites on their missions over Cuba. I helped plan the missions to minimize exposure to the SA-2 SAMs. Sadly, Rudolph Anderson was a casualty of the United States' involvement in the Cuban Missile Crisis.

While I enjoyed flying the B-47 bomber, the T-33 and T-39, my most challenging assignment was flying the U-2 in the handmade partial pressure suit.

Harry N. Cordes,
Deputy Chief of Staff for Intelligence,
Strategic Air Command Headquarters,
Offutt AFB, Nebraska, October 1970

July 1957, Detachment B, TUSLOG, Incirlik, Turkey,
Weather Recon Unit in their "uniforms"
L to R, Harry Cordes, Chet Bohart, Ed Perry, Don Curtis,
and William Kennedy. Harry was the only U-2 pilot in the group.

TUSLOG, Detachment B, Incirlik, Turkey,
Top L to R, Francis Gary Powers, Sammy Snyder, Tom Burkhead,
Ed Perry, E. K. Jones, Bill McMurry, Bill Hall
Kneeling L to R, Chet Bohart, Cy Perkins, Buster Edens,
Jim Cherbonnoux, Harry Cordes

RICHARD GIORDANO
Montgomery, Alabama

Wife: Anita

I had been selected for the U-2 program early in 1956 and had gone through the physical, received my pressure suit and had been though the high altitude chamber tests when I had a T-33 accident on July 19, 1956. That put me in the hospital for seven months. Thanks to Colonel Jerry Johnson, I was assigned to Laughlin AFB in February 1957. I was given a job they made up for me as Executive Officer to Buzz Curry in the U-2 squadron. In between visits to the hospital for continuing plastic surgery I was primarily performing administrative duties in the unit.

Obviously I wanted to return to flying status. The Flight Surgeon said it would be physically possible to return to flying but not in a pressure suit because of the limitation created by the scarring. So I asked to meet a Flight Evaluation Board. It was held on January 27, 1958, almost 18 months to the day after my accident. Given the fact that at that time I looked like death warmed over, I really did not think I had a chance, especially since I had suffered a cardiac arrest during one of my surgeries.

Horace Reeves was the Board Prsident. Members were Floyd Herbert, Leon Steffy, Joe King, Floyd Kifer and Harvey Hertz. Witnesses were Jack Nole, Lloyd Leavitt and Curley Graves. The whole proceeding took about an hour and a half. The Board recommended return to flying status. A. J. Russell agreed and it went to SAC Headquarters. SAC approved it with the recommendation that I not be returned to a combat crew.

I then re-certified in the T-bird. I remember flying guys around for instrument proficiency and even a trip where we took a couple of T-birds to the OL at Ramey for the guys deployed there to practice instrument flying. I thought the trip was unique in that it was the first of its kind and required a stop at Guantanamo, Cuba, where the unit would play a significant role a few years later.

Since my accident was in the T-33, I wasn't particularly crazy about continuing to fly the plane. I asked to get dual qualified also in the U-3A so I would feel more a part of the unit, if only chasing the U-2 around the pattern with a U-2 instructor pilot in the right seat. Nothing exciting there, but I do recall as an instructor pilot, I was almost grounded when I flew too low over Brackettville while John Wayne was filming "The Alamo." Wing received a nasty phone call about my screwing up their shooting since there weren't any airplanes scheduled to appear in the movie about Texas in the 1830's.

I very reluctantly left in September 1959 for two years in Morocco. I knew I would never have gotten by an FEB as easily as I did had it not been held on my home grounds with fellow pilots and friends. It is something for which I am eternally grateful as it allowed me to finish a 32-year career as an O-6 and Wing Commander. Some of my best friends from that assignment have remained best friends to this day.

GERALD E. (JERRY) MCILMOYLE
Venice, Florida

Wife: Patricia

RECRUITMENT INTO THE DRAGON LADY PROGRAM

It all began 50 years ago, in the spring of 1956. I had just returned to my unit from leave at McCook, Nebraska, my hometown. I was flying the F-84F in the 515th Strategic Fighter Bomber Squadron at Malmstrom AFB in Great Falls, Montana. I didn't think I had been gone that long, but the squadron was abuzz with recent changes. A flight commander myself, I found that two of the other flight commanders, Lt. Barry Baker, Lt. Jim Barnes and the Assistant Operations Officer, Captain Frank Grace had departed Malmstrom to enter a super secret program.

I was disappointed that I had not been included in the selection for the program, but my Squadron Operations Officer, Captain Homer Hayes, told me my name had been on the list of candidates for consideration. The candidates were interviewed at a local hotel in Great Falls. They returned and told our Squadron Commander, Major Robert Keene, that they were resigning their reserve commissions; they were discharged immediately. The three of them were directed not to say anything about where they were going or what they were going to be doing; we just never heard from them again.

It was mysterious and disappointing to me on two levels. I thought Frank, Barry and James had been good and close friends. We had all been in Korea together; we partied together, played bridge and poker and camped out together. Christmas rolled around and we received no cards, no phone calls, absolutely nothing from any of them. I really didn't understand why. Subsequently, we have run into each other a couple of times in the past 50 years, but there was no camaraderie, just a handshake and smile, no small talk. I was reminded of the old Pentagon euphemism: those three friends "evanesced".

Scuttlebutt had it that those selected for the new secret program would be flying a new jet aircraft and would be earning about five times our Air Force pay plus bonuses. The rumors seemed to be verified a couple of months later when our squadron commander asked me to lead a flight of four F-84F fighter aircraft to Houston, Texas, to attend the funeral of Frank Grace, my old friend. We learned during that trip that Frank had been killed during a night takeoff from an unlighted airfield, had hit a telephone pole and crashed. We were directed not to ask any questions about the crash, where, what, how, when, and most especially not about what aircraft he had been flying when he was killed. Frank's wife and children were devastated by their loss, as were we all. Frank had been a good friend to all of us in the squadron, both personally and professionally.

After I returned to the squadron, I learned that Captain Louis Setter of the sister 517th Strategic Fighter Bomber Squadron, was reassigned and no one knew where. It happened rather quickly. Setter was a regular officer and had not resigned his commission, another mystery to the mix. An engineer by education, Setter had designed a small handheld computer for use with F-84 flight planning. The Strategic Air Command (SAC) had jumped to put his invention into use.

All the elusive stories surrounding the Dragon Lady stimulated my appetite to be part of it. After a few months of rumors, the squadron was told that all the fighter bomber wings in SAC were to be disbanded by the summer of 1957 due to the limited range of their fighter aircraft. I was well aware that my four-year obligation to the Air Force would be fulfilled near the end of 1956. I did not want to return to the computer programming job I held before I entered the Air Force and my wife, Patty, wholeheartedly agreed.

I applied for and was offered a job flying for United Airlines out of Denver, Colorado. Flying for a living; I definitely found my niche in life. However, another option surfaced when our Wing Commander, Colonel Murray Bywater, called Lts. Buddy Brown, Hank Macklin and me into his office. He announced that we had proven ourselves to be the class of officer the Air Force needed. He guaranteed us that if we would apply for a regular commission we would be approved. A regular commission was attractive to me if I were to make the Air Force my career because I would not be subject to a reduction in force (RIF) which was a possibility as a reserve officer. Patty and I debated about the change and what it would mean to the family. We agreed that I should apply.

Out of the blue, a third choice surfaced. Colonel Jack Nole, the future U-2 Squadron Commander from Turner AFB, came to Malmstrom AFB and I found myself in a room with about ten other pilots. Colonel Nole gave us a sketchy description of a new aircraft President Eisenhower wanted and had funded. SAC needed pilots to volunteer to fly it. The decommissioned SAC fighter wings made available a large cadre of well-qualified pilots from which the still TOP SECRET Dragon Lady program had its choice. We were asked to sign up then and there or depart the briefing room; those remaining would be given a more detailed briefing. Most of us were eager to be part of the new program and raised our hands. The new volunteers pledged an oath of secrecy and signed it. We were now in the program. Patty and I had talked about this program and the possibility I might be selected.

We agreed that staying in the Strategic Air Command where we were known was preferable to reassignment to a new command where I would be the "new guy" on the block.

Not even pitiful base housing deterred us from our new post of duty at Laughlin AFB in Del Rio, Texas, just a few miles from the border of Mexico. Still no details on the new aircraft or its mission had been imparted to us. Despite the lack of information, there was a feeling of excitement among the volunteers that our mission was important and the aircraft would be a challenge to fly.

In the spring of 1957 I traveled to the David Clark Company in Worcester, Massachusetts to be fitted for two partial pressure flight suits. Pilots of this new aircraft required extra protection in an emergency loss of cabin pressure. The Clark Company had been a manufacturer of women's undergarments and the founder of the company had been experimenting on pressure suit design with a degree of success. Ordinarily, funding for anything in the Air Force was a major ordeal; however, the CIA was the source of funding for everything related to the U-2 and money was no issue. The fact that we were visiting where the pressure suits were made put us on the edge of the "spook world." We made the trip to Worcester dressed in civilian clothes, no military uniforms were allowed. The trip itself was by a circuitous route and we had no military documents with us. When we arrived in Worcester, we were met at the terminal by a guy with a sign on which our names were written. We introduced ourselves, received a handshake but no name from him in response. On the drive to our hotel there was no conversation from our driver. All he said when we arrived at our hotel was, "I will pick you up here at 8:00 a.m. tomorrow morning."

With the new pressure suits finished, we were sent to a high altitude pressure chamber at Abilene AFB, Texas for testing. The test was to determine the effects of rapid decompression for the pilots and the suits. We went to this chamber because it would be the one used by my future unit's pilots for required high altitude qualification. Once we were inside the test chamber, technicians evacuated the air until the chamber was the equivalent pressure altitude of 75,000 feet. The pressure suits and pilots passed the test.

Volunteers now knew another piece of the puzzle about the aircraft we would be flying; it flew at extremely high altitudes. The highest I had ever flown up to that time was 49,000 feet in an F-86F in Korea. It seemed inconceivable to me to fly at 75,000 feet. It didn't take a rocket scientist to figure out that I would be flying the same plane in a sister program to the one that Louis Setter, Frank Grace, Barry Baker and Jim Barnes had joined eight months earlier. There were other rumors that I associated with those four comrades-in-arms, such as the one about civilians seen taking off in this weird airplane that went practically straight up from US air bases in Germany, Japan and Turkey.

Those of us scheduled to become part of the Dragon Lady program formed a bond that is still firm to this day. We were filled with anticipation of our future flying a new high altitude aircraft and our relocation to Del Rio. The men and women of the 407th Strategic Bomber Wing one by one departed Malmstrom AFB for their new assignments.

My cousin, Colonel Harvey Hertz, was the Flight Surgeon of the 4080th Strategic Reconnaissance Wing. I contacted him and told him I was being assigned to the Wing there. He invited Patty and me to stay with him and his mother (my great aunt) while we looked for a house to rent. Much of the usual anxiety of our new assignment and finding a place to live was relieved by my cousin's generosity.

I reported to the 4028th Strategic Reconnaissance Squadron the first week of August 1957. On that first day at Laughlin AFB, I saw the U-2 for the first time. I was mesmerized by the sleek appearance. For me, it represented a dream come true. It was love at first sight!

Gerald E. (Jerry) McIlmoyle

Gerald E. (Jerry) McIlmoyle

Jerry McIlmoyle checking his aircraft before a flight.

CHARLES B. STRATTON
9 Mile Falls, Washington

Wife: Ann

MY FIRST U-2 FLIGHT

There may be some that don't remember their first flight in the U-2, but I sure do. I had flown the F-80A and C, the F-84G and F, the B-57C and the RB-57D. Moving over to the U-2 didn't seem like any big deal. I decided that after checking out in the miserable F-80A that anything else would be a walk in the park. So I was miserable again until my first attempt at landing the U-2.

After the usual ground school, simulated landings in a U-3A, cockpit procedures, briefings, etc., it was time for the first flight. My Instructor Pilot (IP) was Ed Dixon, a really cool, calm confidence-instilling pilot. He briefed me on what to expect in flight and repeatedly emphasized the fact that the bird would not land unless it was held off the runway until it stalled and "dropped" to the runway. Dixon drove home to me the fact that if I touched down above stall, I would be airborne again and "bullfrogging" down the runway. This seemed in conflict with his previous admonition to NEVER, EVER STALL THE U-2! I thought to myself, "Okay, okay, enough already. Let's get on with it. What the hell can be so tough about landing this bird?" I had watched several U-2 landings from the Mobile Control chase car and they seemed normal enough. What I failed to realize was that those landings were by experienced U-2 pilots, and not the new guy on the block that I was.

The takeoff and inflight maneuvers were pretty straightforward without surprises, if anything in the U-2 could be called straightforward. When I had completed my pre-landing familiarization flight maneuvers to get the feel of the U-2, I radioed my IP that I had completed that phase and was ready to enter the landing pattern. Ed instructed me to enter the pattern and reminded me of pattern altitudes. He rechecked my pattern speeds with me and computed my remaining fuel load. My downwind, base, and final approach airspeeds were right on. As I approached the runway, I saw Ed initiating a pursuit curve on me with the chase vehicle.

I passed Ed and he started calling out my altitude above the runway: "10 feet, 8 feet, 5 feet, 3 feet, 2 feet, hold it off, hold it off, HOLD IT OFF!" I held off until it started to shudder and I instinctively released some back pressure, touched the runway and bounced back up. Again I hit the runway and bounced back up. I didn't want to get into a "porpoise," so I added power and took it around. Wow, I got out of that one by the skin of my teeth.

Now, I can guarantee you that the first attempt to land an airplane in a "controlled crash" is a sobering experience. The next approach was similar to the first one, and so was my attempt to land when the bird started to shudder. Again, I couldn't help myself and released some back pressure. There I was "galloping" down the runway. On the next go-around with some one-sided discussion with Ed, I decided to hold that sucker off, even if it crashed. On the next approach, as Ed called off "3, 2, 1 foot, hold it off, hold it off," I kept sucking back on the yoke. The bird started to shudder, so I kept coming back and it "flopped" to the runway. I figured this was a disaster and then Ed called out, "Nice landing!"

My next four or five touch and go's went good, but they still seemed like controlled crashes to me. As all U-2 pilots know, after a few landings, you don't even notice the shudder just before the "crash." After that flight, I really knew the meaning of the pilot cliché, "Well, I walked away from another one!"

COMMENTARY BY JERRY MCILMOYLE

What did I feel when I first saw the U-2? It was total, unbridled excitement and I could not wait to get in it and fly. What was it like to take off and climb above 70,000 feet? It was like everything I ever wanted and hoped it would be. It was total euphoria; I was thrilled to the core with absolute and complete focus on what I was doing and making the plane perform. I couldn't get enough of flying this airplane. When I left the U-2 outfit for a staff job after seven years, it caused me real physical and psychological pain to realize I would probably never fly the bird again. Would you believe I still feel that way?

COMMENTARY ON FIRST FLIGHTS OF REPUBLIC OF CHINA PILOTS
BY ANTHONY MARTINEZ

Charles Stratton's account of his first flight brought to mind the critiques I attended as Squadron Operations Officer when the Republic of China pilots were training at Laughlin AFB. The IP was Eddie Dunagan. Fellow pilots knew Eddie sometimes slipped into South of the Mason-Dixon Line lingo when he got real excited.

This particular time, his Chinese student was listening intently to Eddie's explanation of the identical procedure that Stratton described when the bird is one foot above asphalt. Eddie said, "I don't want you to start "crow hopping" from main gear to tail wheel or you're going to be in real trouble. Do you understand?" The ROC pilot answered with a puzzled look, "What do you mean, 'crow hop'?" I not know what is "crow hop?" Then Eddie proceeded to demonstrate with his hand bouncing up and down on the table. We all looked at each other and had a good laugh. The ROC pilots had learned much of their flying talk from the one and only "Muddy" Waters. He and his wife, Marty, really made those young ROC pilots feel at home while they were with us.

Chuck Stratton leaning on the unit's modern, speedy Dodge wagon for mobile control and chase vehicle at Bien Hoa AB, Vietnam, March 1964

CARMINE VITO
(Deceased August 27, 2003)

Widow: Barbara

The following is summarized from the *Austin American Statesman,* Saturday, August 30, 2003.

For decades, the world knew nothing of Carmine Vito and his covert U-2 missions over the Soviet Union. That changed in 1998 when the Central Intelligence Agency declassified the details of the spy flights and their contributions to the Cold War.

"I want to say a special thanks to the pilots, from Carmine Vito, to the U-2 pilots of today," CIA Director George Tenent said at a 1998 symposium on the U-2, the high-flying surveillance plane that debuted in 1956.

"The courage that Carmine and his colleagues showed made an enormous difference to the security of our country," Tenent said. "These men allowed generations of Americans to live in peace and prosperity."

Vito, who flew 65 spying missions for the CIA, was the only American pilot to fly a U-2 reconnaissance mission directly over Moscow. That flight, on July 5, 1956, collected critical information about the Soviet military capacity. Vito's U-2 hangs from the ceiling of the Smithsonian National Air and Space Museum in Washington, along with the Tutti-Frutti gum that he left beneath the canopy.

The CIA flew 24 missions over Russia between 1956 and 1960, when the loss of Francis Gary Powers' U-2 plane halted the flights.

Glen Dunaway, also an Austin resident, was one of the first group of six pilots, along with Vito, to operate the

U-2. Dunaway remembers Vito as an ebullient and thoughtful man who was always ready to fly. "It was a huge deal, and everybody knew it," Dunaway said of their missions. "They also knew the dangers of a mission when you fly in somebody else's back yard and they don't like it. You have to treat it with maximum respect and professionalism."

The photos taken from the U-2 provided the first verifiable data about the Soviet Union's military capacity and was used to debunk rumors that the Russians were much stronger than they turned out to be.

"It was the beginning of a program that allowed the US to have a much better understanding of what was going on in the Soviet interior," said Jeffrey Richelson, a senior fellow with the National Security Archive at George Washington University. "Accurate information about the Soviet military laid the groundwork for future arms treaties," Richelson said.

Vito met Barbara at CIA Headquarters where she was an administrative assistant. They married in 1960 and had four children. Vito spent the remainder of his career in the Air Force, retiring as a Colonel.

FLYING WITH THE LADY

Once you have tasted flight, you will forever walk the earth with your eyes turned skyward for there you have been and there you long to return.

Leonardo da Vinci

JULIAN ANDERSON
Vashon, Washington

My crew was flying our last B-29 training mission the day "The War" ended. In November 1945 a large portion of the crew was transferred to Roswell AFB, New Mexico to be discharged or reassigned. I considered my options at the time; I was 5 feet 5 inches and pilot requirements for commercial airlines were 5 feet 6 inches. Employment as a commercial pilot did not seem to be a viable option for me. I decided I would stay in the Air Force and I became an Administrative Officer in the Base "Pool" Squadron until I received an assignment. I was finally assigned to the 393rd Bomb Squadron, 509th Bomb Wing as a copilot when it returned to Roswell. After 18 months, I was upgraded to Aircraft Commander. A great deal of my Air Force career was subsequently in aircraft safety where I participated on a number of aircraft accident investigations.

In August 1948 Jack Nole was assigned as the Deputy Commander of the 393rd Bomb Squadron. We were deployed to Goose Bay, Labrador for a short TDY. Our new squadron commander had a friend who had been assigned to the Wing and to my crew for that TDY. He was designated as the Wing Fly-Away Kit Officer. The Kit Officer was responsible for insuring that anything required for support of the squadron aircraft on TDYs was stowed in the bomb bays until supply lines could be established. Not only did I fly a combat crew, but I was also the Squadron Technical Supply Officer and Fly-Away Kit Officer. For that scheduled flight, I already had a substitution of other members of my aircrew when the Squadron Commander requested that his friend be assigned to my crew. The friend was to have flown the "test hop" of our aircraft, B-29 S/N 44-86383 on Wednesday, August 11, 1948. However, he did not show up for the flight which was flown with another crew member as co-pilot. On Thursday, August 12, prior to takeoff I briefed the Squadron Commander's friend on his responsibility on the takeoff. I specifically briefed him on the "flap retraction procedure." I explained what the procedure was and why I would call for "flaps 10 degrees" after the aircraft was established in a climb. The last 10 degrees of flap retraction in the heavyweight B-29 would lose a lot of its lift so we would then gain more airspeed. To ensure we had a climb re-established on the flight before retracting the last 10 degrees of flaps, I called for "flaps 10 degrees." About the time I felt the aircraft losing lift, I heard the co-pilot say, "Uh-oh, I forgot to play their coast." A quick glance at the co-pilot's instrument panel showed the flap indicator almost at "zero." My efforts to stop the aircraft from settling were almost successful but it was not enough. The two inboard propellers on the B-29 were six inches lower than the outboard propellers, a fact which played against us that day. I saw a flash of fire and instantly knew we had struck the ground. I concentrated on keeping the wings level and the nose slightly elevated for the next impact. The crash came with such devastation that only eight of the 21 crew on board survived. After the aircraft hit the ground, my left leg extended with the rudder pedal to keep the wings level and I sustained a fracture at the knee joint. I sustained head injuries that I can only attribute to my good fortune and a Guardian Angel to have survived. I was off duty for three months recovering from my injuries. I was fortunate to be among the eight, but to this day I remember those who lost their lives.

Following my recovery and return to flight duty, I attended Air Tactical School and Air Force Instrument Instructor Pilot Training. I transitioned into the B-50s as the 509th Bomb Wing was being converted to the B-50 aircraft.. Then the B-47s came into operation and I volunteered to be reassigned to that aircraft. The original intent was to have the B-47s operated by a three-man crew and all qualified as navigators/bombardiers/radar navigators. The plan was to have the crew members rotate in each of the positions; however, the headquarters decision makers never implemented it.

After a year of training schools, I was assigned in 1951 to the 376th Bomb Wing at Barksdale AFB, Shreveport, Louisiana. I flew the B-29 until our unit subsequently received their B-47s. I was offered a job on the Wing Staff but I declined in order to refresh my proficiency in the aircraft. Part of my flying included testing the newly devised Minimum Altitude Bombing Technique for the SAC War Plan procedures. After transitioning into   B-47s, I became an Instructor Pilot (IP) in the B-47 and accrued 1,000 hours. Later I was selected as the Wing Director of Safety under the new Wing Commander. Part of my new duties was to fly the Wing Commander whenever he wanted to go in a B-47.

One day a B-29 crashed while attempting a three-engine emergency landing. It occurred away from the airfield in the Special Weapons Storage area at Barksdale, but it did not impact the storage bunker. Crash equipment was routinely positioned alongside the runway at regular intervals for easy access in case of emergency. As the aircraft burned, the crash recovery crew had to travel a circuitous route to get to site. There were no survivors of that emergency.

I was a member of the investigative board proceedings for this accident. I recommended to SAC that procedures be revised. The recommendation was—if a B-29 pilot was making an emergency three-engine landing, once he descended through 500 feet altitude above the ground, he was then committed to land the aircraft, hopefully on the runway or within the confines of the landing area where the crash recovery vehicles are positioned, making it more probably for crew members to be safely rescued.

As a result of those recommendations, I learned that Brigadier General Austin Russell, Commander, 4th Air Division at Barksdale was impressed with the accident investigation. Another accident involved a B-47 from Eglin AFB, Florida that crashed in the Mississippi River. The pilot was attempting to "get on top" of a line of thunderstorms enroute to Edwards AFB, California. I learned again that General Russell was again pleased with the board's investigation of the accident.

The 376th Bomb Wing was relocated to Ohio and the Strategic Evaluation Group (SEG) came to Barksdale from MacDill AFB, Florida. It was considered to be a SAC Headquarters assignment and I was assigned as Director of Safety for the SEG.

When it came time for the relocation of the 376th Bomb Wing to Ohio and the SEG to Barksdale, General Armstrong, Commander of Second Air Force at Barksdale made his first visit to the 4080th Strategic Reconnaissance Wing at Laughlin AFB, Texas. The day General Armstrong arrived at Laughlin, his plane was delayed from landing due to a crash of B-57C right on the runway. It took two hours for the crash recovery team to get the runway cleared to permit General Armstrong's plane to land. Rumor was that General Armstrong returned to Barksdale and immediately phoned General Russell and said, "A. J., you are now Commander of the 4080th Strategic Reconnaissance Wing at Laughlin. Get down there and straighten them out."

I recall a conversation with our Personnel Officer who had just returned from Second Air Force Headquarters. He said, "You know what is going to happen to you, don't you?" I replied that I was to be Director of Safety for the SEG when they arrived from MacDill. The Personnel

Officer told me he had seen my name on a message from General Russell at Laughlin saying he wanted me as his Director of Safety in the 4080th. I knew what General Russell expected of me; he expected regular visits, even if it were only to have a cup of coffee.

I was assigned to Laughlin AFB from Barksdale AFB in January 1958. My B-47 experience enabled me to be checked out in the B-57C.

A ground incident occurred in the 4028th SRS Physiological Support area. Due to the extreme altitudes involved with these flights, high-pressure oxygen bottles were included in the pilot's equipment. While handling one of those bottles, one of the technicians inadvertently dropped it. When the bottle hit the cement floor, the valve was knocked off and the bottle became a flying missile, passing through a solid wood door two inches thick. Fortunately, no one was injured, but the incident sure got everybody's attention.

A ground accident occurred during the servicing of the forward wheel on a U-2. Due to the high altitudes the U-2 flew, the wheels had to be serviced with high pressure gas rather than air. The gas was in a two-bottle wheeled cart. The valve system required the sequential adjustment of two valves to put gas in the tire without allowing too much pressure to build up. Sadly, the valves had not been adjusted properly and the unlimited buildup of pressure disintegrated the tire and severely injured the young Crew Chief working on it.

On August 3, one of the Republic of China pilots encountered an engine flameout at 70,000 feet. Rather than bail out, he began descending above an undercast layer of clouds. From 35,000 feet to 17,000 he made four unsuccessful attempts to get the engine restarted. As he approached the top of the clouds at 14,000 feet, he saw an opening and spiraled down through the overcast. As he broke out, he noted the lights of Cortez, Colorado in the distance and the flashing/rotating beacon of the Montezuma County Airport. He retracted the landing gear and the speed brakes to help lengthen his glide distance. He was successful in getting to the vicinity of the airport trying to land on the runway in a southerly direction. He was not quite aligned with the runway so he touched down and skipped a short distance, turning about 135 degrees and slid backwards off the runway where he came to a stop.

Major Mike Hua got himself disconnected and out of the cockpit, retrieved his identification papers, removed his helmet and walked over to the terminal where he found an agent on duty. Major Hua said, "I yust crash land an aircraft on your airport." He then presented his identification papers to the agent who called Kirtland AFB, Albuquerque, New Mexico. The agent told Kirtland a foreign pilot had crashed an aircraft on his airport and presented a packet of papers. The agent asked, "What should I do?" The person at Kirtland replied, "Do what the papers tell you to do" and he hung up.

As soon as the 4080th received notification, plans were made for the accident team to depart the next morning to pick up Major Hua and the U-2 engine. I was onboard the aircraft that day and recalled it was my fifteenth anniversary as a rated pilot. When we arrived at Montezuma County Airport, we met Major Hua and he said repeatedly, "I sure lucky, I sure lucky."

That was the last accident investigation team I participated in with the 4080th SRW. I have many fond memories of my service with that organization and the many life-long friends I made.

An RB-57D accident in the 4025th SRS occurred when one of the most professional pilots I knew was at the helm. With many years between then and now, unfortunately I can't recall the pilot's name, but I think it was Bob Schuler. However, he could always be counted on to touch down in almost the same spot on each of his landings, which resulted in him being awarded a Spot Promotion to Major. On this particular flight, the pilot took off but the nose gear failed to retract. After consulting with the Command Post, he was directed to land. He flew his usual landing pattern and touched down in the same spot. As the weight settled on to the gear, he continued his roll, but the left wing failed at the outboard side of the left engine.

General Russell was on the scene immediately and I was summoned from my U-2 Field Training class. Upon investigation, I saw indications the wing spar had cracked. I told General Russell of my theory of the wing spar crack and recommended that we recall any other RB-57s in flight to check for the crack. My counterparts at Second Air Force Safety told me I was nuts because the wing spar could not have been cracked. When the results came back from Wright Patterson AFB Testing Lab, they proved that the wing spar was indeed cracked.

General Russell left Laughlin in early 1959 and was replaced by Colonel A. J. Bratton. I then tried to get reassigned to a KC-135, hoping it would help me obtain employment at Boeing in Seattle after retirement. I had already purchased property on Vashon Island in order to be near my wife's parents. I had a friend in SAC Headquarters who was trying to guide my application through the Personnel channels. We thought we had it made but one day while my friend was out of the office, a "Hawkeye Sergeant" looked at the application and put the skids on it. He said, "This guy has B-29, B-50, and B-47 bomber experience. He can't go to KC-135s; he has to go to B-52s. It was already in concrete before my friend was able to do anything about it. I was due to leave for transition at Castle AFB, Sacramento, California in early September 1959. I was assigned to a B-52 wing at Sheppard AFB, Wichita Falls, Texas from 1960 to 1965 at which time I was transferred to Yokota AB, Japan as Director of Safety. I checked out in the North American Sabreliner T-39. Part of my job was to fly the Air Division Commander to visit tactical squadrons stationed in South Vietnam and Thailand as well as Japan, Korea, Okinawa and Philippines. I had two TDYs to Vietnam flying the Scatback Sabreliner operations that transported personnel and classified materials.

At Fuchu Air Station, Japan I served as Director of Safety for Fifth Air Force. During my briefing for Lieutenant General Seth McKee, a messenger summoned the General to the Command Post for an emergency. The USS Pueblo had just been seized by North Korea. I was directed to report to Osan AB, Korea as Director of Safety until the Pueblo situation was settled to the satisfaction of those in command in Washington, DC.

After my tour in Japan, I was reassigned as Assistant Deputy Commander for Materiel at Udorn, Royal Thailand Air Force Base for my last year of active duty. The Wing there consisted of two F-4 fighter squadrons, two RF-4 squadrons and an intelligence C-130 in addition to the base flight group. Our R-F4 squadrons were the first to receive the new laser cameras.

Following my reassignment stateside, I retired from the Air Force on September 1, 1969.

**Julian Anderson awaiting his
flight with Air Combat USA, 2005**

Julian Anderson checking the scheduling board for his flight.

BUDDY L. BROWN
Knoxville, Tennessee

Wife: Nancy

MY GREATEST ASS CHEWING

This is a short story about a long ass chewing, which I rightly deserved, by my Detachment Commander, Colonel Forrest W. "Whip" Wilson. I would like to state that the nickname "Whip" was really a term of endearment. He was by all accounts a great leader, an outstanding pilot and most importantly, an officer and a gentleman.

Whip Wilson was one of those dedicated pilot/commanders who, if he had his way, would extend the day from 24 to something over 26 hours. He was our Maintenance Officer at Laughlin AFB, and a Detachment Commander when we were deployed.

The story starts at Barksdale AFB, Louisiana. The Cuban recon program had been moved from McCoy AFB, Florida to Barksdale to operate the U-2 out of a SAC base and to provide better support. The Detachment Commander, Whip Wilson, was assigned four pilots, including Yours Truly. We were flying Agency (Central Intelligence Agency) "C" Model U-2s for several reasons; we could get to higher altitudes and could have an updated defensive system.

It was the middle of August and Louisiana was hot, muggy hot, sticky and nasty and humid. On that particular day I was primary mission pilot. I completed the normal mission planning and briefing in our Operations hangar monitored by Colonel Wilson. I left the Operations building early to start my crew rest for a

3:00 AM scheduled takeoff. This was normal takeoff time for the Cuban mission out of Barksdale in order to arrive at the target area with the right sun angle (approximately 30 degrees) and before the thunderstorms built up over the island. My wakeup call, pre-mission and maintenance briefings all went according to schedule. Colonel Wilson was in attendance during the briefings. I was dressed by the PSD (Physiological Support Division) folks and transported out to my aircraft.

Before I climbed up the ladder to get into the cockpit, a couple of the maintenance guys came up to me and asked if I would do them a favor. Without hesitation I said, "You bet." The maintenance guys said they would all have their cameras out on my return from the mission and would like for me to make a pullup for them. I thought about this request for a couple of seconds and said, "Okay, have your cameras ready." I would be making my first approach at about 10:30 a.m. I had said "Okay" because I knew that Colonel Wilson was never out on the ramp or runway during a recovery, so I felt confident I could pull this off.

I was strapped into my bird, went through the challenge and response checklist, taxied out to the runway and was cleared for takeoff. My takeoff was on schedule and I headed across the Gulf of Mexico for Cuba. For about three hours I photographed targets and flew my return flight back over the Gulf arriving at Barksdale right on time for my 10:30 recovery.

I called Barksdale Tower and requested a low approach prior to landing to verify my gear was down. The Tower approved. I also requested a pullup over the base to approximately 10,000 feet and again the Tower approved. I started my approach, gear down, flying down the active runway at about five to ten feet altitude. I approached the midpoint of the runway. All the troops were in several of our maintenance vehicles, cameras ready. When I was just opposite of where they were standing, I called the Tower and stated that I was going to make a pullup over the field to 10,000 feet. I requested re-entry to traffic for a full stop landing. Again the Tower approved.

I flew opposite the maintenance folks, pushed the power to full throttle and pulled the aircraft to a vertical attitude. With only 200-300 gallons of fuel remaining, the thrust of the J-75 was more than the weight of the aircraft. At 10,000 feet I recovered to level flight attitude and requested a pattern entry for a full stop landing. Again the Tower approved.

I flew my approach, was chased by Mobile Control and stopped on the runway. The maintenance guys ran to install the pogos, the manually installed gear that held the wings level on the ground. The Mobile Control Officer stated that Colonel Wilson had watched my pullup. That was my clue that I was in hot water. After the pogos were on, I taxied back to the hangar. As I stopped the aircraft and was unhooking my equipment, I saw a steaming Colonel Wilson standing at the base of my ladder. I could tell by his expression that he was really "steaming." I thought, "Colonel Wilson never came out for a recovery, but this time he did. Just my luck." I knew I was in for a big time chewing.

I climbed down the ladder and Colonel Wilson ordered me into a "brace" at full attention, eyes forward, no speaking. Remember, it was August in Louisiana and I still had my pressure suit on and it was hot, hot, hot. Colonel Wilson began to chew. The maintenance folks knew what was going on; they looked a little startled when I glanced their way. The chewing continued for what seemed like hours; actually it was probably only about 10 to 15 minutes. Sweat was running down my face and inside my suit. Colonel Wilson was also sweating from the hot sun and from the fierce tirade he was delivering.

There was no regulation against a fly-by pullup for a gear check, but clearly this was not the reason. Colonel Wilson pointed out during his lecture that grandstanding like I did out there would not be tolerated. His primary concern was that I was returning from an operational mission over Cuba. I had a load of exposed film to be removed and processed immediately. I believe his exact words were something like, "When you return from an operational mission, you land the aircraft and download the film. You do not show your ass flying around the flagpole." He was absolutely right on every count. It was really a dumb mistake on my part to make a pullup like that.

Whip finally finished chewing me out and said, "What do you have to say for yourself?" I was still in a brace. I said, "Colonel Wilson, you are absolutely right. I really enjoyed it, but I would never do it again." And I didn't.

When he cooled off, Colonel Wilson told me later that he just about had a heart attack because the J-75 engine makes a lot of noise. He didn't realize when I started my level-off at 10,000 feet I had pulled the throttle back to "idle." The level-off went from a tremendous volume to absolute silence. He said he thought I had flamed out. I think that ticked him off a bit more.

For a couple of days, I received some hard looks from Colonel Wilson, but after a couple more days, our dialog was back to normal. Colonel Wilson was later awarded the Koligan Trophy for his outstanding airmanship in a critical emergency during an operational mission out of Eielson AFB, Alaska. By the way, I repeat, that chewing I received from Colonel Wilson was well deserved.

COMMENTS BY ANTHONY MARTINEZ

I liked this memory of Buddy Brown's "debriefing" by Whip Wilson. I was especially fond of Whip. He was my backyard neighbor in base housing at Laughlin. Whip had the most spacious lawn of anyone on base and he manicured it weekly. As testimony to his fastidious nature, his hangar at the Operational Maintenance Squadron was a showplace at any hour of the day or night. He had set the standard and one by one the other buildings started to look better.

I had the opportunity to spend a week with Whip in 1963. Colonel DesPortes, 4080th Wing Commander, appointed us to survey several SAC bases for the purpose of relocating the McCoy AFB, Florida Cuban Surveillance Operation. We set out in a Lockheed T-33 (T-Bird) with about a week's worth of skivvies. At Barksdale AFB we received the royal treatment from the 2nd Bomb Wing Commanding Officer. The Base Commander there gave us the run of the base and agreed to give us two huge enclosed nose docks for our Physiological Support Division, pre-takeoff kitchen, pilots' briefing room and administration and operations offices. Whip got us all the necessary Aerospace Ground Equipment and vehicles; we were in business in short order. Last time I saw Whip was in Laughlin for the 4080th SRW reunion about ten or more years ago.

Buddy Brown

RICHARD (DICK) CALLAHAN
San Antonio, Texas

Wife: Sharon

It was an uneventful takeoff and initial cruise on my fifth or sixth training flight in the U-2. There had been an unusual amount of emphasis on the possibility of a flameout, the U-2 being a single engine aircraft. At an altitude of 70,000 feet the U-2 can glide approximately 250 miles with a dead engine. That being the case, finding and getting to an airfield is really no problem. We were constantly reminded to be aware of where we were in relation to a suitable landing strip.

I had not yet had my final training flight and Stand Board (Standardization Board) check flight so I was ensuring that I did everything by the book. Every procedure was new, to say nothing for the perspective of viewing the earth and navigating from an altitude of 70,000 feet.

The usual western training route was over El Paso, Texas to Phoenix, Arizona and then north. But on this particular flight that route was not open for NEPHO (photographic) training. Everyone always flew north to Salt Flat then west. Not this time, thanks to Jack Moon, Harding Smith and Ray Pierson who managed to stretch the string and find some NEPHO targets for my training flight. They also planned my day celestial training leg coming back west so that when I finished, I would be close to my letdown and landing at Laughlin AFB, Texas.

Everything was going great. I was experiencing some new and different NEPHO runs other than the usual El Paso, Lordsburg, Tucson, etc. I had finished my NEPHO run over Hot Springs, Arkansas. I turned south for my last run heading towards Shreveport, Louisiana where I would start my celestial navigation leg.

In 10 years flying Air Force single engine jet fighters, I had never experienced a flameout, but my luck had just run out. This was to be my first flameout. I know we had practiced this and had even shut the engine down on an earlier training flight. We talked about the U-2 being prone to flameout at high altitudes, but if you just keep your cool, the aircraft can be restarted.

To restart the engine, I knew I needed to keep the airspeed up, the engine wind milling at about 35 percent on the tachometer and electrical power to the battery. There is definitely no restarting without power. I notified FAA of my emergency, stopcocked the throttle, and set up my glide for Barksdale AFB, Louisiana. Air start altitude was 35,000 feet. I could see Barksdale in front of me so I knew I would arrive over the runway with plenty of altitude in case I wasn't able to restart the engine.

I attempted my first restart at 35,000 feet, with no indication of an air start when the engine tailpipe temperature (EGT) did not come off the stop. With a sinking feeling in my stomach, I recalled how "everyone" had assured me that flameouts were common and after air start, "they said" you just climb back to altitude and continue the training flight. Again I reviewed the restart checklist precisely, carefully checking each and every point. After several attempts, it became apparent this bird was not going to restart.

I was approaching Barksdale and requested FAA permission to go to the Barksdale Tower radio frequency. I informed the Tower that my U-2 had flamed out and I had not been able to restart the engine. I requested permission to make a dead engine landing on their runway and asked them to notify the 2nd Air Force Command Post of my situation. Barksdale Tower gave me clearance for a flameout landing on Runway 12 and advised me their winds were light and variable. Passing through 20,000 feet, I informed Barksdale that I was continuing to attempt air start as I descended over the runway. The Tower had me in sight and informed me that they observed something streaming from my aircraft, probably fuel. Needless to say, I ceased attempting air start.

I set up my flameout landing pattern with left hand orbits over the landing approach for Runway 12. As I descended, the Tower advised me there was construction equipment off the left side of the approach to Runway 12. Since winds were light and variable, I requested and received permission to land on Runway 30 so construction would not be a factor. I arrived at high key over the end of Runway 30 at 1,700 feet above the runway. I started my turn for the left hand pattern and everything seemed ideal until on final. "Oh, shit! I'm going to be short," I yelled aloud to myself. I checked my airspeed and saw it was seven to eight knots high. Whew! I bled off my airspeed to the desired amount and crossed the end of the runway with altitude to spare. I landed 1,500 to 2,000 feet down the runway with no mobile chase car to call off my final few feet of altitude to me, another first for me on this flight. I already had more of those then I needed.

After stopping on the runway, I was suddenly surrounded by more full colonels than I had ever seen before. I turned off all the switches and inserted my seat ejection safety pins, opened the canopy, disconnected my oxygen supply, shrugged out of my parachute and prepared to exit the aircraft. Those terrific maintenance guys put up a ladder to the cockpit. I climbed out and took off my pressure suit helmet. Someone asked if I needed anything. I replied, "We usually are medically prescribed two beers after every high flight." Sure enough, they sent someone to get me a beer.

The Barksdale maintenance guys were unfamiliar with the peculiarities of the U-2. They wanted to put a huge rope around the nose wheel and tow the U-2 clear of the runway. I told them that was a definite "no, no." We would have to unlock the tail wheel and push the aircraft. They did exactly that and parked my bird next to a hangar. Maintenance cordoned off the plane and stationed a guard next to it.

A maintenance team arrived from Laughlin AFB. They found and repaired a ruptured fuel line. I flew the bird home the next day, but I didn't get credit for my celestial training leg and had to do it over. Fortunately, there was no flameout on the next flight.

Sharon and Dick Callahan

ORVILLE CLANCY
Portland, Oregon

Wife: Betty

Orville submitted the following as a summary of a story written by Ray B. Sitton in the Aerospace Historian, June 1978.

In the early morning hours of the late 1950's, a Republic of China Air Force (ROCAF) pilot was on his first night navigation training mission and experienced an engine flameout over southwest Colorado. He went through his emergency procedures and descended to the altitude for an engine restart. As he descended closer to the mountain peaks below, he continued several unsuccessful engine restarts. The pilot decided to descend through the cloud cover and hopefully make a successful emergency landing.

As he broke through the cloud cover, he saw lights of the small Cortez, Colorado Airport, the only airfield for many miles. Without radio contact, he circled the field in preparation for an emergency landing. As he turned on final approach to the runway, he determined that he had sufficient hydraulic pressure to lower the landing gear. With the gear locked into the down position, he then realized he had lined up with the lights of Main Street, Cortez and not with the airfield. He raised the gear and turned toward the field. He tried to lower the gear but was unsuccessful this time. The U-2 continued to descend silently, unannounced and undetected, to a belly landing at the Cortez Airport.

The ROCAF pilot disconnected all his cables, hoses and harnesses, a task usually performed with help from the PSD guys. He exited the aircraft and walked toward the lighted airport office in his pressure suit and helmet.

To the shocked night manager and a friend who was visiting, the ROCAF pilot appeared like a space alien from the movies. In the excitement of the moment, the pilot had difficulty with his command of English. However, he remembered his instructions concerning security of his aircraft in the event of an unscheduled landing. So he yelled, "MAXIMUM SECURITY! MAXIMUM SECURITY!"

The manager's friend knocked over his chair and ran for the back door. The manager shouted, "COME NO CLOSER! COME NO CLOSER!"

After both the airport manager and the pilot regained their composure, they were able to arrange for security of the U-2. The pilot called for a USAF recovery crew at Laughlin AFB to retrieve him and his aircraft. The following day, the U-2 and the pilot departed Cortez inside a C-124 transport with many of the residents of Cortez on hand to witness the departure.

WARD GRAHAM
(Deceased May 8, 2004)

The following was submitted by Ward prior to his death.

MY FLAMEOUT LANDING

September 22, 1965 was a day that has remained etched in my memory. The deep blue sky was peppered with cumulus clouds. It was a vision of tranquility contrary to the imminent danger that I faced. My black, long-winged airplane silently approached the runway at Flagstaff Pulliam Field, Arizona. I circled once and headed in for a dead-engine landing on Runway 21, almost 7,000 feet of asphalt. I glided my Black Dragon down from above 70,000 feet to this field on the high mesa of Arizona, 7,014 feet above sea level.

The probabilities of a successful U-2 landing on such a short runway at such high elevation without power was slight. I thought at the time the odds were against me as I was considering I did not have flaps, speed brakes, drag chute nor communication from the Control Tower. I did not even have communication from another U-2 pilot in a Mobile Control chase vehicle about wind direction and speed.

About 40 minutes prior to this landing, I had been on a celestial navigation leg westbound about six hours into a routine training mission. I had completed a series of sextant shots on the sun and was recording data on my map. I noticed the shadows changing on the chart. I looked up and discovered the airplane in a 60-degree left bank. The autopilot had disconnected. I reached for the controls to roll back to level flight, and I heard the sound no jet pilot wants to hear--the spooling down of the engine. The extreme bank angle had caused a flameout.

My pressure suit inflated and my face piece fogged over. I began to shut down systems in the airplane to conserve battery power for an expected air start of the engine in the denser air below 40,000 feet. I made an emergency call but I received no response from Phoenix Center. I began to make large spirals around a town I saw on the ground. I descended through 40,000 feet, and initiated one of several air start attempts on the normal and the emergency fuel system. With a sinking feeling, I discovered that the engine was not going to start. I was down to 30,000 feet and noticed an airfield that just South of the town I had been orbiting. I did not know what town this was nor the length of the runway, but leaving the "bird in hand" was not an option. Due to the celestial navigation leg and the confusion of the first few minutes following the flameout, I had become lost, something few pilots like to admit. I had no idea how far it might be to a longer runway.

Praying hard to the Lord for deliverance, I continued to descend toward the town's runway. By this time the battery was dead and no communication with the ground was possible. I guessed at the altitude for high key and tried to get some action from the flaps and speed brakes. There was virtually no hydraulic pressure available to operate these systems. The U-2 has no backup hydraulic system. I knew that with the engine dead, the chance was very slim of a successful drag chute deployment.

By what I can only attribute as help from the hand of God, I made a normal, no flap, flameout pattern. I touched down on the first 1,500 feet of a rather short runway at Pulliam Field, the civilian airport at Flagstaff, Arizona. There was no convenient taxiway on which to turn off so I stopped on the runway. After I landed, some firemen and mechanics came to the airplane. We were able to move it off the runway and prop the wings up on 55-gallon drums in one of the hangars on the field.

I had an interesting two days in Flagstaff staying with the firemen at the local station and being interviewed by a reporter from Phoenix. Investigators found a valve had failed in the fuel control. The failure was such that the engine would continue running in the air, but once fuel flow was interrupted it could not be restored. The real mystery to me was why the autopilot disconnected with no previous warning.

Three days later I flew the airplane back to Davis Monthan AFB without further incident. As a result of this flight, I was selected as Strategic Air Command "Pilot of the Month" and received a Distinguished Flying Cross. More importantly, I have been able to credit God for saving my life.

PATRICK J. HALLORAN
Colorado Springs, Colorado

LOSS OF OXYGEN AT 63,000 FEET

After I finished my initial U-2 checkout in mid-1957 at Laughlin AFB, I proceeded through the advanced training in long-range navigation and photo run sorties. Missions of this type were normally six to eight hours' duration and usually involved a number of visual runs on photo targets using pilotage navigation, followed by an extended celestial navigation leg on the return flight.

On one such sortie I departed early in the morning from Laughlin AFB and I climbed to altitude in a northern direction towards Dyess AFB. After reaching an initial cruise altitude of 62,000 to 63,000 feet, I began to concentrate on visual navigation to my first set of photo targets in the panhandle part of Texas. All was going well when I became aware of an increase in my rate of breathing to the point of obvious hyperventilation. This would sometimes occur during the period of pre-breathing preflight preparation while wearing the pressure suit. I think most pilots experienced a degree of claustrophobia and hyperventilation at one time or another in their early days in the pressure suit. For all who did have this experience, it was a very uncomfortable period of anxiety and difficult to control. Definitely it was a "mind over matter" situation. I had been bothered by this phenomenon a few times, but immediately recognized the indications when I encountered it this time in flight--a cold, clammy feeling on the skin.

The recognition of hyperventilation gave me an immediate surge of adrenaline and an awareness that something was drastically wrong and required my undivided attention. I began a quick mental review of my situation and attempted to force myself to return to a normal breathing rate. This procedure normally worked on the ground, but I suddenly felt the breathing bladder of my pressure suit helmet collapse around my head. I knew that I was in serious trouble. I was at 29,000 feet cabin pressure and was OUT OF OXYGEN.

I frantically checked the primary and secondary aircraft oxygen system gauges and valves but everything indicated "normal". My mind was racing to find a fix or an alternative plan but nothing was making much sense. My hyperventilation, while attempting to breathe through the anti-suffocation valve in the helmet, was increasing to the point that I was becoming aware of serious hypoxia symptoms, the "old gun barrel" view of the world as my vision narrowed.

I went through a mental process of looking for a means of immediately getting to a lower altitude. I knew that I couldn't "fly" the aircraft to a meaningful, lower altitude as it would take too long and I wouldn't retain consciousness. I discarded a plan for an autopilot descent. That would take too long and would probably result in a flameout if I wasn't capable of making throttle adjustments. I remember considering either stopcocking the engine and attempting an emergency descent or bailing out. There was no ejection seat then. I realized that both options would have immediately moved my physiological altitude from 29,000 feet to about 63,000 feet. Survival would be unlikely. I probably went through this review process in seconds. The time of useful consciousness at that altitude is short and I could tell I was running out of time.

I was frantic and tried to think of an alternate plan. I reached for one of the cockpit mirrors to check my faceplate. My vision was seriously deteriorating and my physical actions were getting a bit spastic. I reached to adjust the mirror; my arm jerked and I hit the mirror with my hand so hard that it grabbed my attention. The mirror was now aimed at the lower right side of my body where the oxygen hose cluster on the pressure suit was located. Looking in the mirror I was startled to see in the shadows that my faceplate breathing hose was disconnected from the cluster and was dangling free.

With all the concentration I could bring to bear, and with an awareness that this was going to be my last shot, I managed to twist around, and with both hands, reconnected the breathing hose. Relief was immediate as my helmet filled with oxygen pressure and my sight and breathing returned to normal. I had an overwhelming sense of relief that I could continue the long training mission without further difficulty. When I landed seven hours later and relayed the incident to the Lift Support and Safety folks, I was roundly criticized for not aborting the mission and returning immediately to the base. At that stage of our training, what did we know?

The problem, as I learned later, was the procedure for connecting the individual hoses to the cluster. It was a simple "press to insert" and then twist to drop the "dog ears" into a retaining slot. My hose had not been twisted far enough to drop the "ears" into the locking slot. It remained in that intermediate, though still functional position, until my cockpit movements popped it loose. Subsequently, the little spring safety clip was added to the assembly. It could not be installed unless the hose was in the fully locked detent position.

For some reason, I didn't think of activating the emergency oxygen bailout bottle because if I had thought of it, I'm sure I would have done it. However, it wouldn't have been any help because no oxygen would have gone to my helmet anyway. I've had a chilling thought of that incident if I had not been able to correct the problem. I was on autopilot, on a western heading with enough fuel to fly several thousand miles before the plane would have flamed out. I wonder what part of the Pacific Ocean that would have been! The Safety Office would have had one hell of a time trying to figure that one out.

This one scared the hell out of me after the fact, but in those early days in 1957, I suspect that there were lots of incidents like that which didn't get publicized too much. It was part of the "development" of the system I guess, so when someone had a major problem, they just said, "OK, we'll fix that and let's press on."

Marking the one-millionth foot of film shot over Cuba in 1963 are Left to right: Colonel DesPortes, Major Halloran, Jim Combs-Hycon Tech Rep, CM Sgt Max Burns, CM Sgt Willie Haynes, Kneeling: Airmen Jim Lobig, Jim Manis, and Joseph "Rooster" Robinson.

Laverton RAAF Station Australia, 1965. Celebrating 1000 hours in the U-2 for George Bull. L to R: Ray Pierson, Line Chief Okie Barnes, Crew Chief (name unknown), Ed Purdue, Pat Halloran, and George Bull.

Beijing, China, 2004. Pat Halloran views U-2 flown by Jack Chang of the ROCAF. Chang was shot down by a SA-2 on January 10, 1965.

ROGER HERMAN
Fort Worth, Texas

Wife: Monica

WOULDN'T THIS BURN YOU UP?

During the last years the 4080th SRW was located at Laughlin AFB, we were tasked with a project to map a number of areas in the upper Midwest. The project name eludes me but, as best I can remember it, it was in the area of Ohio, Wisconsin, Minnesota and maybe some of the fringe areas next to those states. Clear weather that would provide fine photographic reconnaissance was always a problem in these northern states. Consequently, whenever the weather forecast was favorable, any pilot scheduled for a long duration training sortie would be tasked to plan a NEPHO Run (photo recon) to take high-resolution photographs of as much of the not-yet-photographed area as possible.

On this day I happened to catch such a mission. However, the weather was only forecast to be somewhat favorable early in the day. Therefore, I was scheduled for a takeoff several hours before daylight. I rolled out of bed at "O Dark Thirty", (translation: very, very early). I departed home in the black starlit night enroute to the quiet Laughlin flight line. I had my usual medical check from the Flight Surgeon and then my high protein breakfast of steak and eggs. I always looked forward to that because the cooks in the PSD always sent us off with a wonderful meal designed to last many hours. The PSD personnel helped me into my pressure suit through pre-flight by the Mobile Control Pilot and PSD hookup and check of my life support equipment and system after I was in the U-2 cockpit. Engine start and takeoff were on schedule.

The "as planned routine" ended almost immediately after takeoff when "you know what" hit the fan. I heard a "whoop" followed by a loud "whoosh" and a rush of very warm air. I reached down and placed the pressurization switch to Ram Air. That stopped the rush of warm air, but it also left me without cabin pressurization. That's because pressurization and cockpit heating come from a bleed valve that siphons compressed air from the sixteenth stage of the J-57 engine. My switching to Ram Air shut off that system entirely. Of course, it solved one problem but created another. Without pressurization, I couldn't go to altitude. Recommendation from Ground Support was that I return the pressurization switch to Normal. So, I did that, and it was a really BIG MISTAKE. The extremely hot air was still flooding the cockpit. The air conditioning system had swallowed its bleed air-mixing valve. This meant that no air-conditioned air could be mixed with engine bleed air. I immediately returned the switch to Ram Air but now that did not correct the problem. Within a couple of seconds, I knew the cabin pressurization and heating system was not stuck in full hot bleed air from the engine. Believe me, it was really hot! I couldn't remember the temperature of the bleed air as it comes off the compressor section of the engine, but I believe it was in the 200 degree range. The goal was to maintain absolute minimum power to reduce the bleed air as much as possible. There was no putting down the landing gear, opening the speed brakes and trying to burn off fuel to get to landing weight pronto. Even absolute minimum power produced unbearably hot air.

It was still several hours before daybreak and ground support decided we would try to hold off on the over-weight landing until it was light. Along about this time, probably 20 minutes into the flight, most of which was at a near idle power setting, it was suggested that I might try stuffing my gloves into the air outlet ducts that were accessible. If I had been able to do it, the hot air probably would have burned up the gloves. But I never got that far. When I took my first glove off, I found the yoke already too hot to grip with my bare hand. Fortunately, I had not taken my face piece off. But, even with my face shield in place, my face was still extremely warm. However, thankfully, I was being cooled somewhat and breathing the cool oxygen from my life support system.

I informed the Mobile Control Officer and Squadron Operations about how hot I was feeling. After another 20 minutes, following a discussion with the Supervisor of Flying (SOF), the Flight Surgeon and other consultants, we arrived at the conclusion that it might not be safe, physiologically, to wait another hour or more for a daylight landing. So, even though I still had in excess of 1,000 gallons of fuel, the decision was made to land as soon as possible. Usually the computations of flight speeds for the landing pattern and final approach were computed from the fuel remaining reading and done with little effort by the pilot. On this day, I had a lot of help determining my landing pattern, base leg and final approach speeds. Fortunately, I accomplished a rather smooth landing. During the landing rollout after touchdown, every circuit breaker in the cockpit popped! As soon as I stopped my roll, I opened the canopy. What a relief to feel that cool, early morning Texas air. When my pressure suit was removed, the outsides of my ankles were extremely red. If they weren't considered burns, they were the next thing to it and remained that way for another 10 days. Afterwards, I consumed about a quart of orange juice.

All's well that ends well and I could look forward to my next "exciting" U-2 flight.

GERALD E. "JERRY" MCILMOYLE
Venice Beach, Florida

LOW FUEL WARNING LIGHT

Night celestial navigation training was another challenge in learning to fly the missions of the U-2. It was exciting to enter the navigation training room managed by Lieutenant Colonel (Lt. Col.) Don Todt. In those days there were no navigation aids in the areas of the world in which the reconnaissance missions were flown.

In some respects we were like Christopher Columbus, venturing into the unknown and using celestial navigation to get us into the sky and back to earth. I was excited about knowing how well I would be able to learn and apply godly navigation directly related to mission accomplishment and my own personal survival. Contemplating flying the U-2 on 3,600 nautical-mile flights without navigation aids really got my attention. I understood that celestial navigation would be critical to successful mission completion.

I felt inspired as I entered the navigation flight planning room. I had dreamed of flying since I was in elementary school. I was learning a navigational device that has not changed much from the days sailors used it more than 600 years ago. Quentin Stokes taught me the fundamental heavenly navigation techniques. I was lucky because "Quent" knew his technology. He included the underlying philosophy of celestial navigation and the technique of a good instructor.

Quent was, and still is, a happy, easygoing guy with a ready, wry grin. I sometimes had to give him my "double take" to determine whether he was telling me something factual or if he was pulling my leg. In any case, Quent-the-Expert, taught me well, from basics through sophisticated application of the navigational system. Quent went the extra mile with me, too. He would meet me at night at the squadron to take hand-held sextant fixes on stars from our fixed location. We knew that the U-2 on autopilot was seeking the set airspeed and heading. This "seeking" had a sine wave curve of approximately two minutes' duration. Quent taught me to be patient. We had to keep the star centered in the bubble for a two-minute period and then average out the elevation readings recorded by centering and aligning the sextant's indices.

I never was able to shoot a star and have my reading be precisely my location, no matter how hard I concentrated. Quent's indoctrination made me realize what he was teaching me; my celestial star shots were going to yield my "most probable position" but not my exact location. He thus convinced me that the best navigation approach was a three-star fix with one of the three stars as close to my line of flight as possible. He said this would give me a good speed line. The other two stars should be preferred so that their Line of Position (LOP) formed as close to and equal to lateral triangle as possible. The small triangle derived from dropping a perpendicular from the apex of the triangle to the opposite side would be my most probable position and close to my real location. I don't know why but, to me, this navigation technique was exciting, intriguing and fascinating. I would have the knowledge of being able to navigate anywhere in the world by lining up with the stars. Of course, this gift of navigation was basic to our squadron's mission of flying over the North and South Poles. I could span the oceans of the world and stretch my U-2 over the Amazon jungle. I could traverse the periphery of the Soviet Union, China, North Korea, North Viet Nam, anywhere.

On this special night of flying the U-2, I was "charged up." I was going to test my first attempt to navigate using three star fixes on two separate night celestial legs. Before the flight I had a relaxing dinner with my wife, Patty, and our two children, Patrick and Ruthie. I left them about three hours before takeoff. Most of the squadron was flying or in support of our celestial training this particular night, including the Squadron Commander, Buzz Curry. The wives were going to play bridge into the wee hours of the morning. I had to wait for the heavens to get dark. I told Patty as I left, "If I ever get reincarnated, I want to come back as an Air Force pilot's wife!" Patty laughed. She knew who had the fun job and it wasn't her.

My first stop after leaving home was the Physiological Support Division (PSD), the Flight Surgeon's domain. The Flight Surgeon and coincidentally my cousin, Colonel Harvey W. Hertz, gave me my preflight physical. Harvey gave me the thumbs up and sent me to the dressing room to begin my two hours of pre-breathing oxygen. This pre-breathing oxygen process removes as much nitrogen from the body as is reasonably possible. It prevented the "bends" in case of cabin depressurization at altitude. I walked from PSD carrying my portable oxygen supply to the waiting PSD transport van that drove me directly to my assigned U-2. My U-2 had already been preflighted by a fellow U-2 pilot and was set for takeoff. As I stepped out of the PSD van, I noticed the unique Texas night sky. It was clear and cloudless, with a million stars forming an enormous black dome over Laughlin AFB. What a sight for celestial navigational flight in this high-flying airplane. I was "wired" and I was anxious to get airborne.

Everything had gone so smoothly; I anticipated a flight that would be satisfying in every respect. On climbout, I started trimming up the U-2 so I would have the best possible platform for my celestial training. I was approaching 45,000 feet altitude and was ready to turn on the autopilot when the fuel warning light lit up--a bright orange glow. What the hell? A quick glance at the fuel counter told me I had used 45 gallons of fuel since start engine. The light was correct. I had 40 gallons of fuel before flameout. I immediately retarded my throttle to idle, turned back towards Laughlin, notified FAA and declared an emergency.

Once informed of my traffic and cleared to Laughlin, I cancelled my clearance and dialed our squadron radio frequency to inform Mobile Control of my problem. My eyes were set on the red fuel button; I was down to 35 gallons of fuel. I radioed Control that I intended to set up a flameout landing pattern and land. The calm, controlled voice of the Mobile Control pilot talked to me in a monotone voice—always a monotone voice for emergencies. "Winds are light and variable, no traffic in the pattern and you are cleared to land Number 1."

When I arrived at high key for my flameout pattern, I estimated I had remaining 20 gallons of fuel. I thought to myself, "No sweat! I've got it made." I concentrated and focused on making as smooth a landing as I possibly could. I was at maximum gross weight for landing; U-2 pilots considered that a "no-no." We thought of the bird as being made out of aluminum foil. Touchdown and rollout were smooth and I breathed a grateful sigh of relief. I brought the aircraft to a stop and the engine quit; it was a flameout from fuel starvation. My fuel counter indicated I still had another 5 gallons of fuel. Well, maybe not!

Opening the canopy, I anticipated exiting the aircraft and receiving praise for my absolute skill and cunning. I brought the bird back on the ground without damage, right? But, right then the Squadron Commander jumped above the cockpit railing with a pissed-off look on his face. In a pissed-off voice and similar demeanor, he asked me, "Why did you shut it down?" Through the yelling, he told me emphatically, "We will have to close the runway while we get a tow vehicle out here to tow the airplane back to the ramp." I replied, "Sir, I did not shut it down. The plane flamed out all by itself."

Without comment the Commander's head withdrew and the roar diminished. Was I ever glad that a maintenance inspection found the fuel shutoff valve in the OFF position. I had taken off with only 95 of the 1335 gallons of fuel normally onboard. As I rode my bike home that night, I felt proud of myself for getting the bird back on the ground undamaged. One of the pilots in the squadron burst that bubble the next morning when he informed me, "That's your job!" From then on the maintenance inspection plate was left open and checking the fuel shutoff switch in the "ON" position became a pre-flight checklist item.

ERRATIC AIRSPEED INDICATOR

I had just taken off from Laughlin AFB at about 2230 hours on a night celestial navigation training flight. As I was climbing out, I set up the aircraft so that it was in trim and holding 160 knots indicated airspeed. The string outside the canopy was centered with the airflow indicator line and was aligned with the longitudinal axis of the aircraft. It was just an old simple string on this sophisticated aircraft. The wings were level and the aircraft was holding its airspeed and heading, flying hands off with only a gentle correction now and then.

As I passed 45,000 feet indicated altitude, I engaged the autopilot, checked that my VOR indicator was tuned to the Cotulla VOR and the pointer was dead on the nose of the aircraft. By then I passed about 50,000 feet and started to set up my sextant for taking my first heading star shot. The indicators pitched down. I usually flew with one hand on the aircraft control yoke. I over controlled the autopilot, then disconnected it and did a rapid crosscheck of the instruments. Everything was normal, aircraft attitude OK, vertical velocity OK, but the airspeed indicator was rapidly vacillating between no airspeed and exceeding limits. The altitude and vertical velocity indicators work off the same pitot static system and were indicating normal. Within a few seconds, I decided that I did not want to climb higher. I cut the power back and started a descent, turning back toward Laughlin.

Precise trimming the aircraft was to me critical to a successful flight. It aligned the aircraft so that it flew straight through the air and not sideways. Trimming in the U-2 was even more important because all those aircraft were handmade. None flew straight unless trimmed for straight flight. Trimming enabled the autopilot to better maintain a heading and a Mach number. It also made the indicators from the sextant celestial readings more accurate. Trimming also affected the gravity flow of the fuel stored in the U-2's wings. An out of trim aircraft resulted in uneven flow of fuel because the high wing's fuel drained to the sump pump near the engine faster than to the low wing. A truly simple solution was devised to align the longitudinal axis of the aircraft with the direction of flight. A white line was precisely lined up with the longitudinal axis of the aircraft and then finely etched into the top of the cockpit canopy from fore to aft. Yes, an ordinary string was attached so that when in flight the airflow across the canopy would cause the string to align with that airflow. If the string was not aligned with the line etched in the canopy then the rudder trim tab was used to align the aircraft with the airflow and the string would indicate alignment with the canopy line. A simple string was used to give pilots clear assurance that the aircraft was flying straight through the air and not sideways.

When I contacted the Squadron, the first advice I received after reporting my situation was, "Try not to stall it or exceed 220 knots Indicated Airspeed." Although it wasn't a laughing matter to me, I said to myself, "Shit, I already know that!"

The next problem was how to land without stalling or exceeding aircraft limitations. As I passed 45,000 feet altitude in descent, I engaged the gust control to give me an extra margin of safe airspeeds I could fly. It was a clear night with light winds so turbulence was minimum. As I approached Laughlin AFB, Squadron Commander Hayden C. "Buzz" Curry came on the radio and asked me to describe my situation. I explained my circumstances and we discussed burning off some fuel at 10,000 feet so I would have time to eject if the aircraft became uncontrollable. We decided that was my best option and they would get the U-3A launched. By the time Curly Evans was airborne in the U-3A, I had reduced my fuel load by half and we decided to attempt to land my U-2.

As I made my approach to landing, Curly was to fly formation with me and call out my airspeed. I was afraid of that approach because of the delay in reaction time, and I was uncertain that his airspeed would be precisely the same as mine. I requested to fly formation on his U-3A right down to landing. Curly was to fly five knots above our computed landing speed based upon my fuel load at that time. I also wanted Curly to rendezvous with me, not me with him. That way I would always know my airspeed in descent. I could get out of gust control and set up for landing. It all worked like a charm and we got my bird back safely on the ground. On postflight inspection our maintenance guys found a small flake of rust in the pitot tube.

The next day "Goog" Boyd, from Maintenance, made a formal presentation to me of the offending rust flake. It was only slightly larger than the head of a pin. It was hard to believe something so small could cause such an enormous problem, but it sure did.

CROSSWIND LANDING

Crosswind landings in the U-2 were a real challenge whenever the component was above 15 knots. After reading about crosswind landings in *Plane and Pilot*, I recalled a crosswind landing I made in a U-2 at Plattsburg AFB, NY in 1959. I was returning to base from an air sampling flight near the North Pole only to find a crosswind of 15-20 knots, gusting to 35. The U-2's maximum crosswind tolerance was 25 knots because of the tandem landing gear. The main gear, located just below the cockpit, and the rudder-linked steerable tail wheel, were in line and on the aircraft's centerline.

My ground controller had computed the crosswind right at 25 knots and reviewed the landing procedure with me, the danger being weather vaning upwind. This was due to the high, large vertical stabilizer, rear center of gravity and lack of tail wheel traction (only six inch hard rubber wheels).

The technique was to land with full flaps on the downwind side of the runway in a combination crab and slip to kill the drift. Once I touched down, I was to immediately put the downwind wing tip skid on the runway and hold it with full down wind aileron deflection and full downwind rudder. Luckily, Plattsburg had a significantly crowned runway center which helped counter the weather vaning. I was able to stop my aircraft on the runway though it had slightly weather vaned. My U-2 and I had crossed the centerline and were headed for the "boonies."

I have landed many places in the world, but I still remember every single second of that landing. A crosswind landing in a U-2 can be a memorable event when it is successful.

Jerry McIlmoyle receiving an award, 1960

L to R: Jerry McIlmoyle, Danny Schmarr, Ray Lodin and Ed Dixon, November 1963.

JACK D. NOLE
(Deceased June 8, 1996)

Widow: Celeste

The following was submitted by Robert Ingram.

Colonel Jack Nole, commander of the 4028th Strategic Recon Squadron, had the distinction of landing the first U-2 aircraft at Laughlin AFB. He also earned the distinction of the first military pilot to safely bail out of a U-2. He recorded the highest altitude parachute escape in history on that ejection.

On September 26, 1957 Colonel Nole had been airborne approximately 35 minutes. He was on what was to have been a routine test flight following maintenance performed on the flight controls and the engine. He was nearing 53,000 feet altitude. Colonel Nole was in contact with Laughlin tower as he began his checkout of the various systems. Without warning the aircraft nosed over and began plunging toward the earth. The flap position indicator showed the flaps to be fully extended but he had not selected that position. Corrective action had no effect on the falling aircraft. The tail section separated from the fuselage. He reported the condition to Laughlin tower and their response was "Bail out, bail out!" He thought, "I wonder what they think I am trying to do."

Ejecting from the U-2 was no simple process. Each hose, tube and connector had to be individually disconnected, including the shoulder harness and radio connection. Nole had shut down the engine when he first observed the trouble. His pressure suit had inflated and further restricted movement in the cockpit. He struggled to release himself from the various connections then released the canopy and exited the aircraft.

He faced another problem after he had ejected from the aircraft. At this altitude, he had two choices. One, he could pull the cord to open his parachute and allow himself to get oxygen from his emergency tank. Two, he could free fall and risk suffocation. There was a possibility of freezing to death if he opened the parachute at such high altitude. He remembered his training—any action was better than no action, so he pulled the ripcord.

As he descended, he was swinging alternately face up then face down. For the first time in his 17 years, in the cockpit, he became violently airsick. When he landed, he came down on his seat pack on his bottom. Investigators said it would have broken his back without the pack.

As a result of Colonel Nole's incident, many changes were made in the U-2, the most significant being the ejection seat. The first U-2 did not have ejection seats, but "the powers that be" decided later to install ejection seats. Quick disconnects were also incorporated for all systems and harnesses.

Colonel Nole's survival contributed to the future survival of countless other pilots.

CHRIS POCOCK
Uxbridge, United Kingdom

The following is an article that first appeared in the United States Air Force Yearbook, 1997. Chris has authorized use of this article.

RIDING THE DRAGON LADY

We had been airborne for almost 50 minutes before I really appreciated just how high we were! As we cruised steadily across California's San Joaquin Valley, I glanced down and to the right. Way below, an airliner leaving a thick contrail was intersecting our flight track. As it passed underneath us, that jet seemed no bigger to the naked eye, than if I had been looking up at it from ground level.

In fact, this was no illusion. The airliner was at 35,000 feet; whereas, we were above 70,000 feet!

We were 50 minutes out of Beale AFB, and I was riding backseat in the U-2ST trainer 80-1064, call sign "Pinon 72". From the front cockpit, my Instructor Pilot (IP), Major Brandon King, explained that the Pinon grows at higher elevations than any other tree. The U-2 Dragon Lady is similarly found at higher altitudes than any other flying machine, except the occasional SR-71 Blackbird from the same stable, Lockheed Martin's famous Skunk Works.

The enlarged and improved U-2R model which first flew in 1967, proved to be an unrivalled platform for a new generation of reconnaissance sensors. It offered a stable environment for sensitive, long-range side looking cameras, radars and signals-gathering devices. They could listen and look further from the U-2's lofty perch than if they were carried on more conventional craft. Most importantly, the U-2 could hang around— operational flights usually last for more than nine hours. Blackbirds, satellites and unmanned aerial vehicles come and go, but no one has yet devised a more cost-effective method of airborne intelligence gathering.

Such are the rewards of long-endurance, high-altitude flight. But there are also penalties, and I was wearing one of them, the S1031 pressure suit and helmet. It's bulky and inconvenient, forty pounds of cumbersome restriction to the everyday movements that one takes for granted (including bodily functions). It's also a virtually complete barrier to sensible communication with the outside world, save through the intercom system. But if you want to survive a cockpit depressurization at high altitude, you don't leave the ground without it.

U-2 pilots learn to live with it, and I seemed to be coping quite well too, thanks to the previous day's very thorough induction into the strange world of pressurized protection at Beale's Physiological Support Division (PSD).

Following a stringent medical, I had first been introduced to the S1 ejection seat. This is a zero-zero device for low-altitude escape, but if a high-altitude ejection is ever required, it is designed to descend from the heavens with its occupant still attached, who thus benefits from a continuing supply of oxygen for breathing and suit pressure from two emergency cylinders. At 15,000 feet, aneroids automatically command release of the body-restraining straps, and one floats free as the parachute deploys.

Then I was invited to change into long white underwear, and don the suit itself. This procedure requires the active cooperation of two PSD technicians who do most of the tugging, stretching, attaching and zipping. From the inside out, the suit consists of a nylon inner layer, a polyurethane-coated pressure layer, a restraint layer of adjustable mesh-patterned nylon, an immersion layer and an exterior cover of yellow-colored nomex.

Supervised by Dick Cook, a veteran PSD supervisor, my assistants pulled on my boots and clip-fitted the gloves to the suits' rigid metal attachment rings. Then I squeezed my head with some difficulty into the goldfish-bowl helmet. This too was attached to the suit, and now I was ready to go "on the hose". I flopped into a semi-reclined leather chair next to the oxygen console.

Nothing really prepares you for the sense of detachment which ensues once the faceplate has been latched down and the oxygen starts flowing. People carried on conversations a few feet in front of me, but I couldn't hear them. They sometimes moved out of my limited field of vision. I found that I could only follow them by raising my arms to the helmet and physically pushing or pulling the helmet sideways. The sound of my breathing was amplified through the built-in headset and soon became monotonous.

According to Major King, some prospective U-2 pilots never get past this initial suit up. A member of the 1st Reconnaissance Squadron (Training), King manages the recruitment of the 20 or so pilots who join the Wing each year. "One in ten of them feel uncomfortable and get claustrophobic. They become disconcerted hearing their own breathing. We call it the Darth Vader Syndrome," he told me.

My indoctrination at PSD continued with a visit to the altitude chamber. I was positioned in the chamber and the "climb" began. At 20,000 feet, Cook invited me to remove the faceplate for a demonstration of the insidious effects of hypoxia. Then the ascent continued to 70,000 feet, then down to 55,000 feet, whereupon Cook simulated an explosive decompression. The chamber fogged over, though I could still see the glass of water which had been placed on a nearby ledge and which was now boiling vigorously. My body fluids would have met the same fate had I not been protected by the pressure suit which had now inflated to hold my arms and legs in a vice-like grip. I wondered how a U-2 pilot could physically manage flying the jet if this should ever happen for real.

Still, Major King gave every reassurance when we met later to discuss the next day's flight. After discussing my few essential tasks (pulling the pins, sealing the canopy, etc.), he proffered some culinary advice. On long flights, U-2 pilots take sustenance by squeezing pureed food up a tube inserted into the helmet through a pressure port. King recommended "Peach and Pear" and suggested that I also take at least two bottles of liquid along to help prevent dehydration.

The day of the flight dawned, cloudier than I had hoped. At the office, King introduced me to Captain Steve Reed, another 1st RS pilot who would be our "Mobile" today. He would preflight the black jet while its two prospective pilots were suiting up and pre-breathing. He would also assist the heavily encumbered King and myself into the aircraft and generally supervise the ongoing flight.

Off we went to suit up. A one-hour period of pre-breathing is necessary to reduce the proportion of nitrogen in the blood and prevents decompression sickness. King demonstrated a useful procedure for passing the time: He fully reclined his chair and fell asleep! When the appointed time came, our oxygen supply was switched to portable containers, and we waddled out of PSD onto the van which took us to the flight line.

After negotiating the steps up to the cockpit with some difficulty, I gingerly lowered myself inside, one leg either side of the huge, old-fashioned control column. A long process of connecting man with machine ensued—oxygen hoses, communications cord, seat harnesses, boot stirrups and so on. According to standard procedure, I was a helpless spectator throughout the process which was carried out by two PSD technicians and Captain Reed.

In the four dual-control U-2 trainers, the rear cockpit occupies the space known as the Q-Bay on operational aircraft where cameras or other sensors may be carried. The instruments are conventional with a large attitude indicator at center front. Unfortunately, I was denied the use of a unique U-2 feature, the driftsight which affords pilots a splendid view of the territory beneath them. Shielded by a rubber cone protruding from above the attitude indicator, the viewing optics for this are at head level, but in the two-seaters, only the front cockpit is so equipped.

With some difficulty thanks to the heavy helmet, I glanced down and sideways. Throttle and trim wheel to the left, with radio and oxygen controls aft, next to a recess where Reed had placed my food tubes and drink bottles. Navigation and some environmental controls were to the right. Somewhere behind me were a whole raft of circuit breakers, which could surely only be manipulated by feel.

On the intercom, I heard Major King call for engine start. The brand new General Electric F118-GE-101 turbofan wound into action. We set off for a holding point on the taxiway which intersects Beale's 12,000-foot runway at the halfway point. No need to take the full length in this bird! The departure performance is so impressive that each mission is said to "launch" rather than "take off". And for today's two-hour flight, we would be launching with only a half fuel load.

We taxied onto the runway and paused to allow the ground crew to extract the locking pins from the outrigger wheels known as "pogos". Then King selected 80% power, released the brakes and we surged forward. In no time at all we were rotating into a steep climb that took us to 6,000 feet before we reached the end of the runway!

King had prepared me for this, but it was still breathtaking to watch the altimeter wind up at such a rate. We passed 20,000 feet after only three minutes, and King soon engaged the autopilot in pitch mode. The 30-degree climb attitude seemed more like 60 degrees to me as we turned north to our first waypoint above the Sierras.

As we neared 50,000 feet, King decreased the pitch so that we could establish a speed schedule of Mach 0.72, then re-engaged the autopilot. We were about to enter the cruise-climb, and henceforth the aircraft would rise steadily but more slowly as fuel was burnt off. King bid goodbye to Sacramento control and checked in with Oakland Center on a special frequency which had only another U-2 flying from Beale to keep us company. After 18 minutes of flight, we passed through 60,000 feet.

We turned south over Reno, Nevada, and I caught a glimpse of Lake Tahoe below as the overcast thinned. Right now, though, it was more interesting to look above and to the side. The sky had turned darker as we climbed, and directly overhead it was now almost black, with stars visible. The blue had retreated towards the horizon where it resided as a thin line separating earth from sky. This horizon seemed a long way distant and I could now discern the curvature of the earth quite clearly.

It was all rather peaceful and beautiful, but my reverie was interrupted as Major King invited me to take the controls. I accepted a trifle reluctantly, having heard plenty and written some about the dreaded "coffin corner" or "throat". This is a condition known to all high fliers as they approach the top left hand corner of the envelope. Put simply, the slowest that the aircraft can go comes close to the fastest that it can go, as the margin between stall speed and Mach buffet steadily erodes.

In the original, smaller U-2 versions, that margin could be a mere five knots under certain conditions. Right now our margin was a generous 30 knots, but King warned that we were only a few knots from overspeed, and he told me to maintain 100 knots indicated airspeed, Mach 0.71. I tried a few gentle turns, and the big winged bird responded well. It seemed at home up here.

Now King fell silent on the intercom, and my sense of isolation grew. I could not actually see him in the cockpit forward and below mine because the interior was obscured by its large black sliding sunshade. Some minutes later, I learned that his microphone was malfunctioning intermittently. In the meantime, though, I began to experience something of the "out of this world" feeling which has been described by so many U-2 pilots.

In order to re-establish some relationship with Mother Earth, I peered downwards over the canopy rail. The altostratus had cleared and we were approaching our next turn point at Monterey on the California coast. I had a superb view all the way up the San Francisco Bay. King re-established contact, and after we rolled out of the turn he checked our fuel balance. Soon it would be time to start the descent.

The U-2 is the only flying machine where you routinely extend the landing gear at 70,000 feet, plus the speed brakes. The throttle is brought back to idle, the flaps are set to the gust position, and with luck, the aircraft may now be persuaded to quit the heavens and start a slow descent. King set a direct course back to Beale, but although the base was more than 100 miles distant, we weren't coming down quickly enough. A lazy 360-degree turn helped us lose 15,000 more feet.

As we passed through 30,000 feet, I took control again. In contrast to its earlier performance at altitude, the aircraft now handled like a truck in the thick lower air. I handed it back to King, and since we were now safely below 20,000 feet, unlatched my faceplate and turned the oxygen supply off. For the first time in this entire exercise, I could smell real airplane!

At 5,000 feet, King retracted the speed brakes, faired the gust control, and trimmed the bird for landing. This can be the most challenging phase of flight, especially for novice pilots. The correct procedure is to cross the runway threshold at 10 feet and the correct speed for the aircraft's configuration. With 600 gallons remaining, our T-speed today should (would, dammit!) be 76 knots.

Our Mobile came up on the radio, ready to talk us through the landing and chase us down the runway in one of those ostentatious five-liter Ford Mustangs. We arrived overhead the field and turned downwind at 105 knots. Flaps and speed brake were extended once again.

The "powers that be" had rejected King's request to perform a touch and go, so we performed one low approach before repositioning for a full stop landing. King told me that on hot afternoons in summer, strong thermals rising from the cornfields surrounding Beale can wreak havoc with even the most carefully flown approach. No such drama today, though. With the appropriate adjustments for yaw, pitch and power, we reached the threshold in good shape.

King flared for landing. "Five feet, four, two," called Reed from the Mobile. As we touched down, King retracted flaps and speed brakes, but continued making yaw and pitch inputs until the aircraft slowed to near walking pace. Ground crew re-inserted the pogos, and we headed back to the ramp.

A small reception committee awaited. Later, I was required to seal my initiation into the world of the "high flyers" by drinking a yard of ale in the so-called "Heritage Room". A less distinguished flying outfit would merely describe this place as their bar. But no other wing has a drinking establishment which can boast wall plaques listing every pilot who has ever qualified on type. Even after all these years, the U-2 drivers are still a select band.

Chris Pocock is the author of *Dragon Lady, The History of the U-2 Spyplane; The U-2 Spyplane, Toward the Unknown;* and *50 Years of the U-2.*

Chris Pocock shown after his own U-2 flight to high altitude. Photo courtesy of Chris Pocock and Schiffer Publishing Ltd.

114

FRANCIS G. (FRANK) POWERS
(Deceased August 1, 1977)

The following was contributed by Frank's son, Francis G. (Gary) Powers, Jr., Director of the Cold War Museum, Washington DC.

Frank Powers joined the USAF in 1950 and flew the F-84 with the 468th Strategic Fighter Squadron at Turner AFB, Georgia. He was recruited by the CIA and was a pioneer in the field of U-2 aviation. He resigned his officer commission in the USAF in 1956 in order to fly with the CIA.

Most of the U-2 pilots flew their secret missions with little notice from the Air Force and the country. However, Frank Powers' entry into the history books came on May 1, 1960. His plane was the target of a surface-to-air missile over the Soviet Union. He survived the crash in the Soviet Union and was convicted of espionage. He was sentenced to three years' imprisonment and seven years of hard labor. However, 21 months after his capture, he was exchanged in Potsdam, Germany for US-held Soviet KGB Agent Rudolf Abel.

Following his extensive debriefing by the CIA, Lockheed and the USAF, Powers appeared before the Senate Armed Services Select Committee. During the analysis following Powers' testimony, the NSA acknowledged he had followed orders, did not divulge any critical information and conducted himself "as a fine young man under dangerous circumstances."

Subsequently, Frank left government service and was employed by KNBC television station in Los Angeles. On August 1, 1977, while working as a helicopter reporter, he died in a crash caused by a malfunctioning fuel gauge that was repaired without his knowledge.

Francis G. Powers in his partial pressure suit ready for flight.

Francis Gary Powers Sr. and Francis Gary Powers Jr.

Photos courtesy of Francis Gary Powers, Jr. and the Cold War Museum, at www.coldwar.org.

DANIEL (DANNY) SCHMARR
(Deceased December 9, 2005)

The following was submitted by Danny's widow, Kay.

Danny was in the cockpit approximately 22 years, including pilot training, and he absolutely loved every minute of it. His favorite years flying were in the F-4 although he had been in the U-2 for four years with the Air Force and five years with the CIA. He was the epitome of the fighter pilot, and the F-4 filled those needs in him. He served as Squadron Commander during the Vietnam War at Ubon, Thailand, with the Night Owls. It was the only squadron to do the "dirty work" at night and it was his proudest time.

Danny was the USAF Operations Officer aboard the USS America aircraft carrier when the U-2R qualified on the vessel. They were out of Edwards North Base. He reported the landings on the carrier by the U-2 as a hair-raising experience. However, it was more interesting to watch the sailors when the U-2R took off rolling mere feet before being airborne.

I was so fortunate to have such wonderful life-long friends at each location we were stationed. When the men were TDY, we wives checked on each other frequently, shared rides to the commissary and held our families together. Everything about the U-2 program was so "hush hush" and I knew that Danny couldn't talk about it at home. Like most of our friends, Danny and I had no close relatives nearby; our Air Force friends became our family.

After Danny retired, we had a little Cessna for our own personal travel. He also worked with KHQ Radio/TV in Spokane, Washington. He did traffic reports and became quite the local celebrity. He always said,

"When I become rich and famous..." and he laughed because he had become a local celebrity. He never quite achieved the "rich" part except in the many blessing from above.

Danny Schmarr strapped into the cockpit ready for a flight.

ROBERT M. WOOD
Gig Harbor, Washington

My first landing in the U-2 at Laughlin AFB was successful and I felt good about it. The only comment by the Mobile Control pilot was "After touchdown, hold your yoke back to keep your tail wheel down."

With those comments in mind, I took off and prepared to make my second landing. Approach and landing were normal with tail wheel down as the Mobile pilot had instructed. After touchdown, I brought the yoke back. The next thing I knew, I was airborne again at a very steep angle! The power was in idle and my left wing started to drop. I hit the power to maximum to recover from a most difficult position and to save the aircraft, to say nothing for saving my own butt.

My thoughts at the time were that I had just "bought the farm" and this was it. I was holding back the yoke trying to pick up the left wing to keep it from hitting the ground and the aircraft turned approximately 45 degrees to the runway. So in this nose high, left wing down position, I said to myself, "Where in the F--- is all this power that I have been hearing about?" Just in the nick of time, before impact, the power did kick in and the aircraft started to fly. Then it became a matter of a vertical wing over recovery 200 to 300 feet altitude with a 20 percent power reduction.

The final landing for the day was normal. Debriefing comments by General Russell were, "About average first landings, Captain Wood. You have a nice weekend."

119

Robert M. Wood relaxing at his Gig Harbor, Washington home, 2006

IT TOOK A DEDICATED TEAM...

What the human eye observes casually and incuriously, the eye of the camera notes with relentless fidelity.

Bernice Abbott

WHAT IS NEPHO?

When the Lockheed U-2 was conceived, it became obvious this aircraft would be the most technologically advanced reconnaissance system ever devised. It was not until the advent of the CIA A-12 and the USAF SR-71 that this high tech equipment was updated beyond that of the U-2. The A-12 and the SR-71 no longer fly, but later generations of the U-2 are in the air today. Currently, the U-2S is the primary manned airborne reconnaissance system the US has in its intelligence-gathering inventory.

When the U-2 was designed, Jim Baker, an optical engineer from MIT and Edwin Land, developer of the Polaroid camera, were tasked to design the camera system for the U-2. The specifications seemed impossible to meet: capable of photographing ground areas from altitudes in excess of 70,000 feet, weigh less than 500 pounds and compact enough to fit inside the equipment bay. Baker and Land worked with the Hycon Company of Monrovia, California to develop the camera known as the Hycon 73B, or simply the "B" configuration.

The Hycon 73B camera or B configuration held two sizes of film. Two 4,000 foot rolls or two 6,000 foot rolls were used with the B configuration. The length of the mission was the determining factor for the film selected. One spool fed from the front of the camera to the take-up spool at the rear of the camera; the second spool operated in reverse. This process was critical for the balance requirements of the aircraft. A unique feature of the camera was the film it used. The image on the film would produce a picture 18 inches square.

The purpose of the T-70 Tracker camera was to help the Photo Interpreter quickly find the most important imagery (target). The Tracker also eliminated the need for the interpreter to go through 6,000 feet of B configuration film. The T-70 Tracker camera used a Perkin Elmer prism that scanned from horizon to horizon in order to get a panoramic view of the area below. Perkin Elmer developed a "split prism" that resulted in extremely high-resolution photography.

Baker and Land knew that the most important part of this camera would be the lens and they turned to Perkin-Elmer of Norwich, Connecticut, for the optical lenses. With the precision optical lenses from Perkin-Elmer, the team set about to design a camera that met all of Lockheed's requirements and specifications. Together, Baker and Land engineered a photographic system for the U-2 that made it a success in every corner of the globe the U-2 was directed to fly.

The secret nature of the photography spawned a language spoken by all who were involved in the operation and maintenance of the cameras. NEPHO became the term used to describe the camera and film equipment used in the U-2. TOP SECRET security clearances were required for all personnel who were assigned to the NEPHO operation.

Hycon camera 73B of B Configuration used in the U-2. Photo courtesy of Glenn Chapman.

GLENN R. CHAPMAN
Tucson, Arizona

Wife: Sylvia

GLENN AND THE FLIGHT LINE BADGE

Back in the good old days in 1958 at the 4080th SRW when I was just A2C Glenn R. Chapman, I was a young Nephographics troop in Armament and Electronics (A&E) Squadron. I learned early on the definition for nephography was "study of the clouds." When I first joined the outfit, I had only a SECRET security clearance, but a TOP SECRET clearance was required to work on the U-2. Only a year and a few months earlier the U-2s came to Laughlin AFB at Del Rio, Texas. While waiting for my clearance to be approved, and like many other two-stripers, I was assigned to the A&E coffee bar. I was far removed from the activities that were going on all around us. I spent six weeks there until I finally got cleared for TOP SECRET work.

The Nephography Shop was where all the action with the RB-57D and U-2 cameras took place. My Squadron Security Officer gave me the official "Shut Up and Burn Before Reading" TOP SECRET briefing. He said in no uncertain terms that outside this shop not a word was to be said about what we did or how we did it. Security was so tight and important in Hangar 2 that even the other shops seemed to be in the dark about what NEPHO did. The same attitude went for us at "SFERICS" which was Electronic Countermeasures.

Everyone knew the primary part of our security was the little piece of plastic-laminated paper called a flight line badge. Not only did it allow us into certain parts of the flight line, it also authorized our entry into specific areas, such as NEPHO, SFERICS, Operations, etc; or, rather, DID NOT allow us into certain areas. The badge had a picture of the individual on the front along with a multitude of numbers indicating areas of authorization. Numbers were either visible or punched out prior to lamination. The numbers remaining on the badge were the designation for areas where the individual was authorized entry. The reverse of the badge contained ID information, signatures, and a round, funny looking red inked circle that seemed not to have been inked properly. These "un-inked" properties were intentional and none of us knew what they meant. However, the Air Police, or "Sky Cops" as they were called, knew what those spots on the badge meant.

There were quite a few Sky Cops out on the flight line, each providing security for designated aircraft. When we went out on the flight line, the badge was clipped to the collar or pocket on our fatigues. When we came off the flight line and entered a non-secure area, the badge came off and went into the shirt pocket securely buttoned up. It was each individual's responsibility to take good care of the badge, or else it was "doomsday" for them with the Security forces.

After a year of being cleared for TOP SECRET, I was pretty confident of the procedure. About the same time, the Squadron Security Officer was replaced by a Captain named, you guessed it, Chapman.

One day, Bob Archey, a co-worker in NEPHO, and I decided to go for a cup of coffee so we cut across from the NEPHO Shop in Hangar #2 to A&E Squadron. Normally, the line badge didn't need to be worn on this part of the ramp, but we all wore it. Halfway across the ramp, one of the Sky Cops walked up and grabbed the line badge off my collar. What he held in his hand was only the badge clasp, no badge. This was cause for three blasts on his whistle which summoned just about every Sky Cop on base. I was ordered to "assume the position" on the ground face down, hands over head. A short time later Captain Chapman showed up and I was ordered to stand and answer his questions. It was over almost as fast as it started, and I was turned over to Captain Chapman. We went together to Pass and ID for my new badge. Then another problem surfaced. When they asked for my ID data, I gave them my last name, first name and middle initial. They asked what was my middle name and I told them that I had no middle name, only an initial. The Pass and ID staff really came unglued with that answer. Captain Chapman told them that he knew me well and I was not lying about the middle initial. Then Captain Chapman, still chafing from his humiliation of one of his troop's negligence in proper care of his Flight Line badge, looked me straight in the eye and told me in no uncertain terms: "Chap, one of us gotta change our names and it ain't me!" No, I didn't have to change my name either.

* * * * *

Another memory I have of the Sky Cops was with a three-striper named Ross. I got to know Ross off duty as well as on duty. He was a very nice, gregarious person, but Lord help the individual who crossed him during his official duty.

One day at the base cafeteria, Ross came in and asked to see my badge. He had seen it earlier and something struck him wrong about it. I gave it to him and he asked when I got it. I told him the date and he told me what the problem was. I didn't have the red-inked circle on the back of the badge. It took me a while to convince Ross that there had been a mistake made when I got the pass. He wrote out a citation for me to have the problem taken care of. I went straight to Captain Chapman and he made a few phone calls. The reply he got was that there were a few badges that were made that same day that didn't get the proper stamp on the back. I went back to Pass and ID for the red-inked stamp.

* * * * *

One of our longest serving and most revered 4080th SRW Wing Commanders was Brigadier General John DesPortes. We enlisted guys, depending on whatever outfit we were with or whatever the circumstances, usually were extremely sorry or very glad to see a "Wing King" leave and get replaced by someone else. There was always hope when a commander left that the new Colonel Someone Else would be better than the last or the fear he could be even worse.

Sometime after DesPortes assumed command, somebody in the Wing came up with the name of "Big John" for him. We came to know him as a hard but fair commander who somehow came to know just about everybody in the 4080th by either first name or nickname. This kind of congeniality was the only time in my entire Air Force career that I experienced it. After Colonel DesPortes came to know who the driftsight guy was, he called me "Chap" like everybody else in the unit did.

The driftsight was an upside down periscope placed in the U-2 aircraft so the pilot could view downwards to check a target on the ground. It was a lousy hunk of junk, but I was one of only two or three guys that liked working with the driftsight. I became very good at working on it. Every one of us was extremely competent on systems (Bobbie Black on the 73B camera, Jerry Fogel on the Tracker, Bob Archey on the A-2 camera configurations). Maybe I just wanted to do my best for "Big John". I thought the world of him and still do. Like all the other

127

guys, he was always "Big John" but I never even came close to saying "Big John" where he could hear me.

A few years ago, I wrote a book about my U-2 experiences titled *"Me and U2: My Affair With Dragon Lady."* I had volunteered to conduct a course about the U-2 to a local senior citizen group. One of the attendees was a gracious lady who introduced herself to me as Peggy DesPortes. I had a pleasant conversation with her and I decided I should tell her about the "Big John" nickname. I let her know that it was just a nickname someone came up with because we liked him so well. She told me that DesPortes knew from the first day that we called him "Big John" behind his back because he came home for lunch or dinner and told her, grinning, "They are still doing it!" Peggy said he just loved it, because he knew he was doing things right and that we appreciated him.

A few years ago we lost Big John to Alzheimer's disease. It was a sad ending for one of the greatest guys I ever served. He was a great humanitarian and a good old southern boy. God love and protect you, Big John, from all of us in the 4080th SRW.

* * * * *

For the Chapman family, the tradition of working with the U-2 has continued with my son, Joe. He was sworn in to the Air Force on the same day as my own father and I. I worked on the U-2A through the U-2F and Joe has worked on the U-2R and the U-2S. Joe was with the 9th Recon Squadron at Beale AFB and the 5th Recon Squadron, the Air Force Black Kats at Osan AB, Korea. I was with Operation Crow Flight, the High Altitude Sampling Program. The same program was renamed Project Olympic Race when Joe worked with the U-2 at Beale.

Glenn R. Chapman and his son Joseph Michael Chapman,
a U-2 crew chief at Beale AFB,
with Oscar, the Crow Flight mascot.

ALEXANDER R. (ALEX THE OLD) DULEVITZ
Spring, Texas

Wife: Ann

My early exposure to the U-2 was in 1959 when I was living in Incirlik, Turkey. My father, Alexander Dulevitz, was a civil engineer providing contract support to the USAF units assigned to the base. I was a dependent son who took advantage of my father's foreign employment to see a part of the world that I had not seen, and at age 19 there was a huge world out there. Having lived on US Air Force bases all my life, I was reasonably confident I could identify most, if not all, aircraft in the United States' inventory. I noticed an unusual looking aircraft and I was curious about its location--always on the "other side" of the base. I started asking a few questions about the aircraft and its mission. Upon reflection, I realize I was fortunate that not more was made of my inquiries, but I was told it was a "weather" aircraft. I watched it take off several times, and the sight of that aircraft zooming so quickly into the air was breathtaking and a most memorable experience.

During my stay in Turkey, I met some airmen on the base and bowled with them in their off-duty time. I learned that a unit associated with the aircraft was Detachment 1010. At the time there were three detachments: A in Germany, B in Turkey and C in the Far East. There were veiled references to Detachment 1010, although the official line was that it was all weather related. Knowing the people who worked there did not give me any confidence that they were in the weather business, but I did not suspect that they were "spooks," either. Later I learned that it was the support unit for the

mystery aircraft and a temporary home of the photographic interpretation unit and the collected imagery. At
this time the US was using the U-2 to over fly not only
the Soviet Union but China as well. Actually, I didn't
learn the full story until five years later when I was a
young Air Force lieutenant assigned as an imagery
interpreter to Headquarters United States Air Forces
Europe (USAFE).

When I was commissioned in the Air Force, I passed
the physical exam for flight school. For most Air Force
officers, the ultimate goal was to be a pilot, but I don't
like airplanes. I know it is unusual to be in the Air Force
and not be in love with airplanes. So there you have the
honest answer. I recall meeting the "motivation board"
and they asked me what type of aircraft I wanted to fly.
The correct answer was, of course, a fighter. I responded
that I would like a bomber. When asked by the board
why I wanted to be a bomber pilot, I answered, "Because
they have more engines." That answer told the board all
they needed to know and they sent me into something less
glamorous. Someone decided I might be interested in
Intelligence and there my career unfolded.

I was first introduced to the unique capabilities of the
U-2 in 1963 as I assisted with the development of tactical
targeting materials used by the tactical units in Europe.
The materials were used to develop attack routes to
targets in the former Soviet Union and Eastern Europe. In
1965 the imagery was still within the realm of sensitive
controlled information, but we followed procedures for
release of some imagery at the SECRET NOFORN (No
Foreign Nationals) level. The Tactical Targeting
Information (TTI) sheet used the printed imagery and
specific data about the target. Given that much of the
Soviet Union had not been photographed by the U-2, we
also used German World War II imagery with a much
lower resolution and no explanation for the changes that

occurred over time. The TTIs were of limited value, but gave the pilots some sense that there was a real target at the end of their penetration route. Obviously, it was better when the TTI contained U-2 imagery.

Within the imagery interpretation process, there were generally considered to be three phases. The first was the "initial" in which the imagery was reviewed for coverage of intended targets. The product of the application was called the Initial Photo Interpretation Report (IPIR). The secondary phase was the review done for any number of reasons, but actually involved the more complete use of the imagery for target/installation review and update. The product was called the Supplemental Photographic Interpretation Report (SUPIR). The third phase was generally considered to be the in-depth review done for specific installations. For example it could include detailed reporting on the launch complex at Tyura Tam or the flight test range at Akhtubinsk-Vladimirovka or the Surface-to-Air missile test facility at Sary Shagan where the Russians eventually developed their missile test range. The folks who did the third phase were indeed the experts such as the man who taught antenna configurations at NPIC.

I was stationed at USAFE from 1963 to 1967 at Lindsey Air Station, Building A-17 which housed the Headquarters Deputy Chief of Staff for Intelligence, my home away from home for three of those four years. Most of that time I spent as a briefing officer, or "talking dog," as the common title was known. I briefed the air attachés on a recurring basis, several ambassadors to the Soviet bloc countries and Senator John McCain's father, Admiral John S. McCain, prior to his taking command of our Pacific Forces. Admiral McCain made a tour to get an appreciation of the European threat and I was available to brief him. I recall the event primarily because of the timing of his trip near the Christmas holidays.

My primary duties involved briefing the National Intelligence Estimates on Soviet forces, both offensive and defensive forces, in addition to developing other staff briefings of interest to the Headquarters staff.   I also worked with the Headquarters Foreign Technology Detachment and provided imagery support on such topics as the new Soviet aircraft unveiled at the Domodovo Air Show in Moscow when the Soviets allowed us glimpses of the aircraft they were developing.

One event has remained in my memory on how interesting my briefings were to civilians. One day I was told I would be briefing the Ambassador to Turkey, and I pulled out my briefing slides and awaited his arrival. The briefing room had a huge mosaic from imagery covering East Germany, a rather impressive backdrop.   The Ambassador, Parker T. Hart, was a career diplomat who served as our ambassador in various Middle Eastern countries, including Turkey, Saudi Arabia and Kuwait. He arrived in the midafternoon, and I proceeded with the briefing which was about one hour depending on the number of questions asked. Mr. Hart sat quietly through the briefings and at the end asked only one question: "Are you related to Duley Dulevitz?" I replied he was my father. Mr. Hart nodded, thanked me for the briefing and left. I reflected that out of all the information provided, he was most interested in my name tag.

In 1967 my tour in Europe ended and I was reassigned to Southeast Asia (SEA) and again ran across the U-2. The aircraft was then flying its primary routes and target areas developed to provide information and photography for the National Intelligence Community, a term that refers to certain three-letter agencies in Washington, such as CIA, NSA, etc.   At one time, there was a National Intelligence Board comprised of all intelligence agencies and the Director of the CIA served as titular head of the group.

The tasking for the U-2 in SEA focused on possible Chinese road building in the northern area of Laos. It was estimated the roads were being constructed to provide the Chinese access to the eastern provinces of Thailand. By 1967 the increased sophistication of the North Vietnamese defense environment made U-2 overflights impossible. That chore was assigned to other "air breathers" including the A-12. The term air breathers referred to aircraft that flew within the atmosphere using that same air as a prerequisite for their combustion engines. They were a great deal cheaper to operate than the more expensive satellites.

Additionally, the weather over SEA was abysmal, often cloudy, so it was less expensive to use an aircraft rather than a satellite with limited film supply. Our primary intelligence focus remained the Soviet Union and China. Therefore, our aircraft continued to be a practical and affordable alternative.

When the A-12 passed from CIA control to SAC and became the SR-71, it was modified for a two-man crew. In addition to the U-2 and A-12, we had the remotely piloted vehicles (RPV), little Firebee drones that were launched from beneath the wing of a modified C-130 transport aircraft and flew over North Vietnam. Some of the most startling imagery from that war came from those little drones which, at times, were no higher than 50 feet above the ground.

When I arrived in SEA, the U-2 was tasked with covering portions of Laos and the transportation network known as the Ho Chi Minh Trail into Vietnam. The resolution of the imagery collected by the U-2 was so superior that even camouflaged trucks could be detected as they traversed routes into South Vietnam. Unfortunately, given the jungle environment and terrain, much of the film was of tree canopy.

I used a loupe (same as jewelers use to view gemstones) and on a light table viewed a large roll of film showing the tree cover. The method at the time was to rapidly look over the image for features that were not normal and then, if necessary, use high-powered stereoscopes to magnify the image for detailed study. This would suggest that the imagery was being well analyzed, but I observed interpreters working late at night actually fall asleep as the imagery slowly moved beneath their eyes.

Once again I found myself in the role of "talking dog." As the 7th Air Force intelligence briefer, I briefed the strike and reconnaissance results daily to a range of people, occasionally including civilian officials. I briefed the images that were of interest to the attendees such as successful strikes on convoys, air combat showing successful kills, and often what we called "happy" snaps that gave various general officers a feel for what we were seeing. The U-2 photos were useful because they provided very high quality images of trucks destroyed by US aircraft. At times we even had pictures of bicycles moving equipment down the Ho Chi Minh Trail. The most popular images were from the RPVs which at times flew so low that they captured the facial expressions of the startled North Vietnamese.

One day I was briefing several civilians at the request of the Deputy Chief of Staff for Intelligence. They had been introduced to me by another civilian as "controlled American sources." As it turned out, they were Germans who were going to penetrate into East Germany. I had been tasked to brief them on the installations and terrain of specific areas. During the course of the briefing, one of the men spoke to another in German. Colonel Opper, DCS/I, observed my reaction and told me to continue. Later he told me that we were supporting the Chief of Station in Bonn.

Initially, the U-2 film was sent to the Strategic Air Relocateable Processing Facility (SARPF), a group of specially configured trailers where specialists processed the raw images and several trailers for interpretation. When I arrived in Vietnam, the SARPF was located at Tan Son Nhut. The U-2 film was initially processed by a SAC detachment and then shipped to the US for further analysis at the National Photographic Interpretation Center in Washington, DC. The SARPF was returned to the US in 1967 for refurbishment. When the SARPF left the theater, the imagery then went to the 6470th Reconnaissance Technical Squadron for interpretation and that unit then morphed into the 12th Recon Technical Interpretation Squadron. Primary emphasis was on analysis of imagery from tactical reconnaissance platforms, gun camera film, SR-71 film and the RPVs.

When I was later assigned to SAC Headquarters, I researched the office responsible for the SARPF. I was surprised to learn the extent of the damage to the unit as a result of weather and corrosive chemicals used in the photo processing. The refurbishment costs exceeded the original development costs.

The lack of emphasis on the U-2 imagery within the theater resulted in a real cost. In February 1968, most of the interest was focused on the Battle of Khe Sanh and the recapture of Hue. It was then that North Vietnamese Army units using PT-76 tanks overran a Special Forces camp. I was the 7th Air Force command briefer and I recall the furor that ensued regarding the strike and reconnaissance results. We were taken completely by surprise. We were totally unaware that the North Vietnamese were introducing armor into the battle for the South.

To say General Momyer, Commander of 7th Air Force, was irritated was an understatement. He asked me time and again where the tanks had come from and why we had not known about them. Unfortunately, I was unable to give him an answer. I knew that there had been rumors of armor for several months, but we had been unable to confirm them from the imagery. I subsequently reviewed a great deal of film and was unable to find any evidence of the tanks prior to their introduction at Lang Vei. In 1971 I was assigned to the Air Staff on Project Corona Harvest, an evaluation of air power in SEA. I found a report completed by the NPIC that traced the route of the tanks as they moved down the Ho Chi Minh Trail to Lang Vei. The report, using U-2 imagery, was not distributed outside the Washington, DC intelligence community. I was surprised and then chagrined as I reflected upon the fact that we had the imagery but had failed to use it wisely. The result was the unnecessary loss of American lives.

During my assignment as briefing officer at SAC Headquarters, I was frequently in front of various staff officers, such as the DCS/Intelligence or DCS/Operations. I had a relatively close working relationship with General Philpott, 7th Air Force Intelligence chief, his successor, General Keegan, "Crazy George," and other generals at headquarters. I was a friend of Colonel John Craig, the Commander in Chief's (CINC's) Executive Officer, who picked me to write the narratives for several general officer awards. That assignment gave me special access to the CINC's office, but it also resulted in headaches when things were done discreetly. When I went to the Pentagon, I had relationships with the Director of DIA as one of his budget "pukes" and was honored on my last day of service in 1985 when the director, General Williamson, came to my office to express his appreciation and to wish me good luck.

Following the SEA tour, I was assigned in September 1968 to SAC Headquarters where I became the Collection Requirements Manager for imagery from SAC-operated platforms. It included the SR-71s, RPVs and the U-2s. The 544th Strategic Intelligence Wing operated a "contingency exploitation branch," a small group tasked with assisting in the development of imagery "boxes." Imagery boxes were mosaics made from the imagery acquired by the U-2 or other platforms to assess the success of the B-52s in keeping their ordnance within specified "boxes." This allowed the interpreters to count the number of bomb craters within the box to assess the effectiveness of Arc Light strikes. Arc Light was the project name given to the cells of B-52s operating from Andersen AFB, Guam. There were normally three B-52s within a particular cell. U-2 imagery was regularly used and interpreted to determine the traffic flow south on the Ho Chi Minh Trail and to detect changes in the routing. This same imagery was used to provide targeting for the B-52 strikes on the truck traffic.

The same contingency group worked the Olive Harvest imagery in 1973 collected by the U-2 over the strip between Egypt and Israel following the 1973 War of Atonement. The protocol was established by the US State Department with photos from the missions to prove to the Israelis and Egyptians that each side was abiding by the cease-fire agreements.

The bulk of my time was spent providing a daily listing of requirements objectives to the planners in the Strategic Reconnaissance Center. The listing included the target name, coordinates, priority rated from 1 to 5, requested frequency of coverage. When I started, there were only a few priority targets, but as the war intensified, we faced a listing of over 100 different targets. To discriminate, we used frequency of coverage as a metric. That, too, began to inflate and we had to use other metrics, such as quality of coverage, to provide a sense of real urgency. It was appropriate, I realized, that the target listing we provided was called the Daily Requirements

Objectives List, or DROL. If it had been my choice, I would have found another word beginning with "L" to make the title complete.

There was one event, during the Christmas bombing of Hanoi and Haiphong during 1972 that stood out from all the others. It was the very first time the President had authorized the use of B-52s to bomb Hanoi and Haiphong. The CINCSAC, General Meyer, immediately tasked his recon platforms with assessing the damage his aircraft inflicted. At the same time, we were getting multiple requests from Washington, DC for specific coverage of various targets. The 7th Air Force Commander, General Lavelle, demanded we focus on his targets. Since CINCSAC owned the aircraft, they first satisfied his needs and then the Washington needs. General Lavelle sent a scathing message to CINCSAC demanding better treatment. I was asked to draft a response, not to General Lavelle, but to the Joint Chiefs. I developed a message that clearly demonstrated that our coverage had addressed our Command's needs very successfully as well as those of the Joint Chiefs and the civilian community. Colonel Jerry McIlmoyle signed the message for the CINC since he was the intelligence head of the Strategic Recon Center.

Perhaps what Jerry did not know was that my Directorate Chief, also a colonel, was furious with me for developing the message. I was astounded by his reaction because I had coordinated it with him, but apparently he assumed that either the CINC or the Deputy Chief of Staff/Intelligence, a general officer, would sign the message. He gave me an hour of his time and a significant piece of his opinion of me, and it was hardly favorable. Fortunately, DCS/I, General Brown had also seen the message as I coordinated it within the Headquarters Staff and the DCS/Operations; they were all pleased with it. I'm not sure what lesson I was to draw from this experience except that it is difficult to please all in a crisis environment.

I left the Intelligence career field for about six years and served in the 90th Strategic Missile Wing in the Minuteman program. There I ran across Jerry and Patty McIlmoyle again. During that time an injury I sustained in Vietnam changed my physical profile and I was released from Operations to return to the Intelligence field. I attended the Post Graduate Intelligence Course in Washington, DC where I was awarded a Masters in Strategic Intelligence. Subsequently, I was assigned within the Defense Intelligence Agency as a program analyst supporting the General Defense Intelligence Program staff.

I was tasked with assessing the U-2 portion of the Intelligence budget as a Budget Program Evaluator. The most amazing thing about the U-2 is its durability, from both acquisition and budget perspectives. I doubt that I have the same attachment to the aircraft as its pilots and crew chiefs. However, looking at the U-2 from an Intelligence view, it was one of the most expensive single items in our Intelligence inventory. Despite its mystique, the U-2 is increasingly vulnerable to intercept by the world's fighters, a factor that limits its use in a modern environment. For that reason and its increased operational costs, Deputy Secretary of Defense, Frank Carlucci, decided to cancel the U-2 program. The Air Force argued strongly to retain the program, but the numbers reinforced the decision to cancel the program.

General Jerome O'Malley, former commander of the 9th Strategic Reconnaissance Wing, home unit of the SR-71 and the U-2, launched his own effort to save the U-2. He visited with friendly members of Congress, briefed them on the value of the program and lobbied for its continuation in the modern Air Force. O'Malley's action resulted in the reversal of the Program Decision

Memorandum and his own subsequent reassignment to command the Pacific Air Forces.

It is interesting to note here that General O'Malley's opposition of the Deputy Secretary of Defense's decision was bold, yet it was supported by various members of Congress. With that said, his career was effectively ended with his reassignment. It was in the tradition of the best leaders willing to risk all to support what he considered to be a valuable program. General O'Malley would be the first to point out that the U-2 served to fly the missions over the "no-fly" zones defined at the end of the First Gulf War. Effectively, he was proven right and the detractors of the U-2 proven wrong.

GARY (SHORTY) ERDMAN
Lake Hiawatha, New Jersey

Wife: Ann

After graduating from Patterson Central High School in Patterson, New Jersey in 1960, I considered military service as a career option. At 5"2", I had always been nicknamed "Shorty" but I had tall ideas. Two of my three brothers were in the Navy, but I didn't like the idea of being on ships or submarines. I preferred having the earth beneath my feet. So I approached the Air Force with my own career goal in mind; I told the Air Force recruiter I wanted to become a butcher. The recruiter told me, "You want to be a butcher, we'll make you a butcher." I realized in a minute the recruiter probably told everybody exactly what they wanted to hear.

Prior to entering the US Air Force in July 1961, my only photographic experience was with my mother's old Kodak Brownie camera. There really wasn't a lot of skill involved. I was the photographer for family gatherings. I never dreamed photography would become a career for me.

Once in the Air Force, I realized I would be doing something much different from meat cutting. Actually, I figured out there were no butchers in the Air Force because all meat is pre-cut. I took the placement tests and I was surprised to learn I had a knack for photography.

After basic training, I was assigned to the 4080th SRW at Laughlin AFB, Texas. I trained in all the photographic equipment of that time from 35mm single lens reflex and 16mm movie cameras to studio cameras. When I had all the appropriate security clearances, I was assigned to the photo lab and developed some of the film taken over

142

Cuba by pilots of the U-2. I remember thinking at the time as I saw the missile sites in the completed film, "It looks like we got 'em." The resolution of the film was so precise that we could identify considerable detail.

During this busy time, all of us photo technicians slept in the lab when we were able to catch a couple hours of sleep. Technicians were required to be available immediately for processing the film when it came in with the returning U-2. Most of us in the lab were oblivious to the severity of the crisis because we were confined to the lab without communication of radio, television or newspapers.

I remember CIA agents always watched over the shoulders of the lab technicians. During much of the Cuban Missile Crisis, developing the film took about eight hours. We made five copies of the film and I know one copy went directly to President Kennedy. I believe other copies were sent to various intelligence units for analysis.

My next assignment was also photo related, but with greater risk than I experienced at Laughlin. In late 1964 I was assigned to Tan Son Nhut Air Base, South Vietnam. I flew aboard a C-123 and photographed the area for mapping the extensive tunnel network used by the North Vietnamese. I was so scared that bullets would penetrate the aircraft I sat on my parachute for extra protection.

I enjoyed my time with the Air Force. Specifically, I liked my service with the 4080th SRW. I met a lot of guys who became as close as brothers with me. Everett Owens was my first roommate at Laughlin. He currently lives in Connecticut and we stay in close touch. Larry Pincombe and George Gwilliams IV were also friends from my 4080th days and we remain in contact now.

4080th Wing Lab, August 1962

First row-kneeling, L to R: C. Cook, F. Robinson, R. Dobbleman, E. Branning, Lt. G. Baker, Capt. R. Duggan, W. Williams, E. MacCue, L. Dillon, J. Lyons

Second row, L to R: R. Barfield, B. Burge, B. Brewer, W. Duetta, H. Warrick, J. Hendricks, L. Pincombe, L. Ames, H. Reed, H. Wayman, G. Gwilliams, S. Andrews, A. Robertson

Third row, L to R: G. Stoddard, g. Erdman, B. Payne, A. LeDuc, L. Oberlander, B. David, T. Presnell, H. Eaves, C. Hunt, R. Hall

Fourth row, L to R: B. Nickolls, L. Dennison, L. Robertson, D. Techman, T. Lee, E. Hinojosa, L. B. Castgerline, D. Smith, R. Heintzleman

144

Maintenance Teams **Processor**

August 1962 4080th Wing Lab

Photo Intelligence **U-2 Photo Processing Teams**

Airmen and NCOs of 4080th Wing Lab, 1961

Gary (Shorty) Erdman, 1961

GERARD (JERRY) FOGLE
Sun City West, Arizona

The power and mysticism of the early days of the 4080th was something awesome to behold. Sometimes the mere mention of the organization opened doors otherwise sealed shut.

While on temporary duty at Barksdale AFB, Louisiana in 1963, I was the Non-Commissioned Officer in Charge (NCOIC) of the NEPHO Section when Don Armstrong got sick with some kind of flu bug. We took him to the base hospital for admission and during sign-in, the admitting nurse asked for his medical records. I told her we did not have the records because we were there TDY. Remaining strict in compliance with her procedures, she insisted all incoming patients must have medical records. We were getting into a loud argument when a doctor came by and asked what the problem was. I explained we were trying to get Don admitted for treatment of his illness. His only question was, "What outfit are you with?" When I told the doctor we were with the 4080th he said, "Bring him right on in."

* * * * *

Another time at Hickham AFB, Hawaii in 1961, I went to the Hydraulic Shop to get fittings for nitrogen bottles since my gauges would not fit without an adapter. The nitrogen was used to purge the driftsight to remove any air with water vapor to prevent fogging. When I asked the airman in the Hydraulic Shop about a fitting, he wanted some kind of written authority. I requested to speak with his supervisor. The supervisor looked at me strangely and asked what outfit I was with. I told him I was with the 4080th and he said, "Take whatever you need." When I said I would return the fittings, he told me to keep them.

* * * * *

We literally took everything we needed to launch the U-2 at the remote site when we went TDY. We took yellow jeeps, a blue staff car used as a chase vehicle, fuel and plenty of spare parts. We understood the base personnel had been briefed not to ask us questions about the U-2 and most importantly, not to take pictures of the bird. So there we were going to the BX in our yellow Jeep dressed in fatigues with the 4080th A&E Squadron patch on the right side and the SAC patch on the left side, with an A&E baseball cap on our heads. It seemed everybody we saw looked at us furtively and whispered to each other. Of course, that made us strut a bit more. We were all young guys and so full of ourselves. After all, we were with the U-2 spy plane, the most secret plane in the AF at the time. It was a great time with lots of fond memories.

* * * * *

In March 1964 I was at Bien Hoa Air Base, Vietnam supporting the NEPHO Shop for the U-2 missions. We were instructed not to take any personal photos of the flight line at the base. A message came from SAC Headquarters back in Omaha, Nebraska. The message was that SAC wanted some photos of Bien Hoa to see what kind of facilities we had--where we lived and worked.

Jim Combs, our Hycon Tech Rep, suggested we take a Perkin Elmer Tracker (70 MM, 3 inch focal length camera) and photograph the base. We loaded a tracker in a pickup truck with two 12V batteries and covered it with canvas, leaving only the bubble exposed. Bob Ingram and I sat in the back of the truck and held the tracker on a box. BC Fowler and Jim Lobig drove the truck slowly up and down the flight line and all over the base. At one point during the ride, an Air Policeman stared at our glass bubble and rotating prism. He didn't approach the truck with any questions though.

We returned to the shop and shipped the film directly to SAC Headquarters. The next day, a couple of Air Police came around looking for the truck with the glass bubble. We told them we didn't know what they were talking about.

Three weeks later a message came in from SAC. The message said, "Thank you, thank you. The pictures were beautiful. We now know what kind of conditions you live and work under."

* * * * *

One day we were sitting around in the NEPHO Section office of the A & E Squadron at Laughlin drinking coffee and telling war stories. A call came in from the base hospital that one of our NEPHO men, Harry Magill and his wife, Dixie, had tested positive for hepatitis. We were advised that anyone who had contact with Harry should report to the base hospital. We looked around at each other. Bob Ingram exclaimed that we all had contact since Harry's greeting was a handshake. Tom McClung, the Perkin Elmer Tech Rep yelled out, "Yesterday Harry had a sip of coffee from my personal coffee mug!" So we all went to the base hospital. At the hospital, we were told to drop our pants and a very painful gamma globulin shot was administered to all. As you can imagine, I hold fond memories of that event. Thanks Harry.

* * * * *

At Davis Monthan in September 1964, I was NCOIC of the trackers. After major maintenance, it was customary to test the camera. We made sure the camera was operational before sending it out on a mission. We placed the camera on its side on a portable bench and took it outside the NEPHO Shop. The camera faced the parking lot and the runway. This procedure had been done many times before. On this particular day, we received word that Bob Primrose had crashed on approach to the runway. When we realized that the camera was pointing in that direction, Ron Kupan, the Perkin Elmer Tech Rep who replaced Tom McClung, shouted that maybe the camera had recorded the crash. We terminated the test and rushed the film to the Photo Lab. Sure enough, the crash was recorded and it showed the problem to be the gusting crosswind.

2005 Reunion, Left to right: Al Defilipis, Horace Tanner, Bob Zint, Bobbie Black, Jerry Fogel, James King, B. C. Fowler, Jim Manis, and Bob Ingram.

B. C. FOWLER
Taccoa, Georgia

Wife: Blanche

A FOGGY TAKEOFF

We had an early launch at a northern location and the area was blanketed with dense fog. The aircraft was ready for takeoff at the end of the runway. The pilot called the control tower for permission to take off which was granted. Two or three minutes later, the tower called back to the pilot and stated he was given permission to take off. The pilot replied, "I did take off and right now I'm breaking 10,000 feet and climbing!"

OPERATION LOCATION 20 (OL-20)

It was quite a feat setting up OL-20 in 1964. We island-hopped for a couple of weeks or more awaiting permission to enter the country where we wanted to set up our operation. A few missions were flown during this time. It was difficult, mainly because of the lack of facilities such as an adequate dark room for the photography. We arrived at our destination, but we found a primitive base. Our living quarters were 12-men tents. The building we found suitable for a shop was quite a distance from the hangar where we installed the equipment in the aircraft. We learned to be inventive. We had to haul the heavy equipment on a trailer behind a pickup truck. Two airmen rode on each side of the equipment to keep it stable and to keep it covered. Our biggest problem was getting it on and off the trailer. Si Lewis and I struggled with that problem more than once.

L to R, Silas Lewis and B C Fowler,
loading a camera for a flight in Vietnam.
Note the sidearms.

JOE FRANKLIN
Whitesburg, Tennessee

Wife: Lola

One of my favorite anecdotes about my U-2 association was at Turner AFB, Albany, Georgia. Colonel Beauchamp was the Base Commander and lived in town next door to my own rental house. One Sunday morning he came out onto his front porch and threw a phonograph record off into the distance. One of the other neighbors witnessed this; he then retrieved the record and gave it to me. Well, it was Elvis' "Hound Dog." I kept the record and after about a month in Texas, I dropped it off at his office, telling the secretary that he had left this in Albany. I never followed up but I did get some secret pleasure from resurrecting what was probably the Colonel's overdose of "Hound Dog."

* * * * *

When Lola and I arrived at Barksdale AFB from Ramey, Puerto Rico, the place was buzzing with the news that some airman had been working as a disk jockey at a late-night radio station. He considered himself quite the comedian and would fill in time with jokes and comments on local events. He made the mistake of commenting on the personal appearance of our Base Commander who was helping direct incoming traffic during a SAC alert exercise. The airman's name was George Carlin. He was discharged and for years went on to use that event as his prime comedic delivery.

* * * * *

In September 1955 I was promoted to Master Sergeant and was sent to the 2nd AF NCO Academy. It was a course aimed at improving leadership abilities, and it did just that. I graduated tenth in a class of 120 students and was runner-up for the Commandant's Award. The following day I received orders assigning me to the 4080th Strategic Reconnaissance Wing at Turner AFB.

I had been at Turner less than a week when Gary Powers returned from his induction into the CIA. Everywhere he went, he was surrounded by a covey of "suits." I met him and knew his mother-in-law, a cashier at the BX. On May 1, 1960, almost five years later, I was waiting for him to land.

The entire Wing was transferred to Laughlin AFB in Del Rio, Texas. The big secret about the 4080th was the U-2 aircraft. One Sunday morning I was herding my family, Lola, Donald and Lela, into the Base Chapel. The first U-2 wobbled onto our lonely runway. Minutes later, one by one, U-2s were all over the place. That day church services were delayed as everybody wanted to get a glimpse of the new aircraft.

Laughlin AFB did not have family quarters when we arrived there. Most married personnel lived in the Hunter subdivision on the east side of Del Rio. Captain Roger Cooper and his family shared the other half of my duplex. Our next door neighbor was Colonel Jack Nole, Wing Commander.

From my back yard, I could see to the north and east for what looked like a hundred miles of cacti and stones. My family and friends would watch the wild pigs, called javalinas, grazing and arguing. Quite frequently jack rabbits were also spotted in the scrub brush.

My parents drove all the way from Tennessee to spend a week with us. Dad was a busy contractor. We took them across the Rio Grande to Mexico for a dinner at Mrs. Crosby's Restaurant and then to see Judge Roy Bean's little hamlet at Langtry, Texas.

One Saturday afternoon, Tim and Sandy Nole came rushing over to our house asking for my son, Don. They blurted out, "Dad has just bailed out of a U-2 from over 60,000 feet!" I asked where their Dad was and they said he had just arrived home. I ran to his house to find him sitting in an easy chair, one bandaged leg propped on a hassock and a glass of bourbon in his left hand. He was noncommittal about the whole affair.

I was NCOIC of the Mission Evaluation Unit. In normal times it would be described as Photo Interpreter Unit, but the word "photo" was not spoken and the unit was officially a "weather" squadron. We worked among the birds in a small building down on the flight line. We were a group of five with Captain Bill Ming and Lieutenant Fred Tietbohl. Then came Captain Niemciewich, an ex-Marine we called "Nemo," who was always in hot water with the Base Commander over his beer-guzzling stunts at the Officers' Club. Ming was a Baptist preacher who refused to even join the Officers' Club. He took a dim view of Nemo's antics. All of the photo and electronic intelligence stuff was processed in our building. The few high-risk missions flown by our pilots were planned in Major Ogglesby's shop. On occasion I was called to help with issues related to our operation.

* * * * *

On Thanksgiving Eve, 1958, I departed for Yokota, Japan. Due to the political turmoil threatening an invasion of Taiwan, my family was unable to travel with me. However, they joined me later.

Before we left Del Rio, John Wayne had erected a movie set of old San Antonio for his movie, "The Alamo." This was located north of Brackettville, a few miles east of Del Rio. How lucky we were that Wayne was on the same flight with my family and traveled with them all the way from San Antonio to Los Angeles. He gave my daughter, Lela, his autograph. John Wayne had a soft spot in his heart for servicemen and their families.

* * * * *

I was at the 6594th at Westover during the Cuban Missile Crisis working with satellite coverage when we received film for processing from the U-2 "B." It had come from Homestead AFB and was escorted by a Brigadier General. Sometime during the film processing, the lab chief feared the film was "fogged" and he asked me to look at it. What I saw was the ocean floor off Cuba where the water was transparent and only the sand dunes at the bottom were visible. I had flown over that area in 1954 exactly where that blue hole appears on the ocean floor. When I explained this to the lab chief, he was really relieved. Just then a frame came into view from the processor that had a "Star of David" SA-2 site on the Cuban mainland. This shocked me because my brother was on standby awaiting call on the base with his EB-47 and crew. When he came over to my house for supper, I was really torn apart because I was not allowed to mention what I had seen. As it turned out, my fears were short-lived.

Was that the film from Major Anderson's U-2? Jim Combs, a Tech Rep for Hycon, told me that the film was retrieved from the crash site. Jim had taught me how to measure image resolution at Laughlin. Six months after I retired to Bossier City, Jim came to my house and asked me to give him some "slant-range" data because the mission profile for recon was being changed. He took me on base where I met Major Tietbohl who had been a First Lieutenant in our Photo Interpretation shack at Laughlin. The Image Motion Compensation cams on the camera bed had to be redesigned and they needed slant/range data before grinding them. I was back into the picture as a civilian working for AIL, EW specialists where I did the threat profile for the B-1 under Rockwell International in 1966.

I have worn many hats in my career, but somehow they all seem to be related over time.

Joe and Lola Franklin

ROBERT H. "BOB" INGRAM
Greensboro, North Carolina

Wife: Barbara

For 17 exciting, memorable years I supported the U-2 program assigned to NEPHO (aerial photographic and electronic sensor maintenance). From 1956-1960, I maintained the camera systems, hand control and drift sight. From 1960-1963, I was supervisor of the camera systems in the U-2. I was selected to attend factory training at Perkin Elmer Corp. and Hycon Corp., manufacturers of the Optics and Camera Systems.

* * * * *

One of my interesting memories occurred in March 1958 when we deployed to Eielson AFB, Alaska for the U-2 to fly sampling missions over Russia. Captain Michael Styer flew a mission that took him over Siberia. At that time Russia was testing atomic bombs above the earth. After the Russians exploded a bomb, Captain Styer flew directly through the bomb cloud.

When he landed and taxied in, the U-2 was so hot with radiation, he had to stay in the aircraft for another two hours while ground crew washed down the U-2. He then opened the canopy, jumped out and ran to the building. At debriefing, he said his Geiger counter went off on his return flight, coming out of Russian airspace at 30,000 feet. He reported that two F-89 Alaskan Air Defense planes had him on radar, but could not see him. They ordered him to identify himself or they would shoot him down. Captain Styer said he was on radio silence. He then hit the U-2 throttle, pulled back on the stick and shot up to 50,000 feet. At that altitude he circled around the F-89s and landed at Eielson AFB.

When we finished our post-flight work, we caught the base bus to the Mess Hall. The bus radio was on. All at once the radio blared, "Attention: Two Alaskan Air Defense fighters encountered a UFO at 30,000 feet. Then the UFO shot off to outer space." We smiled at each other as we listened to the radio with the others in the bus. Once off the bus, we had a good laugh; we knew well what the alleged UFO was.

For our work during that TDY, a few days later, the laboratories in New Jersey notified us, "Congratulations. The data you sent was of great value to our Nation and security."

* * * * *

One day in 1960, I was told to get two men, three "B" configuration cameras and be ready to depart in three hours. I chose Bobby D. Black and John Washburn, the best technicians we had.

I went to my home on base and my wife, Barbara, helped me pack. I didn't know where I was going or how long I would be gone. I just gave her the checkbook, kissed her and our daughter, Stacy, goodbye.

When we got to the flight line, a KC-135 was being loaded with cargo and the refueling tanks were being filled for the U-2s. The KC-135 Loadmaster asked us, "How much does the U-2 fuel weigh?" No one knew; we were all camera guys. He said, "Then I'll guess at it," and pulled out his slide rule and did some calculations. The temperature on the runway at Laughlin AFB was a stifling 115 degrees As most AF flight personnel knew, jet engines did not perform well in high temperatures. Colonel T. J. Jackson, Director of Operations, told the ground crew to remove the overrun barrier to allow more runway for takeoff. The KC-135 developed radio problems and there was a three-hour delay on the takeoff.

Finally, it was a "go" and we rolled out to the end of the 8,500 foot runway at Laughlin; the point of rotation was 7,000 feet. That meant no stopping once we started our takeoff roll. At the end of the runway, we were still on the ground and hit the dirt overrun. It's like driving a car at 200 mph on a paved highway and suddenly hitting a dirt road.

We had three backup U-2 pilots on board. One jumped up and yelled, "We are not going to make it!" Dirt flew by the windows. Then we lifted off, clipped some small trees and were airborne into the blue Texas sky. We breathed a collective sigh of relief.

Right after lunch, that same day, my wife, Barbara and our daughter, Stacy, went to the base swimming pool located on a hill overlooking the runway. As they observed the KC-135, everyone at the pool said that the airplane was not going to make it and all ran to the fence for a closer look. Barbara said confidently, "I'm glad my husband is not on that plane. He left this morning, three hours ago." She did not know the full story until I returned two months later.

On our return flight from Kadena AFB, Okinawa in the KC-135, again full of cargo and fuel, we were over the Pacific west of Wake Island. The Navigator went to sleep and we hit a violent storm. Suddenly all the cargo was flying around and the wings were moving up and down like a bird's wing. John Washburn's face turned deathly white.

John turned to me and said, "Bob, we are not going to make it!" The pilot pulled back on the controls and after about 15 minutes that seemed like hours, we got above the storm and landed at Wake Island. When we exited the plane, we observed the SAC insignia and the AF blue stripe on the KC-135 fuselage were 90 percent gone. The pilot said, "Men, we are not supposed to be here!" He then moved the radar indicator where he could monitor it for the remainder of the flight to Laughlin AFB.

* * * * *

In 1960 I was Chief Master Sergeant (CMSgt) assigned to the NEPHO Shop (Sensors), the aerial camera of the U-2 aircraft. My Squadron Commander, Lt. Col. F. M. Shipley, headed up the 4080th A & E. Colonel Shipley's family and my family attended the St. James Episcopal Church in Del Rio and I was aware that he was a diabetic. When his diabetes was not well controlled, he would have some bad days. The most telltale sign that his diabetes was acting up was his very red, flushed face; he became irritated over the smallest things. I also knew that I certainly didn't want to be the bearer of bad news to Colonel Shipley when he was suffering on a bad day.

Lieutenant Dennin was assigned to our shop, his first assignment in the U-2 wing. He was directed to shadow my daily activities in order to learn the operation of maintaining the camera configurations.

When a camera system malfunctioned, Colonel Shipley summoned me to his office and I explained the problem. Lt. Dennin would follow me each time like a puppy tracking my every move. Once in Colonel Shipley's office, the first thing I would do was check out his complexion to assess his mood. If his face was red and flushed, I kept my mouth shut until he spoke. On these occasions, Lt. Dennin seized the opportunity and rushed to respond to the Colonel's questions, always eager to impress. As a result, Colonel Shipley chewed out Lt. Dennin like a Drill Sergeant in basic training. When I was requested to respond to the Colonel's questions, he always treated me professionally.

After a few months of this routine, on the walk back to our shop, Lt. Dennin said to me, "I don't understand it. Colonel Shipley chews my ass when I explain the maintenance problem, and he treats you with respect when you explain the same problem." Lt. Dennin was reassigned to Beale AFB a short time later and I never revealed my clues to the Colonel's moods.

Lt. Col. Shipley was an outstanding leader and a great friend.

* * * * *

In September and October 1962, the 4080th SRW was flying missions over Cuba from McCoy AFB, Florida. Major Richard Heyser was the first to find the Russian missiles on the island. We were flying one mission every three or four days.

At 1:00 AM, Colonel Shipley woke me and said, "We have received orders to fly five sorties today. Can we do it?" I said with absolute confidence, "Yes, sir." We had five U-2s and five Hycon "B" cameras, 36-inch focal length, and five Perkin Elmer 70MM tracking cameras. My team and I started to work.

The flights were scheduled two hours apart, flying offshore, shooting into Cuba on a high oblique flight. Then, we discovered we only had four sets of mounts to hang the "B" cameras in the Q-bay of the U-2. There was not enough time to fly a set of mounts in from Laughlin on one of the T-33s. The way the flights were scheduled, the first aircraft would be landing when the fifth aircraft took off. The sun angle had to be just right for each aircraft to get the best photography. Colonel Shipley stopped calling me "Bob" and started calling me "Sergeant Ingram." That's when I knew I was in trouble.

We decided not to tell Colonel DesPortes, the Wing Commander, until the last minute. He was known to have a short fuse anyway. Jim Combs, the Hycon Tech Rep, took a set of mounts to the McCoy Field Maintenance Squadron. The Squadron got a Sergeant out of bed at 2:00 a.m. and said, "Can you make a set of these?" He replied, "Yes," and then took raw metal on a lathe and carved out a set of mounts. They weren't pretty, but they were just what we needed. Jim Combs gave the Sergeant $50 cash and asked his Commander to write a letter of commendation.

We installed the mounts, closed the hatch and operated the camera to make sure it cleared the heater ducts behind the windows. The mounts worked perfectly. We never had to tell Colonel DesPortes. The last time I saw those mounts was in a box at Davis Monthan AFB, Arizona. I wish I had them to put in the Laughlin Heritage Museum in Del Rio. There was a lot of sweat over those mounts and a vivid memory for a few of us.

* * * * *

In late 1964, I was called to the 4080th A&E Maintenance Supervisor's Office. I was told I would be going on TDY but I was not told where or how long. Jerry Fogel, Charlie Couch, Si Lewis, B. C. Fowler, Jim Lobig and Jim Combs, the Hycon Tech Rep, were also selected for the same TDY.

I went home, told Barbara and gave her our checkbook. She helped me pack and once again I said goodbye to her and Stacy. Saying goodbye to my family was always the hardest part of my military career, especially not knowing when I would see them again.

We were told to prepare three "B" Hycon Configurations (36 inch focal length cameras) and load them in the doghouses. In addition, we prepared three 70 MM tracker cameras in their cases and three "B" configuration hatches (lower hatch with windows).

On this deployment we were taking three U-2s and six pilots. Three pilots flew the U-2s and three pilots traveled in one of the two KC-135s. The KC-135 carried a full cargo load of fuel for the U-2s and maintenance personnel to support the operation. We were designated Operating Location-20 (OL-20) and our commander was Colonel Kenneth McCaslin.

The flight from Laughlin to Hawaii was uneventful. The KC-135 had to land prior to the U-2s in order to recover the aircraft, put on the pogos and assist the pilots in disconnecting the gear and exiting the aircraft. After refueling on the ground, we launched the three U-2s again with three different pilots.

The next stop was Clark AFB, Philippines. I was excited to be in the Philippines for the first time. We NEPHO troops unloaded our cargo, doghouses, test equipment, film and support supplies into a big hangar at Clark. Once we were established at Clark, we only had training flights; no aerial reconnaissance flights were flown.

As I got adjusted to the area, one scene that caught my eye was the huge mountain on a flat plain 20 miles from the base. That mountain turned out to be an active volcano and years later it erupted and destroyed Clark. I was happy God's timetable was for that volcano to erupt after we left.

We learned through the rumor mill the American Ambassador had directed us to leave the country. A short time later the Ambassador flew nonstop on a KC-135 to Washington, DC, briefed the Administration and returned to the Philippines. It had to have been an exhausting trip for him. The result was we were allowed to stay in the Philippines.

One of the most interesting off-base trips I took was to a local Negrito village. The Negritos, the Aborigines of the Philippines, were only about five feet tall, had very black skin and lived in grass huts elevated about 7 feet above the ground. I talked with the Negrito chief, whom I found to be an interesting fellow. He was dressed in casual western style slacks and short sleeve shirt. The remainder of the tribe dressed in colorful costumes like they were in a Hollywood movie. The Chief said his people were employed by the base as guards. Besides their pay, they had a choice of medical care at the base or exchange privileges. They usually chose the hospital care. I was surprised to learn from the Chief that his son was a medical doctor and an officer in the US Navy. Looking at the village resembling something from the Stone Age, it was hard to believe his son was an officer in the US Navy. I didn't ask the Chief how his son made the transition from the village to the Navy.

Theft was rampant at Clark and I asked the Chief why he could not stop the stealing since he was in the security business. He replied, "I could, but the Base Commander turned me down when I asked him for a truck to haul away the culprits."

All of us bought blowguns in the village, actually a hollow tube from a plant with dart. Other souvenirs were bow and arrows. I bought a $2 machete, 16 inches long made out of an auto spring and water buffalo horn handle. I still have that machete; I use it to cut up boxes for recycle. B. C. Fowler became quite proficient with the blow gun. When he returned to Arizona, he said the blow gun tube and the bow and arrows split in the dry Arizona climate.

I was in the Base Exchange when a Crew Chief came in shouting that the President of the Philippines had ordered us out of the country and we had four hours to pack up and leave. We did some fast packing of all our gear and loaded the two KC-135s.

The Crew Chief of the KC-135 I was assigned to fly on told Colonel McCaslin he had a load of JP-4 fuel on

165

board for a training flight with a fighter scheduled for that night. As a result, the plane was overloaded. McCaslin ordered, "Dump it, we have to go!" We taxied to the end of the runway, pointed the refueling boom toward the jungle and shot the JP-4 out of the boom. What a scene! The Colonel shouted, "Let's go, we are out of time and I don't want an international incident." The boom operator said, "I'm not finished." McCaslin responded, "I don't care. Let's go." So the pilot headed the aircraft down the runway spraying JP-4 as we went. Later, I asked Colonel McCaslin why he moved to the jump seat. He laughed and said, "I wasn't sure we were going to make it."

On to Andersen AFB, Guam. We stored our equipment in a hangar at Andersen AFB, Guam. The base housed all of the enlisted men in two-story brick barracks in the jungle at Maroboro, Guam, about 10 miles from the base. Near the barracks was a small store, selling beer and snacks; it resembled a country store in The States. Each day we went to the main base to check in. There really was nothing to do but eat, sleep and drink beer for two weeks. What a life!

Between Maroboro and Andersen was a span of thick jungle. I often wondered if there were any Japanese left hiding in the jungle. When I expressed this to one of our men, he told me I was nuts because the Japanese had been long gone. WWII had been over for 19 years. Would you believe it, two years later, two Japanese left from WWII surrendered on Guam.

Colonel DesPortes, 4080th SRW Commander flew to Guam from Laughlin. He had a yellow envelope with him and he announced, "Here it is, boys. Our orders. Can't open it until we are airborne." We loaded the KC-135 with our cargo and were ready to go. Then Colonel DesPortes learned there was a Russian trawler two miles from the end of the runway monitoring planes taking off from Guam. The Colonel said, "We can't have that." A local KC-135 pilot offered, "I can get rid of the trawler," and he took off with a load of JP-4 fuel. He flew directly over the Russian trawler and started yelling, "May Day! May Day!" As was planned, the boom operator sprayed the deck of the trawler with JP-4. The pilot reported, "The last I saw of that trawler, he was headed out to sea and washing down his deck as he went."

The runway at Andersen was 10,000 feet; it ran downhill, hit a low area and then went uphill. At the end was a 200 foot cliff with jagged rock and the blue Pacific Ocean beyond. The pilot started down the runway and the plane began sinking; it started to vibrate and shake so I felt I had double vision. Si Lewis was in the boom operator's position where there was a large window. He said, "The blue Pacific Ocean came up at us and I felt I could reach out and touch it." I exhaled and the pilot leveled the aircraft and climbed to higher altitude.

I was sitting next to Colonel DesPortes; he said, "Let's see where we are going." He then tore open the large yellow envelope he had brought with him and announced, "We are going to Ben Hoey" which was actually Bien Hoa Air Base, South Vietnam.

It was March 1964 when we landed on a brand new concrete runway at Bien Hoa. A short time later I asked the flight surgeon, "When do we get our plague shots?" He said, "Ingram, you have been asking me that for weeks. Bubonic plague has been eradicated for years."

A local base captain drove up and said, "We only learned you were coming here an hour ago. Headquarters said you have Priority One orders and we should give you anything you need." Colonel DesPortes turned to me and told me to go with the captain and set up the NEPHO shop. The NEPHO guys and I hopped in a pickup truck and headed for the hangars. Bien Hoa was built by the French, taken over by the Japanese in WWII, returned to the French after the war and now the South Vietnamese had custody. The hangars were a sad sight, rusty metal thick with red mud; grease and dirt covered the floor. I told the captain that this hangar would not do. "We need a 30 feet by 20 feet air-conditioned room for our systems and film."

The captain replied that the only air-conditioned building on the base was the NCO Club and Base Communications. I said, "Let's look at the Base Communications building," and off we went to inspect it. It was a brick building with large green doors. The captain pounded on the doors and a Staff Sergeant (SSgt.) dressed in a nice, clean 1505 uniform appeared. The Captain introduced me and explained that we needed a shop for our operation. The Sergeant said, "Well, we can't give up our office." The building was divided by a wall creating two equal size rooms. The Captain and I walked out and he said, "What do you think?" I responded quickly, "That's it!" We turned around and went back into the building; the Captain called to the Staff Sergeant and said, "Move out." We moved our doghouses into the hangar and our film equipment to the Base Communications building. When we saw him again, the Staff Sergeant was stripped to the waist, sweating profusely and sending us a "Go to Hell" look. We flew 33 successful missions before one "B" configuration failed.

Now about the rats; I learned that Southeast Asia is home to an extremely large population of enormous rats. They were about 14 inches long excluding the tail and weighed up to 8 pounds. At night some of the guys would trap a rat in a wire cage and spray paint them different colors each day. The rats only came out at night and once they actually did catch the same rat a second time. One night we heard a loud, horrific scream from the next hut and we learned a rat had found its way in the bed of one of the troops. The poor fellow almost tore the hut down getting out of there. Two days later, we were all told to report to the flight line to get our plague shots. I said, "Hey Doc, I thought you said the plague had been wiped out." He smiled and said, "Next!"

One day Colonel DesPortes came to our shop and reported, "I've been ordered to go to Bangkok, Thailand to brief Robert McNamara, Secretary of Defense, on our operation." The Colonel was slightly inebriated, really tight as a banjo string; he was obviously nervous about the McNamara briefing. Jim Combs our Hycon Tech Rep, went over everything Colonel DesPortes needed and by the time they finished their preparation, a whole bottle of booze had been emptied.

Three days later Colonel DesPortes returned with a smile on his face. He had news that I was glad to hear. In May 1964, Fogel, Couch, Lewis, Fowler, Lobig and I rotated back to Davis Monthan AFB, Arizona. As we left Bien Hoa, I thought to myself, "Boy, am I glad to leave this place." Little did I know that later I would be returning with Bobbie Black to support the Drones. On that TDY we were there for Thanksgiving, Christmas and New Year and saw the Bob Hope road show. I left Vietnam again in January 1965 and vowed, "This is it for Vietnam." I returned to Vietnam 1966 on permanent change of station orders.

I want to thank the Air Force families, my wife, Barbara, my daughter, Stacy and the many friends who supported us during our separations. I am proud to say I can still call many of those fellows friends today.

Air Force attendees at Stanford University,
IRIS camera training sponsored by the ITEK Company,
L to R: Bob Ingram, Instructor, Photo Specialists Jenkins,
Goudy, Johnson, Rodriguez, Washburn, McDowell and Cook

**Foreground Jim Combs-Hycon Tech Rep,
Far right, Jim Lobig-Nepho Specialist at
Bien Hoa Air Base, Vietnam 1964**

**Bien Hoa Air Base, standing in front of a hut that served
as living quarters, L to R Charlie Couch, B. C. Fowler,
Jim Lobig and Si Lewis**

Bunker for rocket attacks at Bien Hoa Air Base.

South Vietnamese Air Force personnel housing.

Clark Air Base Philippines with volcano in background.

Negrito village chief, Philippines, 1964

Mekong River

Residence Huts

Runway

Water Purification Plant

Mess Hall

Base Theater

174

JOSE (LOPS) LOPEZ
Los Angeles, California

Wife: Irene

LIGHTNING BUG MISSION

I was on my second TDY at Bien Hoa Air Base, Vietnam (known as OL-20) in 1966. Somehow I was "volunteered" to go to DaNang Air Base to help with a couple of missions for the Lightning Bug Project. The project consisted of a Firebee reconnaissance drone that was air-launched and controlled from a DC-130 aircraft. The Firebee drone was flown on low level photographic missions over North Vietnam. Following the drone's recon flight, it was directed to a recovery area where its parachute was deployed. The Firebee was then recovered from the landing location, on land or at sea. It was my job working out of the NEPHO shop to be part of the recovery team to remove and safeguard the film magazine from the camera attached to the drone.

On one particular mission, the Firebee was launched toward North Vietnam. A squad of US Army soldiers and I boarded a CH-3C helicopter. I carried my tool bag in one hand and my AR-15 on my shoulder. Our chopper was escorted by six Huey helicopter gunships. We flew from the base over thick green jungle. After we were airborne for a time, our pilot received information from the C-130 regarding the landing location of the drone and we headed in that direction. The remote guidance systems in those days were slightly less than exact. The drone we were chasing landed in a small village in the middle of the jungle instead of a large safe area as planned.

The pilot found a small clearing to land our helicopter and some of the Army troops jumped out and set up a defense perimeter. The remainder of the troops and I headed to the village where the drone had landed. The Huey gunships stayed overhead and circled our location for our protection. We cautiously scanned the village area for VC but the only people we found were a few scared villagers yelling and running around in panic. We found the drone; it had landed in a fenced area near a villager's hut. I went directly to the drone and removed the film magazine while the soldiers attempted to calm the villagers. We returned to our helicopter and headed back to DaNang. The chopper pilot reported that while we were in the village he heard a radio transmission from a flight of B-57s asking the Huey pilots if they had VC's trapped in the area. The B-57s were itching to level something with all the ordnance they had onboard. The Huey pilots replied they had not seen any VC and the B-57s continued on while we returned to the base.

One of the Army soldiers reported the village chief claimed our drone had killed one of his pigs, but I never saw any dead pigs. The chief demanded payment for the pig and one of the officers took care of the payment. Once we were back at DaNang I handed over the canvas bag with the film magazine to a waiting officer; my mission was complete. I was now free to enjoy a cold babi-ba (33), a Vietnamese beer.

Left to right: Jack Owens, Chuck Dreiling, TSgt Dan Reyna
and Jose Lopez.

Getting ready for a mission launch.

Promotion party celebration
Left: Jose Paz (A2C to A1C), second to left Jack Owens
and Jose Lopez, fourth from left.

OL-20, 1965, Barbeque Time

Our main transportation to the town of Bien Hoa, Vietnam.

JAMES MANIS
Waikoloa, Hawaii

During our deployments, one of the U-2 pilots usually flew a C-54 that carried many of us of the NEPHO Unit to our destination. On one deployment to South America, Captain Charlie Knapp was the navigator. He was charged with mapping the flight plan for the pilot, Major Ed Emerling. To pass the time of the long flight, I played cards with some of the guys. We did notice that the plane was circling a lot. Major Emerling called for Captain Knapp to come to the cockpit for a consultation. When Captain Knapp returned to the cabin, I asked him if there was a problem. He rather sheepishly responded that he had mapped the flight over Cuba instead of the destination in South America. That was at the time when there was already quite a bit of activity in Cuba. We wanted no part of that. Captain Knapp had probably mapped quite a few flights to Cuba in previous months. Prior to becoming officers, both Major Emerling and Captain Knapp had been enlisted men. When we landed, in the presence of all of us on the flight, Major Emerling asked Captain Knapp, "I know how you got to be a Captain, but what I want to know is how you became a Staff Sergeant?" Of course, all of us who were witness to this had a good laugh at Captain Knapp's expense.

* * * * *

We were at McCoy AFB, Florida during the Cuban Missile Crisis. When a U-2 pilot landed, he was instructed to remain at the end of the runway while we installed covers on all the windows. On one memorable day, Mobile Control had stopped its van next to the U-2 on the ground while the cameraman raced to install the covers. The cameraman was near the main gear when the Tower called to see if it had cleared the runway. They had another bird on approach. Mobile Control responded to the Tower to let the bird on approach "go ahead." A series of mixed messages unfolded about that time. Seeing the scrambling cameraman trying to get away from the U-2 where he had installed the window covers, Mobile Control shouted to the pilot of that aircraft, "Not Clear." The aircraft on approach heard "Not Clear" which he thought was meant for him. He was told to abort his landing. In his haste to pull up and go around, he almost clipped another U-2 in the pattern. What a close call that was!

* * * * *

While I was at Edwards North Base in 1960, the US trained Taiwanese pilots to fly the U-2. The Taiwanese pilots were housed in mobile homes on the base. They were not permitted to leave the base. On a training flight over Canada, an excited Taiwanese pilot called back to base that he had experienced a mechanical problem. There were a number of remote landing sites that had been used for training flights such as this one. The pilot was directed to the nearest remote runway and a KC-135 took off to locate and recover the U-2. North Base was unable to contact anyone at the remote site tower. The pilot landed his U-2, disconnected himself and walked to the nearby tower building. Seeing this most unusual sight appear at his tower so frightened the operator that he raced out of the building, jumped in his car and sped away to town. The KC-135 landed, repaired the U-2 and everyone took off. The next day, the local newspaper headlines read "Martian landed, area secured by Air Force."

Jimmy D. Manis

L to R: Jerry Fogel, Al Defillipis, Horace Tanner, B.C. Fowler, Jim Manis and Bob Ingram at 2005 4080th SRW Reunion.

WILLIAM L. MING
New Braunfels, Texas

Wife: Virginia

I supported the U-2 program from the time I joined the 4080th SRW at Turner AFB, Georgia, in 1956, following the unit to Laughlin AFB, Texas, through my assignment in Tan Son Nhut AF, Vietnam in 1962. My job at Laughlin was the Assistant Officer in Charge, Intelligence Photographic Evaluation.

The OIC of our operation was Major Harry Oglesby who was later replaced by Lt. Col. Frick. Our team included Captain Carothers and Captain Glen Furbish, and our enlisted staff included Technical Sergeant (TSgt.) Joe Franklin, SSgt. Walter E. Davis and Airmen Green and Reid.

I never got used to going to the base in the morning and then during the day being instructed to go home and pack my gear to go TDY. I would phone my wife to start packing for me. I rushed home, finished packing, rushed back to the base, boarded a KC-135 and departed for an unspecified period. England or Alaska were my most frequent destinations.

The TDY to Alaska was the best. The mess hall treated us as if we were royalty. Anything we wanted, we received. Once a week, the Officers' Club served King Crab, all we could eat for $1.25!

There was a nice side benefit of going to Alaska. The U-2s would come up to Eilson AFB configured for their mission. When they were to return to Laughlin, they were "light." We would load the empty bays with frozen King Crab which would stay frozen all the way to Laughlin. When the U-2 was about an hour out, Base Operations called the wives and simply said, "Mrs. Ming, will you come out to Base Ops and pick up a package?" She would pick up her frozen crab and happily head for home.

This was an exciting time and we were working with a classified aircraft. Challenges abound. The camaraderie was great and we knew we were gathering intelligence for a purpose.

William Ming receiving an award from Colonel Bratton, 1958.

LOOMIS L. "ROBBIE" ROBERTSON
Oxford, Mississippi

When I reported for duty to the 4080th Wing Lab in April 1958, I was one totally confused and rather unhappy airman. I was "hand-picked" by my former supervisor to go to Laughlin AFB, Texas. The only thing he told me was I would be working in a "Weather" organization. That didn't make any sense because I didn't know anything about predicting weather. I was very happy with the 70th Recon Tech Squadron at Little Rock AFB, Arkansas. I was asked to volunteer, but since I didn't want to leave, and I didn't find going to a weather outfit very exciting, I refused to volunteer. Well, you can guess the rest of the story. The Air Force was kind, however, and since my wife was six months pregnant, she was allowed to stay in Little Rock and she was given an additional 90 days to recuperate. My son was born on January 14, 1958. To the day I was on my way to Laughlin exactly 90 days later.

I arrived at Laughlin and I was told that I couldn't go to work because I would have to have additional clearances. That was confusing because I already had a TOP SECRET clearance. In the meantime I would be working on the Tower just below the Air Traffic controllers photographing with a motion picture camera all the takeoffs and landings of two types of aircraft. One of the aircraft was a B-57D, but the other didn't have a name. I was just told to be on the lookout for something that slightly resembled a glider. The Major doing the briefing told me how important the job was, but I still wasn't excited. He also told me they had never had a crash on takeoff or landing, but he said, "If they do and you don't get a record of it on film, you might as well jump off the Tower, because you've had it." That got my attention, but then I thought, "How difficult could this be?" and for the most part forgot the matter. I was still trying to figure out how "weather" factored into it.

As it turned out, it didn't take long for things to get exciting. I reported for duty the first morning at my makeshift office one floor beneath the Tower room. I saw a B-57 starting its roll, so I panned it until it was airborne. With one eye on the runway and the other on the sky in the direction of approach that morning, I turned the camera off and relaxed. Later the B-57 came home; I caught him as he broke the horizon and panned him until he almost stopped. Then I caught a glimpse of this weird-looking apparatus on approach, and I thought, "Yep, that's got to be the glider." I caught him in the same area as I did the B-57 and panned him until he was safe on the ground and had completed his roll, I thought. I reached over and picked up my cigarette and was feeling pretty good about the whole picture taking thing when all of a sudden I looked at the runway and this weird thing was lying on its side! I just about had the "big one" as I vividly remembered what the Major said about missing a crash. I thought before jumping off the Tower, "Let me check with the controllers and see if they can tell me what happened."

I rushed inside the Tower room and asked them, "What just happened?" First they looked confused, and then I pointed to the "thing" lying on its side. In unison all of them started to laugh. They explained about the "thing" not having any wheels under the wings and they let me know that was normal. They even mentioned something about "pogo sticks," but I didn't know what they were talking about. I was happy to know that I had not missed anything. Of course, I wondered if this thing that flew was somehow connected to this weather outfit.

Three months later I got the clearances I needed to work the job and was given a tour of the Wing Lab. I knew what was going on; it was exciting and everything was new. I had never seen any of the equipment and never heard about the film. Even with the newly granted clearances, I was told not to ask too many questions. I finally understood and I couldn't thank my former supervisor enough for handpicking and volunteering me for this obviously challenging job. I was told, "Don't ever mention the word 'photo' in the same breath as the U-2." As I look back over the years, it seems that I was told something to that effect on countless occasions.

I never did anything with the program that I didn't find both rewarding and challenging. There was plenty of excitement that came packaged with every assignment. It seemed to me that "professionals" just came out of the woodwork. One super person would leave and be replaced by another equally proficient professional. I can truly say that I have been blessed beyond measure to have the opportunity to work with the U-2 program and its myriad personnel.

Like most of my friends, I did not like being separated from the family on some of the long TDYs. I firmly believed what I was doing made a difference, so I gladly made the sacrifice. My wife didn't like the TDY's either, but she still raised the family and supported me 100 percent. Hats off to our officer cadre who did an excellent job of instilling the importance of the Wing mission to all the troops.

I still maintain contact with several of the old troops, and many of the officers from the program. Tony Bevaqua and Pat Halloran are just a couple of the dear friends that I've known for years. The camaraderie with this organization was unequalled with any of my other units.

JOSEPH (ROOSTER) ROBINSON
Tucson, Arizona

Wife: Barbara

I was assigned to the Nephographic Shop of the 4080th SRW at Laughlin AFB in April 1959 and the equipment at this duty station was new to me. Before Laughlin I was with a recon wing at Little Rock AFB, Arkansas. I needed to have a Top Secret security clearance with complete background investigation. (That meant some investigator would be knocking on doors all over my hometown.) I was a stranger in the NEPHO Shop for a while. I was allowed to work on the RB-57 aircraft assigned to the unit until my clearance approval came through.

Once my clearance was approved, I was busy learning the ins and outs of the new photographic configurations flown on the U-2. My first TDY with the U-2 program was in 1962. I received a call about midnight instructing me to report to duty immediately and to bring all my mobility gear in preparation for a short excursion. I boarded a C-123 transport with other members of my unit for a mission at an unknown destination. Our instructions were not to ask questions, do as we were told on a need to know basis, which was actually very little. I was at Homestead AFB, Florida for three days before I knew where I was and what our mission was. I was there in support of the Cuban Missile Crisis.

It was a sad day in my life when one of the pilots from our wing, Major Anderson, was shot down while photographing over Cuba. That was the second time I was in the area when a U-2 was lost. In 1960 I was TDY at Incirlik AB, Adana, Turkey with the RB-57s when

Gary Powers was shot down and captured over Russia—another sad day.

The thing I remember most about the Homestead TDY was the day President Kennedy came to visit. All of the aircraft were on static display, the U-2 parked among them waiting for the President's arrival. Our commander, Colonel DesPortes, had to briefly leave the area but he said he would return soon. He gave me explicit instructions that absolutely no one was allowed to view the inside of the cockpit until he returned.

Shortly after Colonel DesPortes' departure, a staff car drove up with the most generals I had ever seen. They said they wanted to look into the cockpit of the U-2. There I stood, an Airman First Class, telling a group of generals that I had instructions from my commander that no one, including the President, was to look into the cockpit until he returned. Fortunately, Colonel DesPortes wasn't gone long, but it seemed a lifetime. When he returned, the Colonel congratulated me in front of the group of generals for standing my ground and following his instructions.

The planes were readied to depart Homestead after viewing of the aircraft on display. Right then a young Major passed by and made a comment that the C-124 aircraft that he flew could beat the U-2 off the ground on takeoff. At that time the big lumbering Douglas C-124 Globemaster II was the largest transport in the aircraft inventory. Getting that fully loaded aircraft off the ground took all available runway. The brash comment was overheard by one of the U-2 pilots and the challenge was on. The U-2 pilot accepted the challenge and told the Globemaster pilot to stick around and see how quickly the U-2 would be off the ground. The pilot of the U-2 instructed the crew chief to remove all the fuel from the wing tanks and get the bird ready for a max takeoff. Word spread. The U-2 was going to put on a show and that is just what we witnessed. The ground crew hand launched the aircraft shortly after rolling a few hundred feet down the runway. The pilot pulled up, sped toward the heavens and went completely out of sight. It was a beautiful. Several guys there found it hard to believe what they had seen that day. The C-124 pilot stared with surprise as the U-2 disappeared above the clouds only seconds after liftoff. That C-124 pilot was probably grateful he had not bet a lot of cash on his aircraft.

* * * * *

I had always enjoyed sports and I played on several teams at Laughlin. Sports passed the time because there wasn't much for a single airman to do off duty. On a TDY to Carswell AFB, Fort Worth, Texas I joined the basketball team. One of the Carswell players made a comment that I ran up and down the court like a proud rooster. The following year I was on another TDY and was unable to participate in the game against Carswell. They asked about the "Rooster" but the Laughlin team didn't know who they referred to until a photo was produced and I was then identified. From then on everyone started calling me Rooster and the name stuck. Some people I worked with actually thought that was my real name. To this day, some of the guys from the old days still call me Rooster.

* * * * *

I had a great 26-year military career, several years in the 4080th and the 100th. I traveled all over the world with the U-2 group, sometimes not even knowing where I was. I always managed to meet people and made a lot of lifelong friends. As a result of those friendships, I could get almost anything I needed to get a job done. I could get a piece of equipment up and running or a case of steaks for a cookout at a TDY location. It's who you know. People asked how I always had connections, but I kept a tight lip about my connections as I did about my job. For me it was always important to maintain trust and confidence from the people I worked with.

I often found it difficult not being able to tell my wife and kids about my job in the Air Force. All they knew was that I worked around the U-2. When folks asked about my job, I would jokingly reply, "If I tell you what my job is, I'll have to kill you." That usually put a stop to further questions.

The people of the 4080th were a very special group. Our normal situation at Laughlin found us typically understaffed when half of our unit was away on TDY. A routine day could change quickly and we had to prepare for another TDY. The camaraderie and professionalism in the 4080th were unequalled in other units and I am proud to have served with these men.

**Joseph (Rooster) Robinson,
with trophy for Airman of the Month**

Joseph Robinson, standing, fifth from right, with his unit.

CHARLIE ROGERS
Montgomery, Alabama

Wife: Myrtle

I was fresh out of basic training and I arrived at the 4080th SRW at Laughlin AFB when Brigadier General DesPortes headed the organization. My first assignment was in A & E with SFERICS and camera NEPHO. One of my memories during that time was the quality of the leadership; I considered this leadership to be the absolute best. Two of our young airmen and I were summoned to General DesPortes' office to receive an award. The General, being from North Carolina, learned that I was also from the South and he offered good naturedly to "translate" whenever I needed help with the language. We both smiled.

I was married with a young family living in Del Rio. Stretching my airman's pay was always a challenge. For a time I worked nights washing dishes at the Officers' Club and walked the seven miles to my house in Del Rio when the club closed.

I was in the Air Force 30 years and consider it some of the best years of my life and my time with the 4080th a highlight.

GENE STODDARD
Schenectady, New York

Wife: Virginia

As an enlisted photographer, I did get to see a little more of the total operation than the average aircraft mechanic. I covered a variety of official events, newsworthy items and routine base photo duties.

I joined the Air Force as a 17-year-old high school dropout in November 1959. After four weeks basic training at Lackland AFB, Texas, I went by train to Lowry AFB, Colorado. At Lowry I attended the Still Photography School and in June 1960 I arrived at Laughlin AFB assigned to the Base Photo Lab.

The Base Photo Lab NCOIC was Master Sergeant Eric McGough, a no-nonsense Georgia native with a thick southern drawl; next in rank was SSgt Jack Dempsey Lyons from Florida. Both were later reassigned to the Wing Photo Lab, as were most of the airmen there at the time. The base lab was the place to be while awaiting TOP SECRET clearances required for work at the Wing Photo Lab.

Others I recall at Laughlin were Airman First Class (A1C) Mike Bevz, A1C Ernie Libertore and the remainder, like me, were junior airmen in training. Some of those in the group were Alfred Robertson, William Duette, Jimmie Hendricks, Larry Ames, Paul Sharp, and Gustavo DeLa Garza. Some who joined the lab later remained after Air Training Command took over support functions. TSgt "Nick" Nickerson did join us at the Wing Photo Lab, but Cecil Dean, Eugene Monaghan and ex-Marine Richard Thrun remained at the Base Lab along with Bevz and Libertore.

* * * * *

During a night alert, one of our U-2s went down in the desert area near the base. A1C Jimmie Hendricks was on duty that night and accordingly had the job of photographing the crash area. Upon returning to the lab, he took the initiative to call for help. Together Jimmie and I worked through the night processing film and making finished "contact" prints which were on the Wing Commander's desk by the start of the workday. Jimmie did a bang-up job. The Colonel was pleased enough to send a Letter of Commendation for us. Of course, the Colonel didn't have our names so the letters somehow found their way into the promotion packets of two other airmen. Jimmie deserved to be credited with a great job at a crucial time.

Jimmie told me that while he was photographing the crash site, at one point he needed to stand in the cockpit to shoot the instrument panel. The officer in charge of the site cautioned Jimmie not to move "because the idiot didn't replace the pin in the ejection seat." I didn't have any idea who the officer in charge was or the "idiot" he referred to. I guess the pilot had thoughts of ejecting and then changed his mind. I'm sure the officer in charge didn't really think the pilot was an idiot but it was one of those times when everyone was very excited and stressed.

* * * * *

There were so many camera assignments it is difficult to single out any one as a career highlight. However, there was one I considered as less than stellar. I had been sent to record the return of our birds from a TDY in Australia. I went out with standard equipment for a daylight shoot. The arrival was delayed and when the

195

planes finally came in, it was almost dark. My assignment was to photograph the returning pilots beside their aircraft with their families and friends. I only had flash bulbs suitable for fill work and they were not very powerful. The result was photos that showed the people and planes reasonably well but with a completely black background. To my horror, three or four photos made the front page of the *Del Rio News Herald,* the local newspaper, with my name as the photographer.

I enjoyed my assignment in the Photo Lab and I was giving serious consideration to my career after the Air Force. Photography seemed like a very real possibility for me until President Eisenhower visited Laughlin on October 24, 1960 while in the area to meet Mexican President Lopez Mateos. The occasion was to mark the opening of the new international bridge that spanned the Rio Grande between the two countries. On the previous day, I had photographed the arrival of Secretary of State Christian Herter. For me that was a life-changing experience because I decided then not to pursue a career as a news photographer. It was an unpleasant side of the news world as the "pros" jockeyed for position.

When our TOP SECRET clearances were approved, most of us were then transferred to the Wing Photo Lab where the precision processing of aerial roll film was done. The lab itself was in a windowless building near the flight line with a convenient walkway to the flight line coffee shop. At times an armed guard would be posted at the main entrance of the building, such as during the Cuban Missile Crisis. Admission to the building was strictly controlled.

The Officer in Charge of the Wing Photo Lab was Captain Roy B. Duggan, a real interesting character. I was told he was a survivor of a WWII paratroop platoon and his rank was established through a field commission made permanent by Act of Congress. My account of his record is strictly hearsay. His confidence was perhaps evident by one half of a phone conversation I overheard. It involved a dispute with a superior officer regarding base policy of additional duties for lab personnel, such as kitchen patrol or KP. It negatively affected the ongoing lab operation during the Cuban Missile Crisis. I can still see the Captain as he tipped back his chair, put his feet on the desk and drawled, "Well, Colonel, that's not the way it's going to be." I believe he was talking with the ATC base commander, Colonel Byerts. The end of the story was that Captain Duggan did indeed get his way.

During the Cuban Missile Crisis, two state-of-the-art prototype Kodak machines were installed to speed up processing of duplicated films. After October 1962 we were extremely busy until we stood down for removal to Tucson in 1963. At times we operated for long periods without sleeping, the longest such period I recall was 52 hours. There were breaks and catnaps, but no bed rest. All of our equipment was pressed into service, including the mobile unit, which we had taken to Hawaii for Operation Dominic. We also had a contingent of extra TDY photo personnel from other bases to help handle the heavy workload. Two of the TDY personnel were Stanley Knutson, whom I'd met in photo school and Eugene Mock.

One of my additional assignments was filming U-2 training flights. I never saw any of the movie film I shot; I can only assume it was okay because I never heard a complaint. The idea was that the pilot trainees could see and evaluate their landing and takeoff skills. The filming was done from a level-on position below the control tower.

A few highlights of our off duty life came as improvements were made to the base recreation facilities. The addition of a bowling alley, Airmen's Club and library probably created havoc in the economies of Del

197

Rio and Cuidad Acuna bars. The new swimming pool was directly across from my barracks and was a Godsend on some of those brutally hot summer days. Even when we were not at the pool, we could enjoy some of the more attractive female swimmers a short distance across the road.

I was assigned a TDY as part of a large operation called Joint Task Force 8, also known as Operation Dominic. It took place in late spring of 1962 and the objective was in support of atomic tests over Johnston Island in the Pacific. For this operation, a large, unused section of Hickam AFB, Hawaii was opened for our use. We lived in pre-WWII barracks that boasted patches covering the bullet holes from the Japanese attack on Pearl Harbor and Hickam Field. Surprisingly, the barracks had small individual rooms, rather than an open bay construction.

There was one detonation over Johnston Island that I watched with others from the ridgepole of our rickety old barracks. The remaining operations were delayed and then cancelled. After several weeks in beautiful Hawaii, we packed up and went home ahead of schedule. I never visited the Arizona Memorial, something I regret to this day.

One fun thing at Hickam was a design spray painted on our shirts. Oscar the Crow, a four-foot cigar-chewing model of the Old Crow Distillery symbol, became the mascot of our Crow Flight detachment. One of the flight line crew was an artist and he had devised a set of stencils with a special version of Oscar the Crow in native attire. The shirts caused something of a stir at Fort DeRussy and Waikiki. I'm afraid my shirt disappeared after my discharge.

In September 1962, I was sent to Guam on another TDY. The announced purpose of the TDY was support of high altitude weather sampling, but who knew. Two of us were sent out. Our only function was to set up a field photo lab from standard field issue. This would be done only in the event we were sent to an un-named forward position. My only duty was to inventory my equipment and wait.

Once we arrived, Airman X (as I refer to him here) and I had no real functions but were assigned "make-work" duties. I was assigned to an air-conditioned Quonset hut where our pilots suited up. All I had to do was drive the pilot to his plane in the air-conditioned truck. Most of my time was spent drinking coffee and playing cards with our private cook, Airman Arby, who had been temporarily assigned from the main mess hall. As I recall, he made perhaps the world's finest coffee.

Guam was beautiful, the climate was ideal, and I had a great duty assignment. Then Airman X struck and the tides turned. He was a unique person with a Bronx, New York, attitude and an abrasive personality. I figured the Wing Lab had probably sent him for the express purpose of being rid of him for a while. He had been assigned to do errands for Lt. Col. McCaslin and the Operations Center staff. I'm not sure what he did to irritate Colonel McCaslin or the staff, but he certainly messed things up for me. The upshot was he got my cushy job and I got his in the hot, un-air conditioned operations building with no cook and no world-class coffee.

Lt. Col. McCaslin was a tall man who barely fit in the cockpit of his U-2. I was told his head was in a forward position and his helmet contacted the canopy when he flew. He seemed an affable person and I never experienced a problem with him or anyone else. I concluded then that Airman X had been at fault. My new duties then became mainly the destruction of classified data and making up the weekly football pool.

An interesting side note concerning Airman X— before we departed on that TDY, we were both issued some travel equipment. Among the items was a B-4 bag. On his B-4 bag was the name of the previous user, Second Lieutenant (2Lt) Powers, Francis G.

While on this beautiful island, I purchased my first 35mm camera and began taking some personal photos. I swam at Tarague Beach, played pitch and generally enjoyed the scenery. There were inter-service football games and even cheerleaders.

An interesting feature of our rooms was a live gecko-lined ceiling. They became a little noisy but in general caused no problem. In fact, their presence significantly reduced the bug population. The shower and other facilities were conveniently located between two bays. The rooms had no windows, just louvers. The barracks building was three stories high, built of sturdy concrete, which would shortly be put to the test of Typhoon Karen.

One evening in October we received a general alert. Everyone was to report to their duty station immediately. There was a mad scramble and for a time it looked as if we would soon learn the location of that un-named forward area. Our gear was put on transport planes that were loaded and idled on the runway. We were lined up and given shots for some unusual destination. Luckily, the alert status was changed and not only had I been fortunate to miss the shots, we were not leaving for a combat zone. We learned later the reason for the alert was the discovery of missile sites in Cuba.

A couple of weeks later we were warned of an approaching storm. It turned out to be one of the most powerful typhoons ever recorded for the area. November 11, 1962, Typhoon Karen came ashore with devastating effect. As I recall there was no loss of life on Guam, but there was tremendous loss of property.

After the initial storm warning, Lt. Col. McCaslin informed the area commander that our two U-2s were incapable of taking off if the winds reached a certain velocity and evacuation would then be impossible. The evacuation order was delayed and later the storm trackers predicted a direct hit. By that time, wind velocity exceeded the U-2's limitations. The planes were put in a hangar by the runway. Unfortunately, the storm destroyed the hangar and the planes inside were too badly damaged to fly. After some scary work removing twisted and swinging girders, we removed the U-2s, crated them and flew them home on transports.

Without planes, our operation had ended. We didn't leave immediately and therefore, we enjoyed the pleasures of post-typhoon life, such as K-rations, no showers or potable water. The storm had changed weather patterns and it didn't rain for several days. When it finally did rain, most of us rushed out on the lawn with a bar of soap. Although we could see the Pacific Ocean, the beach was off limits due to dangerous and poisonous creatures washed ashore in the storm.

Only slightly more pleasurable than my rain shower was my first cup of Hobo coffee. It was produced on a paint-can stove and boiled in a #10 can mooched from the mess hall, along with the coffee grounds. As much fun as this had been, we packed up and left for home.

Things were pretty much work and sleep for a while when I got back. We were processing film hot and heavy. Although I never knew many details, there was no doubt from the film of the existence of missile sites in Cuba. The only breaks we had were the results of too much cloud cover over the target area and no film to process. Sadly, we learned one of our pilots, Major Rudolph Anderson, was shot down over Cuba while filming those same missile sites. May a grateful Nation never forget him.

Another unforgettable character was Headquarters Squadron First Sergeant Russell Field. He was a powerfully built man who was a serious weight lifter. I was told he had once competed in the Mr. California Competition and came in second to Steve Reeves of the Hercules movie fame. Perhaps this was an exaggeration, but I never knew for sure. I do know that nobody messed with the "First Sleeve" in our squadron. While I'm sure it wasn't strictly legal, Sgt Field would make small, short-term loans of 5 for 6 on payday. Everybody always paid up. I'm almost sure he made more in his "loan" business than the Air Force paid him.

Sadly, the only time I was ever in the Base Chapel was on a photo assignment. I did occasionally attend the Lutheran Church in Del Rio where a youthful Reverend Ahlert J. C. Strand had a way of making me feel I was the subject of his sermon. Perhaps it was my conscience working on me, as it might well have been, but I think he was really a very good preacher. No fire and brimstone mind you, just strong lessons in personal conduct.

Between TDY's in 1962, I played on the lab's slow pitch softball team led by TSgt LeDuc and SSgt Loomis Robertson. While we lost every game, a good time was had by all. One game started off with a bit of excitement when a small rattlesnake was killed at home plate.

Events eventually wound down and I received an early discharge due to the 4080th SRW's move to Tucson. Had the move not forced an immediate decision on my part, it is quite likely that I would have re-enlisted and made the Air Force a career. That being said, I took the other fork in the road.

Gene Stoddard, 1961

Photographic Lab, Group 1

Photo specialists at Bien Hoa 1964, Standing L to R: John Washburn, Larry Wachter (Tech Rep), Sgt McDowell, Airman Rodriguez, Kneeling L to R, Airmen Salisbury and Clampit

JOHN W. WASHBURN
(Deceased December 12, 2006)

The following information was submitted by John prior to his death.

I was with the U-2 program for 12 years and thoroughly enjoyed the camaraderie of the men I worked with. I was assigned to the NEPHO unit and worked with the cameras that were installed in the U-2 for the photo recon missions. During many operations, we worked around the clock to prepare, load and unload the cameras. I made a lot of life-long friends during that time, too many to list. Like all the other fellows, I went on TDYs with the unit but I felt badly being away from my family for long periods.

BUCK YOUNG
Baytown, Texas

Wife: Claire

On April 1, 1957, the 4080th SRW moved from Turner AFB to Laughlin AFB, and the first U-2 flew into the base on June 11, 1957. I watched the plane land, but even as the Base Information Services Officer, I did not know what to make of this unusual plane. I certainly had no idea about its mission.

My wife, Claire, and I had made arrangements for Space No. 29 at the Rio Vista Trailer Park off Gibbs Street in Del Rio where we set up our Hicks mobile home. Rio Vista in English means "River View" but there was no river within sight of our home. In fact, the railroad ran behind the trailer park. I didn't have a clue how to set up a mobile home, but fortunately for me, there were a number of Air Force personnel already living there. Everybody pitched in to help get our mobile home connected, propped up and leveled. The wives brought over a pot-luck supper while the men worked on setting up our home. We immediately felt welcomed into the trailer park.

My job as Information Services Officer at Laughlin got off to a fast start. Colonel Willard Beauchamp summoned me for a staff meeting. I had the competent assistance of A1C Reginald "Dub" Lawley who had been best man at our wedding. In addition, my staff included SSgt. Larry Miller, A1C Dick Oakerson, and four airmen fresh out of basic training: Roger Newell, Alfred Warjas, Bill Hillard and Dewey Griffith and photographer TSgt. Jasper (J.J.) Derouen. This staff was responsible for publishing the eight-page tabloid called *The Laughlin*

Recon printed by contract at the local newspaper, *Del Rio News Herald*.

I was also responsible for community relations and with Colonel Beauchamp attended monthly meetings of the Good Neighbor Committee in Del Rio. In the summer of 1957, the Committee decided to hold a fundraiser for the planned October Festival. The fundraising event was to be a "bloodless" bullfight in Acuna, Mexico, across the border from Del Rio. Colonel Zemke, the Wing Commander, his Deputy Commander Colonel Nate Adams and Colonel Beauchamp joined six local citizens in the bullring at La Macarena to taunt, poke, provoke and generally intimidate the bull before running from it. Jim Thatcher and I were the wheelbarrow and shovel crew to clean up after the bull. The predictable result was that the bull was declared the winner, but it was a fun event enjoyed by all who attended.

In March 1957, almost a year after my arrival at Laughlin, I was reassigned to Sondrestrom Air Base, Greenland.

My first opportunity to return to Laughlin some 41 years later was the 2005 Reunion of the 4080th SRW. I attended with my daughter, Lila. It was an enjoyable weekend renewing old acquaintances and showing my daughter where we lived so many years ago.

1/Lt Buck Young

Supervising the base newspaper prep Nov 1957.
L to R: A3C Roger Newell, A3C William Hillard, 1/Lt Buck A. Young.

DRESSING UP AND STEPPING OUT

Experience teaches slowly and at
the cost of mistakes.

James Frounde

THE DEVELOPMENT OF THE PARTIAL PRESSURE SUIT

David G. Clark started working with a knitting company in the 1930's and later left the company to start his own business manufacturing two-way stretch fibers used in women's girdles. Although his formal education ended at age 15 when he left school to work full time, he attended evening schools for courses in accounting and business at the insistence of his father. He earned no diplomas or degrees after grammar school, but he had an insatiable interest in science. By age 39 he had been granted six patents for items related to the knitting business.

Through his friend, E. J. Baldes, head of Biophysics at the Mayo Clinic, David Clark began research into the development of "G" or pressure suits. The pressure suit, required for flights above 65,000 feet were vital in saving a pilot's life if the aircraft lost pressure. Without a pressure suit to provide supplemental oxygen, the pilot had 60 seconds maximum before he became incapacitated. During his research, Clark became acquainted with a Navy flight surgeon stationed on the aircraft carrier USS Franklin Delano Roosevelt. He was asked by the flight surgeon to make an ear protection device for the men on the flight deck of the carrier; they had nothing but their hands covering their ears to keep out the jet engine noise. Through that contact, Clark pursued his production of the pressure suit and the company began blitz production for the Navy.

When the end of WWII came, the company anticipated an order from the Navy to cease production. However, the order was, in fact, just the contrary and the Clark Company continued production of the pressure suit.

In 1946 the Air Force became interested in the pressure suit for its own pilots. The future of aviation had a special niche to be filled by the David Clark Company. With a budget of $20,000, the Air Force ordered 20 pressure suits from the Clark Company. Through much trial and error and reviews by Wright Patterson, a final pressure suit was approved. With modifications over the years, the Clark Company has continued to make pressure suits for the Air Force and NASA.

Until recent years, all pilots went to the Worcester, Massachusetts factory to be measured and fitted for their custom made pressure suit. Now the company has 12 standard sizes of patterns for the suits with the exception of a couple of female astronauts who had to be custom fitted due to their petite size.

The Clark Company also designs and manufacturers helmets and ear protectors with microphones. Their ear protectors are in use by military and civilian aviation pilots and flight line support personnel.

4080th SRW PHYSIOLOGICAL SUPPORT DIVISION

The Physiological Support Division (PSD) consisted of two groups to support the U-2 pilots in their flight preparations. The Personal Equipment Group consisted of about 30 technicians and the Medical Group consisted of about 25 fully qualified flight surgeons and medical technicians. The technicians in both groups were cross trained to support each other on TDYs. It was not unusual for only four Personal Equipment technicians to be on duty at Laughlin when all others were on TDY.

Pilots scheduled for flights were given a physical by the flight surgeon on duty. (See Dragon Lady Doctors for additional information.) PSD operated a fully equipped kitchen and supplied the high protein meals each pilot ate prior to flight. Steak and eggs, the most common meal, was cooked on the spot and served to the pilots.

When the pilots were cleared to fly by the medical team, they came to the Personal Equipment unit where technicians assisted them in suiting up. Each pilot was assigned a locker for storing his gear—the long johns, pressure suit, parachute and helmet. Each parachute received an inspection every 90 days and was rechecked once a year.

Fully suited up, the pilots went to a room with recliners where they pre-breathed 100 percent oxygen for one hour. Once suited up, the pilot carries approximately 35 pounds of gear. The medical technicians were on hand to monitor the pre-breathing process and connected each pilot to a portable oxygen bottle for the van ride to the aircraft. Once the pilot was seated in the cockpit, the technician unhooked the portable oxygen supply and connected the pilot to the aircraft system. At that time the technician goes through an audible checklist to ensure that all hoses, belts, and connectors are at the appropriate setting. When the checklist was completed, the technician patted the pilot's helmet, climbed down the ladder and was replaced by the Mobile Control Officer to perform his checklist with the pilot.

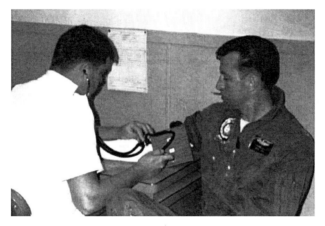

Buddy Brown beginning the preflight physical exam with the Flight Surgeon.

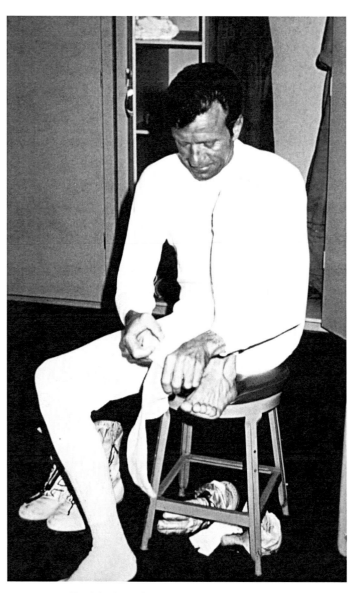

**Buddy dressing in the long underwear
worn under the pressure suit.**

**PSD specialist assists Buddy
with his pressure suit.**

**PSD specialist assists Buddy putting
on the outer garment which
protects the pressure suit.**

217

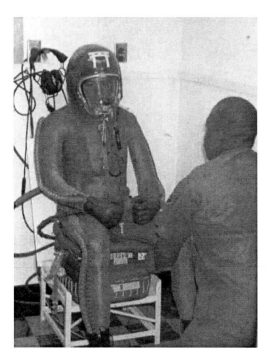

Buddy hooked up to the seat kit system. Next procedure is pre-breathing 100% oxygen for one hour.

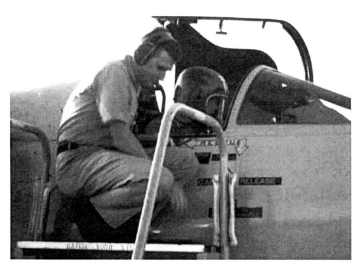

Buddy in the cockpit going through pre-flight check with the Mobile Control Officer.

218

JAMES W. MAY
Mesquite, Texas

Wife: Patricia

Naturally, all of my time at Laughlin AFB was not spent on base. I recall a fishing trip I went on with a Del Rio friend, Gordon McGonigle. The Air Force had a recreation facility at Lake Walk where we could rent boats.

Gordon really knew where to find the best fishing holes, but this particular time was rather scary. There was an upper dam and lower dam on the lake and we went to the upper dam. On the right side of the dam was a discharge tunnel about 10 or 12 feet wide, with water rushing from it into the lake. Gordon headed the boat at full speed into that dark hole in the dam. The water flowed so fast we inched our way inside about 20 feet. Our lantern was bright and Gordon tied the boat to what looked like hitching post rings on the walls. We had to use very heavy weights on the fishing line to compensate for the swift current. I had watched Gordon a few nights before make the weights from the lead in busted up old car batteries. He melted the lead and poured it into a large spoon.

We did catch a bunch of fish that time but I never wanted to go into that hole again. I don't know what Gordon does now but I heard his brother is a fishing guide at Lake Amistad. That love of fishing must run in the family.

I went fishing with a bunch of guys on the Devil's River before Lake Amistad was built. I liked to fish next to the old steam plant where the water was the clearest and cleanest I had ever seen. I caught bass, perch, crappie, catfish, garfish and even an occasional green turtle. When we got tired of fishing, we would go hiking around the countryside and look for wild javalina hogs running in packs.

After two years at Laughlin AFB, I was fortunate enough to meet and marry a Del Rio girl, Patricia Tabor. After a one-year courtship, we married at her preacher's home and was that a story worth telling. Sgt. Hand and another sergeant I worked with showed up drunk and crying, "James don't do it. You're messing up your life." The preacher made them stay in the kitchen during the ceremony.

After the ceremony, we headed out on our honeymoon to Dallas. We had gotten 31 miles to Brackettville when Pat said she'd forgotten her straw hat. It went with a certain outfit, so she made me turn around and go back for it. That's 31 miles driven, 31 miles back to get the hat and 31 miles again to Brackettville, a total of 93 miles for a bonnet. Was that what Sgt. Hand was trying to tell me?

We were married one year before my discharge from the AF and in that year, I went TDY to England for four months. TDYs were rough on the married guys and families.

On days off from Laughlin AFB, everyone learned by word of mouth where to go for fun. Paul Arnold and I played billards at a pool hall next to the City Café on Main Street. We also spent time at the bowling alley. Then there was the Rita Theatre in town or the Gay 90 Drive In Theatre on the highway to the base. Between paychecks, when money was short, the trunk of my car could hold three guys who would sneak into the drive-in. I guess the theater ticket seller thought I drove a "low rider" but we never got caught. Having a car made it nice to hang out at the local restaurants that had drive-in service such as Ceasar's or the High Hat.

Another fun place I found near Del Rio was Garner State Park which had a pavilion with a large outdoor dance floor. That's where I learned the Texas two step.

On one three-day pass Clem Francis and a few of us guys rented a cabin on the Nueces River north of Brackettville. We spent a time fishing and had a big fish fry on our last night out. During that weekend we stopped at the Devil's Sink Hole which wasn't a state attraction yet. The guys lowered me and another small guy by rope into the huge, deep natural hole. It was approximately 40 yards across and over 1000 feet deep. I was last to be brought back up, but at first the guys couldn't lift me, so they tied the rope to the rear axle of the Jeep Wagoneer and I was up and out fast. Before the Jeep was brought into the mix, I made a lot of promises to the Lord as I was hanging in space. I probably haven't kept all of them.

* * * * *

While on a stop over in Hawaii enroute to Australia TDY, we were assigned to set up and receive our U-2s coming in to Hickam. We were all told the bad news that one plane had a "flameout" over the ocean about 500 miles out.

As the story was told to me, the pilot was asked for his coordinates so any ships in the area could do a rescue. To their amazement, he said he was coming on in. Now, I call that gliding! He would only make one pass to land which he did with all of us watching. You don't forget stories like that.

Hawaii was beautiful. A couple of guys and I went to Waikiki Beach, wearing our swimsuits under our jeans, and swam in the clear waters of the Pacific Ocean. Then donning our jeans over wet swimsuits, we went into town for a couple of very expensive beers. It was still a fun experience though.

221

When we departed Hawaii, we were island hopping; first to Cantoon and then Fiji. I have a very scary memory of Cantoon. The runway there is very short and with our fully loaded C-130 Globemaster, it took three attempts to get airborne. Each time the pilot would rev up the engines for a long time then the big giant would shoot off like a race car. Twice he hit the brakes with a lot of smoking and groaning from them. We would stop, turn around only a few yards from the waves coming in. After that experience, I am convinced--you pilots have brass ones!

After a fuel stop on beautiful Fiji Island, we reached our destination of East Sale, Victoria, Australia, about 200 miles southeast of Melbourne. We arrived at the end of winter and beginning of spring, October and November 1960. Their seasons are opposite of ours.

The people of Sale treated us very well. It was embarrassing being asked for an autograph. Some of their customs are a little different from ours. On my first day in town, another airman and I learned one such custom. We went into a pub for a cool one (no "cold" ones there). Before finishing our mugs, two more were set in front of us, courtesy of some blokes at a nearby table. The bartender said it was a custom to buy them one in return which we did. To make a long story short, we kept this exchange going until I'd had 7 or 8 mugs. I'm still unclear how that 19-year-old got back to the barracks. From then on, I was more careful with the ale.

Before our tour called Crow Flight VI was over I went to a sheep ranch for a big cookout of lamb chops, naturally. A local farmer took me kangaroo hunting. It was neat to see the kangaroos bouncing over fences.

Later I went on a two-day R&R to Melbourne. What a great city! There was an open house on the RAAF station for the local community, Royal Australian Air Force personnel and the press. My contribution to the event was to suit up in the high altitude pressure suit and helmet for a four-hour demonstration.

I thoroughly enjoyed that TDY; for me, it was a sad day when we packed up and returned home.

* * * * *

Late one day down at PSD the last U-2 pilot landed and was brought in to be undressed from his pressure suit and debriefed. Before he landed, the pilot, whom I refuse to name, was still airborne and needed to relieve himself most urgently. He got out the "pee" bottle, unzipped the flight suit but couldn't find the opening in his long-john underwear. After trying several times with no luck, he got out his survival pocketknife and cut a hole in the underwear. That's needing to go bad.

While we were undressing him, the large hole in front of his underwear had blood all around it. In his haste to take care of business, he had cut the end of his "you know what." He insisted on no stitches and a medic just cleaned the wound and put a band aid on it. I guess that's why he got hazard pay.

* * * * *

My second TDY was quite different; I spent four months at Eielson AFB, Fairbanks, Alaska. I have never been so cold or seen snow that deep in my entire life.

We arrived in the middle of March and returned home in the middle of July. That's really a good time to go there because we had an opportunity to see winter, spring and part of their short summer. Experiencing 24 hours of darkness and then 24 hours of daylight was strange.

On my one day off, I went up to the ski lodge to learn snow skiing. On the bus I talked with a guy who wore a big leg cast. He said he had broken his ankle a couple weeks back when he tried to ski for the first time. That's all I needed to hear and I no longer wanted that adventure.

One day while on duty, I had to go with the pilots to watch a survival film. The film actually showed how to build an igloo by cutting snow blocks. If the weather was bad, the film said to just dig a hole in a snow bank resembling a bear den and close up the hole. The film reassured us help should be on the way. I know that our country owes a lot to these pilots for all the dangerous places they fly.

Late one day, I noticed something was causing the pogos to stay on the wings of the U-2 on takeoff. To avoid aborting a flight because of the pogo problem, I was told to hold up one wing and another airman would hold up the other wing. As the pilot started his takeoff, we were to run like h--- with him until he could balance it. We only had to run about 15 or so steps before "Kitty Hawk" took off.

When we were leaving for home at the end of the TDY, we loaded aboard the C-130 for a nine-hour flight to Seattle, Washington. Every time I looked out the windows, all I saw were snow-capped, wicked-looking mountains. About three hours out, we had one engine catch fire. The pilot shut it down, and we continued on to Seattle.

After one more hour, an engine on the other side started smoking and it was shut down. We then returned to Fairbanks. We never unloaded the plane; we slept in chairs in the base terminal while a dozen engine techs overhauled both engines for about eight hours. One of the techs showed me a burned valve from one of the engines. I asked him, "What if two engines were lost on the same side?" He said it could still fly but would need to have the load lightened.

I was a little nervous getting back in that old C-130 so quickly, but we flew on safely to Washington and then to

Laughlin. I was returning to marry my fiancé, Pat Tabor. I thank all those pilots and engine technicians for knowing and performing their jobs so well that day.

* * * * *

Down at the Physiological Support Division, better known as PSD, after all the flights were in, one of the U-2 pilots asked us not to undress him. He said he wanted to see if, in a survival situation, he could get himself out of it.

Well, we all stood back, gave him some room and watched what kind of looked like Houdini getting out of a straight jacket. After about 20 minutes and a lot of sweat, he asked us for help. Since this was a serious matter to him, no one uttered a chuckle until the pilot was gone.

* * * * *

Many unusual things happened after the U-2 pilots came in from their flights. On one occasion, a pilot returned from a flight and was getting undressed as usual. Poor fellow must have had a stomach virus because he had completely soiled his pressure suit.

I was on duty that day but I got lucky because Senior Master Sergeant Clem Francis picked my roommate, Bob Wilson, to take the suit into our latrine and clean it. The outrageously expensive suit could not be laundered. Bob cleaned on it for quite some time but Clem smelled it and sent Bob back for more cleaning. Three checks of the suit after attempted cleaning and Clem finally said, "Condemn it!"

* * * * *

One lazy Sunday while I was on duty alone down at PSD where we stored the parachutes and flying gear, I was called and told to hurry up and bring out 25 parachutes to our C-123 cargo plane. The plane was carrying our baseball team somewhere for a game that day.

It took me a while to get them loaded into the van and out to the flight line to the C-123. Since they were in a hurry, the ball team was told to help me get them loaded in the plane. How was I to know they thought that metal D-ring was a carrying handle? As I recall, they popped open about six parachutes before they learned that the D-ring was not a handle. I returned to PSD for more parachutes and finally sent the team on their way.

James W. May, 1962

James and Patricia May, 2004

GERALD E. (JERRY) MCILMOYLE
Venice, Florida

THE PRESSURE SUIT

The David Clark Company in Worcester, Massachusetts, made the first partial pressure suits for us. This entire process was done "in the black" with CIA directing every aspect of the trip. The company also made full pressure suits for astronauts, helmets, earphones, mikes and other devices used by our bomber and fighter aircraft crews.

I went there in late 1956 or early 1957 with instructions not to bring military ID card or dog tags. We were told to bring only civilian clothes and no GI issue underwear. I went to David Clark Company to be fitted for two partial pressure suits. In my mind's eye, I can still see the humongous room with row upon row of sewing machines operated by women sewing bras and corsets, the original products of the company. In the middle of the room was an oldtime wooden stairway leading to a basement where the corridor ended at a green door. Behind the green door were a few people sewing what looked to me like flight suits. At the back of the room was a black door leading to the next room. Inside this room were only a few people and I was instructed to remove all clothes except undershorts. I was told to climb on the two-foot high elevated round platform and stand at a brace.

A stoop-shouldered, wizened old man entered the room. With a tape measure dangling around his neck, he wore a white shirt with sleeves held away from his hands by black armbands. This skillful man proceeded to measure every inch of my body, and I mean every inch.

He even used a cup that he could adjust to determine the volume of my "you know what apparatus"! Then he said, "Okay, we are through. Come back in the morning. A car will come again for you. We will then determine any adjustments that must be made."

The next day I returned to the company. Again I was instructed to strip down, don a set of inside out "long johns" and then put on the pressure suit. The company people hooked it all up, showed me how it should be worn and proclaimed no adjustments were needed.

They gave me two bags containing two partial pressure suits and handed me a folder of airline tickets. The company rep told me, "The first ticket takes you to New York and you will stay at a designated hotel for two days. Go see all the sights, a ball game at Yankee Stadium, Statue of Liberty, Empire State Building and Grant's Tomb just like you are a tourist."

I did the tourist routine. On the third day I presented the tickets at the airline counter and flew all over the country, changing planes and airlines. Casper, Wyoming was experiencing a blizzard and I almost got stranded there, but continued my journey and finally arrived back in Great Falls, Montana where I had begun. This was a memorable trip for sure.

JOSEPH (JOE) RUSECKAS
Worcester, MA

Wife: Marcia

My own flight career began during WWII from February 5, 1942 to February 24, 1946. I served in the Air Force Reserves until my honorable discharge with the rank of Major.

Following my retirement, I was employed by Civil Aeronautics as a flight check pilot and had the opportunity to meet David G. Clark when I flew with him for his own check flight. That meeting was the beginning of a new career for me. Mr. Clark offered me a job as a pattern maker with his company. The current pattern maker was leaving the company for maternity leave and a vacancy was open.

I was then employed by the David Clark Company. Inc. in Worcester, Massachusetts. The company had a Government contract and it designed, furnished and supported the pressure suits the U-2 pilots and astronauts wore for high altitude flights. The company was awarded the NASA contract for all Gemini flights. I was not assigned to the 4080th SRW but was "adopted" into the organization because of the close association with many of its personnel. Pilots came to the Worcester facility of David Clark Company to be measured and fitted with the custom-made suits. I accompanied them to Wright Patterson AFB for chamber flight qualification. It was very special for me being personally involved in the pressure suit project from design to implementation.

I had the opportunity to work with the Air Force and Navy to design and make full pressure suits for X15 pilots. Chuck Yeager was the first to be fitted and I was responsible for his measurements and fitting. The Navy was set to make an altitude record in 1953 in a Douglas 553. I went along on the flight in the bomb bay and recorded the altitude of 83,000 feet.

The Air Force got into the X15 project with Scott Crossfield. He did a test in a Clark suit that I measured and fitted for him. The U-2 program came along and pilots required a partial pressure suit. Every U-2 pilot came to the David Clark Company in Massachusetts. I accompanied the early pilots to Wright Patterson AFB to see that the suit passed testing before the pilots were assigned to the program.

Mr. Clark started out with a knitting company in the 1930's and later left to start his own company that made a two-way stretch fiber used in girdles. He became acquainted with a Navy flight surgeon stationed on the aircraft carrier, Franklin Delano Roosevelt. As early as 1946, the Air Force contacted the Clark Company about developing early model pressure suits.

Mr. Clark's flight surgeon acquaintance again contacted him and requested the company's help to provide ear protection for flight line personnel. Mr. Clark asked me to design the ear muffs and sent the early model to Pratt & Whitney for test. The end result was so successful a half dozen were made and sent to the carrier. A call came back almost immediately to make more. The Clark Company earmuffs have distinctive green domes with the letters "DC" and are presently used by many flight personnel. We later put headsets and microphones in the earmuffs and we were the first to produce the headsets for football teams. It all started with the call to Mr. Clark from the flight surgeon aboard the carrier Roosevelt.

At the time I worked to support the U-2 project, my wife, Marcia, understood that I could not tell her where I was going or what I was doing due to the security classification. Like military wives, Marcia accepted my career choice and she ran the household and cared for our daughter, Connie, in my absence.

Marcia has suffered some major health problems in recent years that have left her incapacitated, but she was in those days, as she is now, my "Co-pilot". My "Co-pilot" was unable to attend the 2005 reunion with me, but my daughter, Connie, accompanied me and shared in the many memories we all recalled those many years ago. It was also a pleasure to meet some new friends as well.

Joe and Marcia Ruseckas

DRAGON LADY
DOCTORS

The art of medicine consists in amusing
the patient while nature cures the disease.

Voltaire

ROBERT W. PARET
Knoxville, Tennessee

In 1952 I flew 100 missions in Korea in the F-84A, C and G. When I was a physician, I transferred to the Medical Corps of the Air Force and became a Flight Surgeon. I regained my pilot rating and became dual qualified shortly before I left active duty and joined the Texas National Guard. Through the ANG I was appointed as Assistant to the USAF Surgeon General for ANG Affairs with the rank of Major General USAF MC.

I was one of the Flight Surgeons who supported the 4080th SRW through the Physiological Support Division. There were at least two and sometimes three Flight Surgeons assigned to the Wing. First names that come to mind are Bruno, Doug, Bob Self, one other whose name is lost to memory, and myself. One Flight Surgeon was required to remain at Laughlin AFB to support the remaining pilot cadre when temporary duty units were in action.

Before every flight, the pilots began their preflight at PSD. The first item on the preflight was a physical exam consisting of the usual vital signs. Through questions and observation, the Flight Surgeon would determine if any additional exams were necessary to approve the pilot for flight. If there was any problem identified in the exam, the pilot would be grounded and a replacement scheduled. Following the exam and clearance to fly, the pilot went to the dining area for his high protein meal. After dining, he was given some relaxation time before getting into the partial pressure suit with the help of the PSD technicians. Oxygen pre-breathing followed. The technicians then connected the pilot to a mobile oxygen tank and he was transported to his assigned aircraft in an air-conditioned van. The pilot was helped into the cockpit by the same technicians who quickly connected his suit to the aircraft oxygen system.

Most TDYs required a Flight Surgeon to accompany the detachment if high altitude physiological support was not available at the remote location. When time was critical, a PSD technician took vital signs freeing the Flight Surgeon to proceed with the physical exams. I went on TDYs to Howard AFB, Panama, East Sale, Australia, Alaska, Fiji Islands and Hawaii. Some of the other Flight Surgeons supported the Cuban Missile Crisis from MacDill AFB, Florida.

Robert W. Paret, MD

235

Bob Paret preparing for a flight.

DRAGON LADY CAREGIVERS

Ask not what your country can do for you;
ask what you can do for your country.

John Fitzgerald Kennedy

MAINTENANCE

Once there was a very pretty young thing nicknamed "Dragon Lady." She was extremely lithe and graceful, yet gorgeous and ugly at the same time. Her personality could go from the fairest lady in the world to the biggest screaming banshee one could imagine. The guys who gave her this strange name were themselves called "Dragons." Some liked to take her up, up and away to glory and beyond. Some had the enviable job of being with her every day. Dragon Lady was also mysterious and tried her best to hang around all those handsome Dragons. Ah, what a lady! And, at over 50 years, the Dragon Lady is aging gracefully and hanging on to her loveliness; she is still one heck of a girl. The Dragons, most of whom have not aged nearly as gracefully, still love her deeply.

--Glenn Chapman, TSgt. (Ret.) USAF
Author, Me and U-2, My Affair With Dragon Lady

It took a team of well-trained men and specialized equipment to support the U-2 program. Although the job duties varied greatly, no one took their work lightly. The 4080th SRW consisted of only 900 people comprised of pilots and navigators, in addition to the operations, maintenance and support staffs. The Wing Commander was directly responsible for the entire cadre of personnel. He reported to the Strategic Air Command Headquarters. In 1962 Air Training Command (ATC) assumed control of the base, and support units then rolled to the new command. However, units directly involved with the U-2 support (food service, motor pool, finance, personnel, civil engineering, etc.) had a TOP SECRET area called

"Warehouse B". Direct duty of operations and maintenance squadrons were the primary units of the 4080th SRW. The 4080th also had its own Security Police and Medical Units separate from the ATC support unit.

In addition to the 4080th Wing Headquarters, these support units were Operational Maintenance Squadron (OMS), Field Maintenance Squadron (FMS) and Armament and Electronics Squadron (AEMS or also known as A&E) which performed direct maintenance on the U-2 aircraft. Assigned to each of these maintenance squadrons were civilian Technical Representatives (Tech Reps). They were employees of and supported contracts for such vendors as Lockheed Aircraft Company, Pratt and Whitney, Hycon, Perkin-Elmer, and TRW. They were not specifically "hands on" maintenance workers; they were the "answer men" when problems arose in the equipment of the company they represented.

ORGANIZATIONAL MAINTENANCE SQUADRON: OMS was responsible for all Airplane General (APG) maintenance ensuring the aircraft was always fully flight ready prior to being scheduled by Operations. With exception for a few administrative, supply and support staffs, OMS was made up entirely of specialists known as Crew Chiefs. Two Crew Chiefs, a primary and assistant, were assigned to each aircraft and ensured that their designated aircraft was fully flight ready.

FIELD MAINTENANCE SQUADRON: Jet Engine Build Up (JEBU) was comprised of specialists who worked on the J-57 and J-75 engines of the U-2. This was not a flight line function, but was performed in the shop. Engine changes were the primary work performed by JEBU which could be the result of periodic maintenance required and certain inspections. Changing an engine was a difficult job. It required precision teamwork to complete the job correctly and safely.

Sheet Metal: Sheet metal specialists spent most of their time working on the aircraft itself. Repairing damage or replacing pieces lost in flight were things the specialists dealt with daily. Sheet metal specialists worked with very precise tolerances. They took great pride in their skills and were indispensable to the program.

Machinist Shop: Almost 100 percent of the machinists' time was spent on the aircraft or the ground support equipment. It was a common occurrence for specialists to strip a screw head while attempting to replace a panel on the fuselage. A machinist would be dispatched to remove the screw so the specialist could finish the work order.

Hydraulics Shop: The hydraulics specialists actually had the dirtiest job. Everything they touched used hydraulic fluid that leaked on them regardless of the precautions they took to prevent it. There was a Murphy's Law at the Hydraulics Shop that stated, "The hydraulic fitting that was leaking was always the most difficult to see, access and repair."

Pneumatic (O2) Shop: The responsibility of the Pneumatics Shop was to repair anything to do with air supply system difficulties. The biggest responsibility of that shop was pressurization of the cockpit. If the cockpit lost pressurization, the pilot's partial pressure suit would instantly inflate to provide 14 pounds per square inch artificial pressure.

Instruments Shop: Technicians of this shop maintained all instrumentation in the aircraft, including the Optical Sextant, which was the primary navigation reference for night missions.

Egress Shop: Better known as the "ejection seat" that hurled the pilot from the aircraft in an inflight emergency, the Egress Technician's primary area of expertise was the maintenance and operation of the ejection system.

ARMAMENT AND ELECTRONICS SQUADRON (A&E):

Radio Shop: The Radio Shop, better known as Comm, maintained all radios in the U-2.

Radar Shop: Like Radio, Radar had only a few units that were their responsibility. The primary unit in the early days was the ARN-6 Radio Compass Unit. It was a small unit set in area. It used conventional AM radio stations as a navigational aid.

Auto Pilot Shop: When the U-2 came to the 4080th, there were no auto pilot specialists in the Air Force. In 1958 the Air Force authorized a new Air Force Specialty Code (AFSC) called Automatic Pilot. The auto pilot system was considered more electrical than electronic so the personnel were assigned to FMS and later became part of A&E.

SFERICS: This was the cover name for the electronic countermeasure equipment carried in the U-2. In reference books it was described as "the study of lightning." However, with the 4080th SRW, it was the gathering of electronic intelligence or ELINT. The main SFERICS platform that went into the equipment bay was System 4, a more passive ELINT system. System 9 and System 12 were also used but carried a higher level of security classification.

NEPHOGRAPHY: See Section "What is Nepho?"

IVORY TOWER: Ivory Tower was the name of a weather platform that was carried in the U-2 equipment bay. It appeared quite primitive to the naked eye. It was nothing more than a piece of three-quarter inch plywood cut to fit inside the Q-Bay with a variety of weather equipment on the platform.

HAROLD A. (BROWNIE) BROWNBACK
Oklahoma City, Oklahoma

Wife: Mandy

I was a Staff Sergeant at Forbes AFB, Kansas when I was assigned to the Black Knight Project in October 1950. Enroute to Lockbourne AFB, Ohio, I detoured for jet engine training to Chanute AFB, Illinois. I was assigned to the 26th Strategic Reconnaissance Wing at Lockbourn until April 1956 when I was reassigned to Turner AFB, Georgia. At Turner I was ordered to the 811 Air Bomber Group and later reassigned to the 508th PD Maintenance Squadron, SAC. In May 1956 I went to the 4080th Strategic Reconnaissance Wing and transferred with the Wing to Laughlin AFB in May 1957.

We became a close-knit unit at Laughlin and everyone worked well together in support of the U-2 aircraft. I was an engine technician in field maintenance, and supervised a crew in engine change and test run of the aircraft.

Considering the difficulty finding housing, we were extremely happy in Del Rio. The local citizens were friendly and we became acquainted with quite a few people there. Our daughter, Judy Colleen, was born in the downtown hospital in August 1957.

In July 1958 I was transferred to England. Although our assignment with the 4080th SRW was rather short, we left with a lot of fond memories. We made a number of friends there and we continue to keep in touch with them today.

242

Harold Brownback, 1956

Harold and Mandy
Brownback, 2005

SWINTON BURROUGHS
Indialantic, Florida

Wife: Betty

RECONNAISSANCE

It had its beginnings for me in 1954 when I was assigned to an RB-47 wing at Lockbourne AFB, Ohio. No more P-51s, P-47s, F-82s, F-80s--just big cameras in big aircraft. In 1956 I was informed that I was being assigned to the Black Knight program. Black Knight? What was that? Where was that? What was the mission?

Enough with the questions. Here are your orders. Get a flight to Baltimore. There, call this phone number and "they" will provide transportation to the Glenn L. Martin aircraft plant. "They" also gave me a briefing on a new aircraft "they" were building, a high-altitude craft. It was derived from the British Canberra which itself was no slouch on reaching higher altitudes. The first test flight was a couple weeks away.

During the daily training sessions on what was inside this craft (what made it go, how to maintain it) the other trainees and I were given tours of the plant to see how it was being put together. We were astonished to see workers smoking in the cockpit and around the assembly areas. Martin's view was that those guys would sneak a smoke every so often and the cigarette butts would end up in critical parts of the plane. By allowing them to smoke, ash trays were kept handy and the employees would police up the area at the end of their shifts. On one tour I asked to see their Engineering Department. Years earlier I thought I might become an aero engineer. They showed me an area with about 500 engineers all appearing to be chained to their worktables. I spoke with one of them whose sole job was to do all the calculations for the design of the small nose landing gear doors of another aircraft Martin was doing. He marveled that I could "tolerate" being in the Air Force and being told what to do all the time. "All in one's perspective," I told myself.

With the training completed my group at Lockbourne was transferred to the 4080th Strategic Reconnaissance Wing at Turner AFB, Albany, Georgia. Once there we became the 4025th Strategic Reconnaissance Squadron (SRS) complete with pilots, maintenance team, Squadron Commander Colonel Mulloney, and finally, some black and white RB-57Ds.

Early training flights out of Turner had the usual glitches. One was a recurring problem for Bill Shuman whose radio communications gear developed a glitch each flight at altitude. Maintenance responded each time with "ground check-OK." Colonel Mulloney said that wouldn't cut it and Maintenance responded that maybe Bill didn't know how to operate the radio. An infuriated Colonel Mulloney told Maintenance to NEVER say one of his pilots didn't know how to operate his equipment.

Some time later Tech Reps reported that Martin found the problem—aluminum wiring that had apparently cracked at some time during installation; upon reaching cold temperatures at high altitude, the wiring shrank causing a gap in the wire. Upon returning to low altitude, the wire expanded and closed the gap, thus the "ground check - OK."

In August 1956 a TDY for six RB-57s was cobbled together for a classified operation at Yokota Air Base, Japan, with Colonel Mulloney as Detachment Commander. Maintenance people stopped at Hickam AFB, Hawaii to service and prepare the birds for the next leg to Yokota. Only one aircraft had a problem that had us all shaking our heads. Keith Lindsay reported an opposite reaction to what he expected on the horizontal stabilizer trim. How could this malfunction have escaped the notice of other pilots on other flights? If the trim was hooked up in reverse, had it been that way since it left Martin in Baltimore? There was no record of maintenance ever done on the system. Regardless of all possibilities, we reversed the wiring and on the leg to Yokota, Keith reported all was well.

At Yokota the skunk-like appearance of the RB-57s attracted some attention, but guards around our parking area kept out the curious, except for one. A Lieutenant Colonel thought because he was in the same Air Force, he was entitled to know what these birds were all about. Early one evening he ignored the guard's order to vacate the area. A shot fired over his head quickly made a believer of him, but the next morning he stirred up a hornet's nest with the Inspector General's office, the Base Commander and the Base Provost Marshal. He was asserting his right to look closely at the RB-57s. Colonel Mulloney and Colonel Johnson, from SAC Headquarters, brought this whole episode to quick closure. Rumor had it the curious Lieutenant Colonel was promptly transferred to another base.

Somewhere along the way news reports said the Chinese had issued the 256th (or some such number) "serious warning" to the US regarding overflights. We heard this occurred frequently.

On one night flight Bob Chalmers returned to the Yokota area and was reporting difficulty in maintaining proper balance between his left and right wings. A sump pump automatically pumped fuel between the left and right wings whenever fuel consumption was greater in one wing than the other; but the pilot could control this situation. In Chalmers' case, nothing worked so he elected to land immediately. The Martin Tech Rep, Michael Vince, went with me and the ground crew to the now parked plane. We could hardly believe what we saw.

The largest honeycomb panel on the bottom leading edge of the left wing had split away from the forward edge of the wing and was curled backwards, leaving the fuel cell looking like Niagara Falls. The jet fuel was cascading to the ramp below. It kept the fire trucks busy washing down the ramp, and the next day we moved the plane to a hangar. After a lot of conference calls, Martin decided to send a replacement panel, another tech rep, drawings and special tools, and design for trusses to support the wing while replacing the panel. In effect, we did depot work under field conditions.

What caused the panel to separate was a reason for alarm on all the RB-57s. It seemed an air leak into the honeycomb allowed the comb to exhale when the plane went to altitude, then to suck in air <u>and</u> moisture when descending. The moisture built up with each flight until so much had accumulated in the comb that it then froze at low temperatures while at high altitudes. With each freezing, the expanding ice caused skin and comb to separate. Inspections of wing panels became routine to try to detect any separation.

* * * * *

In the Spring of 1957 replacements arrived and we headed home. Back at Albany we learned that the Wing was moving to Laughlin AFB, Del Rio, Texas. A C-123 carried a group of us to Del Rio to check on housing. There had been a seven-year drought in Southwest Texas and the area looked bleak. There was one live bush at the entrance to the Officers' Club. It had flourished due to the Club rule to empty whatever remained in a drinking glass, ice and drink, on that bush.

A month later I drove my family to Del Rio and, amazingly, the drought had broken. All kinds of cactus and sage were blooming. When the rains first came, the

247

water couldn't even penetrate the "caliche" soil. Rain had accumulated into a tidal wave that eventually reached US Highway 90 just in front of the main entrance to the base. On each side of the entrance road was a shallow swale that paralleled Highway 90. Local reports were that a car with three women passed the entrance road just as the tidal wave rolled across the highway and in moments the car was washed into the swale. Two of the women drowned.

* * * * *

Once the RB-57s were on base the U-2s began arriving from the Skunk Works with their pilots and ground crew. We used the hangar at the south end of the ramp for the RB-57s. It was only a matter of time before a rivalry developed between the U-2 folks and the RB-57 folks.

One day Bo Reeves, a RB-57 driver, asked me to ready an aircraft for him with "splash fuel;" he wanted the plane as light as possible. That day we observed a U-2 that took off and headed for the heavens like a homesick angel. "Pretty good," we thought. "Now, Bo, take that 57 skyward." Bo was on his brakes winding up his engines when Colonel Wyman, our Squadron Commander, unobserved by me walked up and slapped me on the shoulder. He said, "Burroughs, how much fuel did you put in that plane?" I told him and he responded, "You fool. Don't you know that won't cover the sump pumps in a climb out?" He raced for his staff car to chase down Bo just as he released the brakes.

In about 500 feet the bird was airborne then nose up. As Bo later told us, at 13,000 feet directly above his takeoff point, he decided he better level off while he still had fuel feeding the engines. We declared the 57 the unofficial winner, but Bo and I were declared losers for the day by Colonel Wyman.

248

* * * * *

Colonel Beauchamp replaced Colonel Wyman as Squadron Commander. His office on the second floor of the squadron operations building faced the big hangar doors. One day Colonel Beauchamp called the Operations Officer and me into his office with a complaint. The 35-gallon garbage containers clustered on the ramp were used to collect and separate various pieces of metal. The Colonel didn't like their appearance and he wanted those cans painted. Sergeant Murphy in my unit had wanted to transfer to the U-2 squadron, but because he was an outstanding Crew Chief, I turned down his request. I called him in and offered to approve his transfer if he could pretty up those cans that belonged to Maintenance. The next morning when I arrived at the hangar, I was horrified to see the cans. They were an indescribable color, something resembling baby vomit. It didn't take long before I had a call to report to Colonel Beauchamp. I was sure my career was on the downhill slide. The Operations Officer was also there and we reported to the Colonel. To my utter amazement, the Colonel said how pleased he was with the appearance of the cans and he directed the Operations Officer to do the same with his garbage containers. After this brief meeting, I found Sergeant Murphy and asked him what paint he had used on the cans. His answer: "All the left over paint in all the cans in the paint locker, blended together to give that 'beautiful' tone." It worked and he got his transfer to the 4028th SRS.

* * * * *

One day two of our most experienced pilots were doing touch and go landings in B-57Cs, landing at the south end of the runway, then rolling on again for a takeoff. There was a rise near the south end of the runway, putting it out of sight to those of us watching from near the hangar. On one approach one 57 touched down out of our sight. Then we heard the power poured to the engines but no plane appeared over the rise in the runway. The persistent sound of power but no visible plane was an ominous sign. I grabbed a vehicle and raced to the south end of the runway. Lo! A perfect "wheels up" landing!

A much chagrined crew, Keith Sims and Al Simpson, admitted the belly landing was so smooth they didn't realize at first they were wheels up. The timing of this incident was poor to say the least. The nearly two hours it took to clear the runway added to General McConnell's already infuriated state of mind. His plane circled overhead waiting to land for his first visit to the 4080th SRW since taking command of 2nd Air Force at Barksdale. The incident, combined with several earlier U-2 accidents, resulted in Colonel Zemke's dismissal as Wing Commander. He was replaced by Brigadier General Austin Russell.

* * * * *

In September 1958 Colonel Swofford, Major Stu Spragins, Captain Yates and I went to Taiwan to affect the turnover of two RB-57s to the Republic of China Air Force (ROCAF). Each day we held classes with a translator to teach the Chinese maintenance troops how to look after the aircraft. All the Chinese officers spoke English, but none of the enlisted men did. Spragins worked with the Chinese pilots who had received training in the RB-57s back in Texas. Colonel Gabreski, a WWII ace, arrived with a squadron of F-104s. Members of his squadron had some pretty unkind things to say about our "big winged gliders." One day while Colonel Swafford was occupied somewhere else, we prevailed on Stu to make a max takeoff to show what our bird could really do. The F-104 drivers stood open-mouthed in astonishment. From then on, there were no more smart-ass remarks from them about our birds.

The Chinese pilots hosted a dinner for the four of us US officers and revealed their great sense of humor. Each food dish was brought to the table after a round of toasts to each other. Then one of the Chinese pilots would raise his glass and give a toast to the new dish. The Chinese were particularly jubilant because they had shot down four MIGs that very day with their F-84's. When the next dish arrived, one of the Chinese called for a toast to the new dish, MIG 21. I asked what that meant and my host responded, "Dead duck." And duck it was, a tasty dish indeed.

Interestingly, the Chinese had a couple of large gun implacements near the end of the runway. To assure no Communist Chinese maneuvered their way on base trying to steal an F-84, the ROCAF installed a system of lights from the tower: green light meant the plane was cleared to go, red light meant shoot the plane down immediately.

We had replacements coming for each member of our detachment. Colonel Swofford had arranged for a building to use as a barracks that was located near Taoyuan Air Base, about 25 miles out of Taipei. When the new guys arrived, I had a GI bus take them to the hotel. The hotel was already full, mostly with GI's and their girlfriends. I had to distribute the poor innocent fellows fresh from Texas into a couple of rather unsavory hotels. The next morning they regaled me with lively stories; they said it was the first time they had ever been billeted on per diem in a "cat house!"

Back at Laughlin, I watched as a RB-57 piloted by Bob Schueler came in for a landing. While still rolling in front of Base Operations, the right wing slowly drooped and fell to the ramp. I think this incident precipitated the demise of the Black Knight program. In due time the RB-57s were assigned to other organizations such as the weather service. When the last of them left Laughlin, the flight line maintenance operation was consolidated into one squadron with a branch for the U-2s and a branch for base flight aircraft. Forrest "Whip" Wilson became the Squadron Commander.

While he was commander, Forrest promoted a landscaping improvement project for the desolate, barren "caliche" soil that surrounded the hangar. Our coffee fund bought oleanders and other plants plus grass seed. The result was such an improvement that it inspired like efforts around other buildings, notably the 4028th Operations building. Pilots contributed to help improve the appearance of the grass. That improvement inspired the production of an anonymous treatise spelling out the procedures to follow in removing weeds from the grass. For example, grasp weed tool, hold at 40 degree angle to ground, insert at root of weed, remove weed, etc. The commanding officer of the 4028th was not amused.

* * * * *

What was the price of maintenance? I had a call about midnight from a Crew Chief who informed me they had damaged a U-2 tail wheel strut while moving it. If they had to go through supply to get parts, they feared the repercussions. However, there was an alternative. Field

252

Maintenance had a welder and a sheet metal specialist who said they could fix it quietly if I approved, and if I sweetened the deal with a case of beer. I made a trip to the San Felipe area of Del Rio and found a bar where a case of Mexican beer could be bought for about $3.50. The beer stayed in my car until the repair job was done. Sometime around 3:00 AM the job was finished and the beer was duly delivered. That was the last we heard about the incident.

* * * * *

In mid-September 1960 when the Del Rio area received a storm warning, five U-2s were airborne. They were directed to Laredo AFB and I was instructed to get a team together to go to Laredo to prep them for the return flight the next day. We drove through the night to reach Laredo with several flight line mechanics and a couple of medical personnel. Because Laredo did not have pogos to support the U-2 wings, Operations there dispatched a bunch of Second Lieutenants in flight training to support the wings and push the aircraft all the way to the parking ramp. At the parking area, they used 55 gallon drums under each wing tip skid, then used 50 pound sacks of fertilizer to hold the wings down in the event of high winds. They were unaware, though, the damage the sacks of fertilizer could do to the aluminum surface of the wings.

We brought pogos with us from Laughlin and they were installed as soon as we arrived. It turned out that the base had planned an Open House the next day for local folks in the Laredo area. Having the U-2s come in unexpectedly made their day. They got the word out to local residents by radio and flyers. Saturday morning was a beautiful sunny day and visitors thronged the flight lines. The pilots and I decided to give them a good show.

253

The Personal Equipment crew did everything with a flourish. I borrowed a flight line van for our "acting" Line Chief to go through all the motions of preflight with each Crew Chief who then saluted the pilot. I went from plane to plane, trying to look important. Each takeoff was a max effort event for benefit of the visitors. We were rewarded with a lot of "ohs" and "aahs."

* * * * *

On another weather encounter Bill Shuman was flying near the base and reported that some strong winds were headed our way. For some reason his report was not acted upon, and those of us along the flight line watched as harsh winds buffeted the parked U-2s which were not tied down. A couple of them were pushed around and banged into each other resulting in some skin damage. After that dire incident, all U-2s not requiring work in the open had to be hangared. This imposed a heavy burden on Maintenance. They shuffled aircraft to fit in the hangar and removed those scheduled for flight each day.

An additional task was levied on me to check with the Weather people every evening to assure that the flight line was in shape for whatever winds or rain may be forecast. I usually did it by phone, but one evening I walked to Base Operations where the Weather people prepared their forecasts. Complex charts hung on the walls, teletype machines clacked away and maps covered the desks. I asked the "head honcho" what he had for the forecast. He studied the wall charts and gave me a "Hmm." He walked to one of the teletype machines, looked at it while it typed and then gave me a double "Hmm." He consulted with one of the other guys there and shuffled some papers around on a desk. Finally, he walked over to a door that opened to the rear of the building, stepped out, looked up to a perfectly clear sky, then said, "Major, I don't think you have anything to worry about tonight."

* * * * *

One day Sergeant Fred Covert and I went to check equipment inside a small hangar whose doors opened to the flight line. The doors were only opened about 10 feet and, as we discussed a problem, a tug used to tow aircraft went chugging past the opening. To our absolute amazement, no one was driving it! We both raced for the door opening to catch the wayward tug before it rolled toward an aircraft. Troops were running from several directions to catch the tug. Fortunately, one guy jumped aboard and brought it to a halt just yards away from an aircraft parked on the ramp. I recall that someone got a good chewing about properly setting the brakes on the tug.

* * * * *

Taiwanese Air Force pilots were trained in the U-2s at Laughlin. One of these pilots was on a night mission over New Mexico when he had a flameout. Futile efforts to restart cost him considerable altitude so he referred to his flight manual to locate a suitable landing strip. He chose a strip that had minimum facilities, and in the darkness of the rugged New Mexico desert, he made a silent landing. There was only one light on in a single building. With one wing tip on the ground, he managed to get himself disconnected and exit the plane. He headed toward the light but he was still in his pressure suit and bubble helmet. As he approached the building, he could see a man seated at a desk pouring over paperwork. The Taiwanese pilot entered the door and the building occupant looked up in disbelief. "My God," he said, "If the Chinese have taken this place, they've surely taken the whole West Coast!"

* * * * *

SAC had a management system applied to every squadron which awarded points based on the squadron mission. Every month points were totaled and the Wing Commander got all the Squadron Commanders together to review the standings. The squadron with the fewest points had the "honor" of tethering a goat in front of its headquarters for the coming month. One month the Hospital Unit was awarded the "honor" and the goat was transferred to the hospital commander. For a couple of weeks, we all noticed the goat grazing whenever we passed the hospital and then soon forgot about it. About the third week into the month, the hospital folks put on a feast around the Officers' Club pool featuring "cabrito," barbequed goat. It took a while for it to sink in; we had all eaten the goat.

* * * * *

In January 1962, Colonel Paul Rix and I were sent to Guam to assess facilities for handling three U-2s at Andersen AFB. Paul established needs for the Operations part of the planned detachment and I sought facilities for the required ground equipment. One facility designated for our use was a T-hangar originally built to accommodate one large aircraft except its tail would extend through a cutout area in the doors. It could house three of our U-2s. I asked the civil engineers what wind velocity it would withstand. They spent a day going through their old "as built" drawings to finally give me a response—135 knots. This went into my final report back at Laughlin. Several months later, we had a three-plane detachment at Andersen and a powerful typhoon headed for the island. Forecasters erred on the projected winds until it was too late to evacuate the U-2s. The typhoon hit with winds in excess of 140 knots. One of the large hangar doors fell inward and damaged two U-2s.

* * * * *

In September 1962 concern arose over the Soviets shipping some weapons into Cuba. One dark night I called my Maintenance crew to get three U-2s prepared immediately for a takeoff. I alerted the crews for those aircraft plus the Line Chief. It started to rain and all of us at the flight line were soon soaked. We received a directive to tow the planes out to the end of the runway where they would be positioned for takeoff. The Physiological Support Division guys got the pilots to the planes about the time the rain became a "gully washer." With all the electrical cables exposed to rain, I feared someone would be electrocuted; but the hookups and startups went well. After the first plane was off, a search was mounted for the pogos that were left in deep puddles of rainwater on the runway. We wasted a lot of time searching for the pogos. We decided to remove the remaining pogos on the waiting aircraft; ground crew held the wings and raced along with the plane until the wings maintained lift on their own. This procedure worked well and within a short time all three aircraft were airborne and became the first U-2s involved in the Cuban crisis.

* * * * *

The SAC Inspector General paid us its first full-blown inspection visit by a team who was not fully aware of our mode of operation. Because of the frequency of TDY's, usually comprised of three U-2s and support crew, I maintained a board with all ground crew members' names, aircraft numbers, and personal data such as whether the wife was pregnant or sick. This added bit of information enabled me to select crews that were available and ready to go on a moment's notice. The board resembled a typical organization chart but that's where the similarity ended. The Lieutenant Colonel member of the SAC team assigned to Maintenance found some things he didn't like, but he reserved most of his wrath for the TDY chart.

The Lieutenant Colonel and I walked out into the hangar still arguing about my need for the TDY board. He was insisting that our flight schedule should be firmed up so many days in advance so that everyone knew well ahead what was coming up. He quoted regulation SAC 66-12.

One of the U-2s was parked in the hangar and we circled it while he decided he would go to Maintenance Control and straighten out this scheduling matter. While he belabored the issue, a Flight Chief came up and asked us to clear the area; the aircraft we circled had to be prepared for a special mission. "No, it was not scheduled for a flight," I told the Inspector, "But when SAC Headquarters said it must go, then it would." With that said, he just threw up his hands and walked out of the hangar. That's the last we saw of him.

Swinton Burroughs at the 2002 4080th SRW reunion wearing a plaid blazer that each of the group acquired during the 1957 TDY to Japan to "distinguish" themselves from locals at Yokota Air Base.

JAMES E. (SOUP) CAMPBELL
Mifflinburg, Pennsylvania

Wife: Linda

From 1958 to 1973 I supported the U-2 program with the 4080th SRW at Laughlin AFB and then with the 100th SRW at Davis Monthan AFB. I served as Crew Chief and later a Line Chief. I had an opportunity to see a lot of activity with the Wing and I worked with a lot of good men.

* * * * *

It was an unwritten rule that whenever a pilot blew a tire on the aircraft, he owed the Crew Chief a case of beer. We were in Alaska in July 1962 when Major Rudolph Anderson blew a tire on his assigned aircraft. Sure enough, he paid up promptly and I shared with the rest of the crew.

* * * * *

In 1963 at Davis Monthan, one of the Taiwanese students crashed a U-2 and bailed out safely. He later was assigned another flight on the day before Thanksgiving and subsequently reported to the Tower, "Flameout, bailout." Before the Tower had a chance to tell him to glide the U-2 in, he had already bailed out. I spent Thanksgiving Day picking up pieces of the aircraft over a huge area of the Arizona desert.

In February 1964 I was at Davis Monthan and I passed the Maintenance shack as I left work about 4:30 p.m. I was asked if I wanted to go on a ten-day TDY and I was instructed to get the other guys on the crew to be back at 6:30 p.m. I rushed to the mess hall to get the rest of the crew and we reported back to the flight line on time.

We loaded the aircraft until midnight and the KC-135 tanker that transported the 30 or so support crew took off at daylight. We arrived in the Philippine Islands at midnight their time with U-2 missions scheduled to take off early the next morning. We had only been there three days when the Philippine government demanded that we get out. We were once again loading and fueling the aircraft for a rapid departure.

A captain from the alert hanger chewed on us for taking their fuel truck. While he chewed on me, I continued to fuel up the U-2. He demanded my name, rank and serial number; I responded courteously and professionally. Of course, I knew I wouldn't be around long enough for him to do anything beyond his chewing. One hour later we were airborne with no plans to return to the Philippine Islands. In the haste to depart, two or three of our crew members were left behind in the Philippines, but they were recovered on a later flight. Once airborne, we were given orders to go to Guam.

The KC-135 with all our equipment and gear then went to Guam. I rode in the boomer and observed the flight over the water. Prior to landing on Guam, the pilot had to dump thousands of gallons of fuel out over the ocean in order to get to landing weight. We stayed there three weeks. One evening at midnight we got the word to load up and we departed the next morning, destination unknown to us. Colonel DesPortes, the 4080th SRW commander, was along on the flight and he made a big deal of opening the envelope that contained our orders. He announced we were going to Vietnam. Most of us had never heard of the country. By the time we arrived at Bien Hoa Air Base, Vietnam, I had been up for a full 24 hours without sleep.

* * * * *

I vividly remember the day we landed at Bien Hoa Air Base, Vietnam on March 5, 1964, my 29th birthday. I had always heard about the "outback" and I thought this was it. The support team normally landed ahead of the U-2s and would be issued a truck for Mobile Control; however, this "Follow Me" truck driver refused to give us his vehicle. So we explained to him what he would have to do. Because of the U-2's bicycle gear configuration, the pilot holds a level position until the aircraft comes to a stop and one wing gently falls to the runway. We told the driver that the crew then go to the high wing first and pulls it down to insert the pogos. The first U-2 came in and the pilot dragged the wing the normal distance. Before we knew what he was doing, the "Follow Me" truck driver jumped out of the truck and raced toward the aircraft and grabbed under the skid to keep the wing up. Poor fellow, he absolutely fried his hand and to make matters much worse, there was tar embedded in the wound. I really felt sorry for the fellow but he just didn't listen to us.

We got the bird parked and we were soon in for another surprise. Here came a bunch of Vietnamese GI's holding hands! Now that was sure different for us to see. We learned it was a custom of their culture. Then they tried to climb all over the aircraft, but we quickly stopped that.

After getting the planes bedded down, we got on the bus to go up to the Compound. On the way, we passed a little building which must have been a civilian house; a young woman, probably a teenager, came out, squatted down and peed right there with not the slightest bit of modesty as our bus passed in clear view. Being young and slightly immature, all the guys rushed to that side of the bus; I thought for sure that bus was going to turn over.

We finally got to the Compound and we were told to walk around the hut until we found an empty bed. I found one, but not in the same hut with the other guys from the 4080th. The next day we scouted around until we found an empty hut, put some beds in and proclaimed it ours. In the hut next to ours were some Vietnamese Army guys. They were sleeping two or three in a single bed; now that really was a bit too crowded. There was nothing in our hut to use for storage so a couple of us went in search of a locker. We walked through the rows of huts and came upon the transient officers' hut. There was evidence of only three or four occupants. We found the locker we were looking for and away we went. For a long time, we were the envy of our hut with that locker.

We lived in huts, 12 men to a hut, with a Vietnamese maid assigned to each hut. For a box of Tide, a can of shoe polish and $5 a month, the maid kept the hut clean, did the laundry for all the residents, made beds and shined shoes. She would take the shoes to a long table outside the hut and gather around it with maids from other huts. They would start shining shoes and chattering away while they worked. It was a mystery how the maid could get the right shoes and clean laundry back to the right bed.

There was no place to get safe drinking water except at the mess hall. Our maid filled up liquor bottles with drinking water and brought an extra block of ice she managed to scrounge for us. During that first trip to Vietnam in 1964 the food was good, but in 1966, I returned on separate rations (paid for my own food) and the quality was not as good. There was no place to buy snacks except the BX, and there was always a long line when snacks were in stock and they sold out in a short time.

A swimming pool was under construction by Vietnamese workers when we arrived at Bien Hoa. To say their construction methods were primitive was an understatement. Instead of digging the hole with heavy equipment, there were a number of people out there using a hoe and short handle shovel to put dirt in a five gallon bucket. The bucket was then carried off by another worker, dumped and returned for another load of dirt. One day I saw that they had a small cement mixer on the edge of the hole and watched as it toppled over the edge into the hole. There was a lot of chattering and hand motions as they tried to figure out what to do next. The completed pool was finished a couple months after we arrived. I seriously doubt it would have passed any US construction inspections.

I was at Bien Hoa over 100 days before I had a day off. We reported for work at 3:30 a.m. and finished the day when the aircraft was finally bedded down by about 6:00 or 8:00 p.m. Even with all those inconveniences, that was by far the best TDY that I ever had and I did quite a few.

I remember writing letters to Linda, then my fiancé, from Vietnam. I would write a big "O" every few words; the "O" marked each time I heard gunfire or mortar shelling explosions. I didn't count the O's until I finished the letter and I saw that every two to four words were followed by a big O. I finally explained to Linda at the end of the letter about the O's.

* * * * *

The U-2 could not land in a crosswind. If an aircraft could not land at Laughlin, their alternate destination was Altus, Oklahoma. We then would gather a crew from Laughlin and fly to Altus in a C-123 to recover the U-2 and get it ready to turn around and fly back to Laughlin. On one particular flight to Altus, we had flown from Laughlin in the very early hours of the day and we finally launched the U-2 for its return flight. It was mid-morning and we had not even stopped long enough to have a snack, much less breakfast. We asked the bus driver that was taking us to the C-123 to make a stop at the convenience store for us to buy some drinks and snacks. A bunch of the guys came back to the bus with 6-packs of beer. Once we took off in the C-123, the ground crew gathered in a circle in the back of the plane and started having "breakfast." There was then the problem of eliminating the evidence before we arrived back at Laughlin. Fortunately, there was a small hole in the door that allowed someone to reach through to the outside. The opening was just big enough to toss those cans through; we left a trail of cans raining across Texas. The Navigator came running back to tell us to scatter because we had too much weight in the tail of the aircraft.

* * * * *

I remember one particular U-2 incident while I was TDY at Barksdale AFB that had a rather humorous exchange with a local resident, although the pilot who lived through it might have a different opinion.

It was in 1967. U-2 #708 flew to 45,000 feet altitude when it experienced an explosion. The pilot ejected safely and free floated from 45,000 to 10,000. During that free fall, he got into a spin, but managed to pull his chute at 10,000 feet. He landed in a rural area around Pineville, Louisiana, and disconnected himself from his chute. He began walking down a nearby road still dressed in his pressure suit. A car drove toward him but sped on when the driver got a good look at the pilot in his otherworldly looking gear. The pilot finally came to a mobile home and knocked on the door. A young woman opened the door, looked at her visitor and immediately slammed and locked the door. He yelled through the door, explained who he was and asked her to call Barksdale AFB. After a few minutes, the young woman returned and spoke to him through the door. She said, "Barksdale said they wouldn't accept the charges!" The pilot pleaded again, "Ma'am, if you will just call, I'll give you the money back for the call."

Once we were notified of the accident, I was requested to accompany a Major from our unit to go to the crash site. Barksdale was responsible for the accident investigation, but most of the investigators had never seen a U-2 and weren't too sure what to do. I knew before we arrived at the site that my job was to get to the aircraft and remove the TOP SECRET communication box. There were a lot of people just standing around waiting for instructions. I just went directly to the aircraft, took off the outside panel and removed the TOP SECRET box. I headed back in the direction I came from. On the road I saw a pickup truck and I asked the driver for a ride to the nearby store where I met up with the Major again. I showed him the box and he said, "Let's go. We got what we came for."

* * * * *

In the early days, the U-2 was involved in air sampling over Guam, Alaska, Panama, Hawaii, Australia and England to test for radiation. The device used to capture the air for testing consisted of basketball-size balls installed in the Q Bay. The balls were metal wrapped in wire and pressurized with outside air. Following each sampling flight, the balls were shipped to a lab for testing. The ball racks used during those flights from the 1950's to 1968 had gone back into storage until we learned that France was going to set off some test bombs, so the US started air sampling again. Out came the ball racks, but we needed the special cords to tie down the racks. Lockheed put in a rush order to make the special 6-foot long extension cords needed. Then there was a lot of test hopping when one aircraft crashed in 1968. One of the colonels told me to get the cables off the crashed aircraft, so off I went again with tools to remove the cables. I knew the rules about removing evidence from a crash site, but I had a ranking officer directing me to do it. When the chopper came back to get us, I was stopped by a different colonel who said I could not take those cables. I then reported to the first colonel about the location of the cables and he said he would take care of it.

* * * * *

When I was single, I volunteered to go TDY and enjoyed the traveling. After I married, I knew there was an Air Force policy that would not send a man TDY if his wife was pregnant. I was called about a TDY back to Barksdale but reported that my wife, Linda, was pregnant with our first child. Sgt. Ross took my place on that TDY. Then I was told about a TDY to Argentina for air sampling and I did go on that one because I knew I would be back before our son was born. So, I got the balls and cables ready for another mission in Argentina.

We flew night missions from a civilian airport in Mendoza, Argentina. All the crew wore civilian clothes and nobody there knew we were military. The ground crew had left the hangar after the aircraft took off; we knew it would be seven or eight hours before it returned. Being the Crew Chief, I was required to stay until the aircraft returned. I ran the night shift and I was there with a couple other guys when the phone rang. When I answered, there was a burst of Spanish and the words, "May Day, May Day". I couldn't understand anything except the words "May Day" so I quickly got in touch with our commander who contacted airport officials. We learned that a pilot had reported a loss of electrical power; however, he survived.

* * * * *

Line Chief Wayne Smith and I were sent to California for training when the U-2 engine was upgraded from the Pratt and Whitney J57 engine to the J75 model. The upgrade increased the thrust from 10,500 to 17,500 pounds. We went to Lockheed to learn about the proposed modifications. However, our attendance at that training had the stipulation that once we returned to the Wing, we would volunteer for Vietnam. So once again, off I went to Vietnam.

There was a huge infestation of rats on the base and I learned that plague was still a very active disease in Vietnam. We had received inoculations for the plague prior to departure from the US. The disease, we were told, was spread by fleas carried on the rats and the fleas needed a warm body to thrive. So if the rat died, the fleas went in search of another host, which could be a human. Rats were not poisoned because the theory was that if the fleas then left the rats, we would be at risk.

In the huts, rats walked on the overhead beams like they owned the place, and I guess maybe they did. I had nailed a box to the wall with a few things I wanted to protect from the vermin, such as writing paper and cigarettes. One day I saw something go into the box and I quickly slapped a writing tablet against it. The rat poked its head out of the box and made a hasty retreat right over Wayne as he slept in the next bunk. Wayne never woke up and the rat kept going.

I created a rattrap from a C-130 water separator; it was cone-shaped with the pointed end cut out. I wired it to a 10-inch board and placed a beer can in the homemade trap. The rat climbed inside the can and could not retreat. The Soup Trap reduced the rat population in our area by at least half.

* * * * *

L. Mendel Rivers was a powerful member of the US House of Representatives from South Carolina and Chairman of the House Armed Services Committee in the 1960's. His nephew was a member of our outfit when we went to Argentina. We were told there was a very dangerous bug in the country called "Achuga." If we were bitten, the bug could cause heart damage years later. One day Rivers' nephew came in with a nasty-looking bug in a bottle and asked if this was the bug that was so dangerous. He reported that he was bitten by that same bug. No one really knew what the Achuga looked like. Rivers' nephew got the brushoff by a lot of people. Finally, he invoked the name of L. Mendel Rivers and he was immediately sent downtown for medical treatment. As it turned out, the bug he found was not the dreaded Achuga, but Rivers' nephew still got quick response to his question.

Soup Campbell, left, 1961, Thanksgiving at Laughlin AFB.

Soup Campbell, 1964, outside his hut at Bien Hoa, Vietnam.

Soup Campbell, 1990, with "his" U-2 #707 on static
display at Laughlin AFB.

JOSEPH (JOE) CHAPMAN
Tucson, Arizona

DAD'S EPILOGUE THING

The U-2 Dragon Lady program was, and still is, one of the most prestigious units in the Air Force. In 1994, after seven years of bouncing around in A-10 units as a "crewdawg," I had the privilege of being assigned to the U-2 Periodic Inspection Dock in the 9th Maintenance Squadron at Beale AFB, California. For some guys, this would have been just another assignment to an aircraft maintenance outfit. For me, it was more than that.

About three decades earlier, my dad had been a member of the pioneering unit I was bound for. So I had a little bit of the living history of the unit that began with the 4080th Strategic Reconnaissance Wing (Light) in 1957, later morphed into the 100th Strategic Wing and eventually evolved into today's 9th Recon Wing. Pretty cool. So that's where my story begins.

Anyone who has been involved in Air Force maintenance knows that our Technical Orders (TO) change frequently. Most of the changes come about when maintainers develop faster or easier methods to perform a given task. Throughout the relatively short history of the USAF, one common denominator has always been present—the desire to get the job done in the fastest time possible with the least amount of work. This phenomenon is known in aircraft maintenance circles as the "shortcut," and is the root cause of a large number of the dreaded TO changes.

Every maintainer I have ever known has asked the burning question: Who the hell decided to put the ____ behind the ____? What were they thinking? Damn engineers!" However, there are two sides to everything. While I've heard the "damn engineers" comment on procedures numerous times, usually between a few expletives, I've also heard some rather surprising comments. For example, "Who was the brilliant individual who came up with this idea? Now there is some ingenuity."

Invariably when a maintainer performs a task day in and day out, in addition to just plain getting good at the job, he'll usually come up with subtle deviations that make the job easier. Less time on the job equates to more time at the club, or anywhere that isn't in the shop. Some of the methods and procedures will eventually find their way into a TO or locally designed checklist, while others are handed down through time from one maintainer to another. So, here are a couple of my favorite examples of how the maintainers of yesterday have impacted those of us who have come since; and some who have yet to meet this elderly but graceful machine known as "Dragon Lady."

THINGS AREN'T ALWAYS AS THEY SEEM, BUT SOMETIMES THEY ARE!

Since the U-2 was originally the brainchild of her designer, Clarence "Kelly" Johnson, it seems only right that my examples begin with him. In the mid-fifties the CIA and the USAF needed a new intelligence-gathering platform. The wish list went out and the contractors began vying for the opportunity to be the winner of the latest lucrative government contract. Lockheed Aircraft Company's "Skunk Works" unit was awarded the contract, and the rest is history, or is it? In the interest of keeping costs down, Kelly had the foresight of using an already existing airframe for the basis of his design. Looking at a U-2 from various angles, the many similarities between the "Deuce" and the F-104 Starfighter would be obvious. The similarity arises because that is exactly how the CL-282 first began. It is better known to us today as the U-2A.

Some of the similarities are blatant, while others are more obscure. One of the obvious examples is the canopy of the early production U-2 mirrors that are on the F-104. In fact, the identification tag on the part itself is identical for both aircraft.

Because my Dad was a 4080th SRW Dragon, I found myself talking to him on the telephone about the Deuce on a regular basis. He'd ask me questions like, "Hey, do they still have _____ in the engine bay over by the ___?" Armed with my newly acquired knowledge from Dad, I'd set out to find out if "_____ was still in the engine bay over by the ___." Sometimes I'd learn that the part wasn't installed anymore. However, more often than not, I'd learn that not only was it still used, but it was still in its original location.

One of the times Mom and Dad came to Beale to visit my family, I took Dad for a tour of the dock I worked in. Needless to say, when I introduced him to my co-workers as a 4080th Dragon, the questions flowed. After hearing the myriad answers, a few co-workers seemed to walk a little taller because it wasn't just the boss telling them about the importance of their jobs. Dad was a living history book, at least that was my observation. Moral of this story is: Any former Dragons who have the patience to listen to our questions or to tell a few good war stories, we always appreciated. With a former Dragon dropping in to the shop, we could get "the rest of the story."

HEADS OR TAILS? THIS ONE'S A COIN TOSS!

From the time I was knee high to a grasshopper, I liked to think of my Dad as the most important guy in the world. In grade school, we would say something like, "My Dad can do (enter any silly challenge) better than yours." Later in middle school, it sounds something like, "My Dad can kick your dad's ass!" That's why this story has so much meaning to me; it's how he saved the day.

During my Dad's time on the U-2 from July 1958 to April 1966, he was a Specialist. Yep, that's right; Dad's a "Grinner" and I'm a "Knuckle Dragger." For a little explanation of some maintainer lingo, a "Grinner" is a Specialist who works in the recon system arena. During the launch of an aircraft, the Grinners stand over to the side with big grins on their faces. When one of their systems has an "uh-oh", the Crew Chief usually turns to the Grinners who promptly fix the problem.

"Knuckle Dragger" is one of the nicer nicknames for a Crew Chief. There are others that are waaay more common, but I really can't mention them here. Most Specialists think that Crew Chiefs are lacking in the smarts department, otherwise they would be Specialists. However, those of us who are a little off the deep end would still be Crew Chiefs.

All this has made some very interesting conversations between us. Any Crew Chief or Specialist will tell you that the two cannot peacefully co-exist. Personally, I think the concept is obsolete because in all my time in the Air Force I've had pretty good relations with the Specialists. We're all on the same team and that's it. Maybe being raised by a Specialist had something to do with my outlook, but I think Grinners and Draggers can get along just fine, most of the time.

Dad was a camera guy, and before he gets the chance to correct me, he was specifically a "Nephographics

Technician." His job was to keep the optical intelligence gathering systems and the pilot's NEPHO System control equipment in top-notch working order. One of the tasks all the NEPHO guys dreaded was the alignment of the driftsight and hand control. The driftsight was essentially an upside down periscope the pilot used, for example, to track drifting patterns of the aircraft.

Control of the driftsight was maintained through an instrument like the exterior mirror control on newer automobiles. The hand control had to be calibrated or aligned for precision accuracy. This was a task that the NEPHO guys would rather not have to do because it meant working in a very tight area, and according to the manufacturer's instructions, the aircraft had to be on a fuselage cart. That was a lot of work and a lot of time spent contorting the human body of the unlucky NEPHO guy was who selected to perform the task.

There was one NEPHO guy, however, the other guys must have thought was absolutely insane because he actually enjoyed twisting his body into every imaginable position, or more likely just enjoyed the challenge. Or, maybe it was because he had a "shortcut" that made the job a little bit easier. After a few years working on the system, Dad did in fact devise a method of aligning the hand control that made the job easier. Trouble was, there was no tech data to support his method. The 4080th SRW Commander, Brigadier General John DesPortes, learned about Dad's "unapproved method," so he proposed a showdown between the manufacturer's tech rep and my Dad.

Dad was allowed to take the hand control out of alignment and the Tech Rep performed the procedure according to the manufacturer's guidelines. When he came out of the cockpit, General DesPortes climbed in and inspected it. Using a stopwatch to time both the Tech Rep and Dad, he told Dad to do it his way. The General took a look at Dad's handiwork and found everything to be exactly as it was supposed to be. General DesPortes demanded to know, "Chap, how on earth did you finish the task so rapidly?" I wish I could have been there to witness all this when Dad reached into his pocket and pulled out the tool issued by the US Mint. That's right, a simple United States twenty-five cent coin was the device used for the precision alignment of the driftsight. He proceeded to lay the quarter on the ground beneath the driftsight, clambered up into the cockpit and pointed out to the General how he did it.

General DesPortes climbed back in the cockpit and announced what Dad already knew. The hand control was exactly as it should be. He also asked the Tech Rep why one of his blue suiters (the uniform the NEPHO guys wore) had a much better grasp on the unit than an employee of the manufacturer. The tech rep immediately instructed Dad to have a checklist written outlining his "shortcut" as soon as possible so it could be implemented as an authorized procedure.

The story doesn't end there though. Years later while I was deployed with the Deuce, I lived in a hootch (hut) next door to the deployed photo guy, Keith Haas. Maybe it was fate that Keith and I were to meet, maybe it was just that our hootches were next door and we liked to play guitars together when we were off duty. Either way, Keith and I became instant friends with a lot of time on our hands to shoot the breeze. When I told him about Dad being a NEPHO guy, he expressed interest in meeting him. After we returned to Beale, Mom and Dad came for a visit. We invited Keith to come play guitars and meet Dad. We didn't do much pickin' and grinnin'; quite the contrary. I sat on the couch listening to the two photo troops swap stories for the rest of the evening. It was interesting listening to them compare their likes and dislikes about the job. An observer could believe that these two could be related, and they actually are two birds of the same feather.

Before he left, Keith invited Dad to tour his shop and meet some of the other Photo Dragons. Of course, Dad quickly accepted the invitation. I'll spare everyone the flattery and the "I remember when…" of most of the tour, and I'll fast forward to the final few minutes. Keith took Dad and me into a back room of the shop and Dad's eyes welled up. There on the bench in front of him was the newest driftsight and hand control. As if almost 30 years hadn't passed, Dad proclaimed, "I could still work on this. I probably couldn't keep up with you new guys, but I could still do it with my eyes closed."

Keith then reached into a small toolbox, known as a mini-kit, and pulled out a small round slug about the size of a quarter. Attached to the slug was a red and white "Remove Before Flight" streamer and the slug was etched with the words, "Hand Control Alignment Tool." If Dad's eyes weren't totally welled up by now, they were close when Keith proudly said, "Mr. Chapman, we always wondered where this came from. Now we know."

HEY, JOE, CAN YA GIVE ME A HAND OVER HERE?

The U-2's mission is what we in the Air Force call "Real World." That's one of the reasons I've always said that the U-2 is the most important aircraft in the inventory. I like to tell the fighter guys, "Without the Deuce, the F-16s, A-10s and F-22s would just be a gun flying around with nothing to shoot at." Anyone who knows me understands what my preference is: Recces win hands down.

Because of the critical mission of the U-2, every second spent on the ground is precious. But it doesn't end after the aircraft breaks ground. The U-2 uses a set of outrigger gears called "pogos." The pogos keep the aircraft balanced with wings level during towing, taxiing or just sitting on the ground.

While pogos are supposed to stay installed on the ground, there is only one reason that they would stay in for an entire flight and that would be when a pilot is learning to fly the U-2. I personally have never seen a pilot use the pogos for this reason, but I've heard that it has been done. When the pogos are used in this sense, they act as a set of training wheels. However, this doesn't take long and just like a kid who is learning to ride a bicycle, as soon as the pilot has gained confidence that he can keep the aircraft level, the pogos will only be used for ground handling.

The last thing a U-2 ground crew does before the bird launches is to pull the pogo pins so they will fall out as soon as the wings begin to lift. This takes a couple of seconds, but when a mission is critical, seconds can seem like hours. Sometimes a pogo will fail to fall out of the wing causing a "hung pogo" and can cost not only precious time but a hazard to the pilot. To rectify the situation, the pilot would have to try to land the plane or fly to a designated area to shake the pogos loose from the aircraft.

During the 1962 Cuban Missile Crisis, missions were more important than ever. The ground crew looked for any way to save time without sacrificing safety. A young Assistant Crew Chief named Joe Kent had the solution. Everybody probably thought he had lost his mind, but nobody had any better ideas. The boss approved and said "Let's give 'er a try." The way these ideas work is when someone comes up with a great idea, they also get to be the first person, or guinea pig, to try it out. At the next morning launch, Joe was set to demonstrate how it would work.

After performing the preflight checks and getting the forms documented, Joe gave the signal for "give me air" and the powerful engine came to life. Hydro pressure came up and they pulled the gear pins. The Grinners did their preflight checks and the pilot taxied to the end of the runway. The pilot lined his Dragon Lady up for takeoff roll and Joe's show was about to begin.

Joe grabbed the wingtip and held it steady while the pogo crew scrambled to pull the pogo pins, and this time they pulled out the pogos completely. The pogo crew gave Joe the signal, which he relayed to the pilot, that all was okay. The pilot responded by stomping on the brakes and increasing the throttle. The powerful jet engine slowly revved up to takeoff speed and with a nod, Joe got ready to sprint.

The pilot released the brakes and within seconds the aircraft was picking up speed. Joe took a few more steps and the wing began to fly. Joe let go of the wing and bent to a crouch giving a big thumbs up. Joe Kent had just performed the first hand launch of a U-2.

To this day, when time is essential and the mission is critical, the very same hand launch procedure is used to shave seconds off the takeoff and ensure safety of the crew, and of course, the aircraft. Everybody knows, including the pilots, that the airplane belongs to the Crew Chief. Joe Kent, a Crew Chief's Crew Chief, was the imaginative individual who came up with this idea. Thanks, Joe.

THERE'S GOTTA BE A QUICKER WAY
TO BLEED THIS AMAD*
(Airframe Mounted Accessory Drive)

I'd like to close this epilogue by demonstrating how the guys listed above, and God knows how many more that I simply haven't met yet, have impacted my generation of U-2 maintainers. As I've shown with the examples above, when the pioneer guys started working on the U-2, they had to find their own "tricks of the trade" to make the job go smoother and to save valuable time during a critical launch. But the legacy doesn't have to end with them. They can be proud to know that their ingenuity has fueled a whole generations of U-2 maintainers.

One such story comes to mind while I was working in the Periodic Inspection Dock at Beale when Lockheed began the "sex change" of the R model U-2. Among the modifications was a major change in the engine. After 40 years of using a turbo jet engine, Dragon Lady was about to receive a turbo fan power plant. This story is about the Airframe Mounted Accessory Drive or AMAD.

Whenever the oil lines came off the AMAD or when the oil cooler came out, air would get into the system and would need to be filled and bled. I remember all too well the many nights we spent trying to get the air out of the oil system using the method outlined in the tech manual. Remember, I said earlier most good ideas stem from a desire to get the job done quicker and easier. Most of us resolved to the idea when we were briefed at shift change that we had an AMAD bleed, we were gonna be there all night.

One fellow, Craig Felty, wasn't resolved to that fate. He studied the blueprints and the tech manual, then observed how the system worked as we performed the task. It wasn't long before he got a machinist involved and built a simple hand crank. Little did we know that Craig's brainchild was going to change the way we bled an AMAD forever. Once the boss found out about Craig's tool, he insisted it become a legitimate process. Craig submitted his idea along with a sample tool and it was approved. In 2003 as a Blackcat in the 5th RS in Osan, Korea, I observed that Craig's tool was still being used.

281

THE LEGEND LIVES ON!

I can't speak for every member in the current U-2 program, but I think they'd probably agree with me. I am very proud to have had the opportunity to serve in a unit with the prestige, honor and mission that was started over 50 years ago. I consider myself fortunate to have my name on the rolls of a unit that includes, Major General Pat Halloran, USAF (Ret.), the Crew Chief's Crew Chief Joe Kent, and especially my Dad, the Driftsight Dragon, Glenn Chapman.

To all the old Dragons who paved the way for those of us who came later, and for those yet to come, thanks for setting the benchmarks that we've come to follow. Hopefully, along the way, we've set a few of our own.

Joe Chapman standing beside a U-2 display in Tucson, Arizona.

GEORGE DEBINSKI
(Deceased May 14, 2000)

The following was submitted by George's widow, Terry.

George came to Laughlin AFB from Georgia in 1957 and was assigned to the Sheet Metal Shop in Field Maintenance. His supervisor was Sergeant Ted Guthrie and Sergeant Marcos Villarreal was his First Sergeant.

I grew up in Del Rio, but I knew that the town was oblivious about the activities at the base. George said that occasionally when he went to a bar in Acuna, the Mexican town across the border from Del Rio, there were local guys there who always asked what he did at the base. He always made up something to tell them that was far from the truth, and it satisfied the curious fellows for a while.

We married on October 29, 1960 and George's First Sergeant promised him that he would not be sent TDY for at least a year. We bought a trailer and lived at the base trailer park. When I taught school at the local Catholic elementary school, I rode the bus with the base children bound for the local public school. Some of the base children were at my school.

George went to Alaska once and to Australia twice. He told me where he was going but never what the unit would be doing there.

We left Del Rio when the Wing moved to Davis Monthan AFB, Arizona, and we were at Tucson about 18 months. Many of the families who lived in the Laughlin trailer park ended up in the The Desert Breeze Trailer Park in Tucson. I remember Guthrie, Monge, Lockhart, Gabriel, Doria, Deliberto, Gomez, Ancira; there were so many others but time has faded my memory.

George was reassigned to Okinawa and our daughter, Elizabeth Ann, was born August 24, 1966 at Camp Kue Army Hospital. Our son, Roger Eugene, was born on October 18, 1968 at Cannon AFB, New Mexico, where George was reassigned once again.

George and I enjoyed his tours of duty with the Air Force, but our time with the 4080th SRW at Laughlin and later at Davis Monthan was very special to us.

George Debinski about 1964

CARLTON L. (LYN) FITE
Odessa, Texas

I was assigned to the Aerospace Ground Equipment (AGE) at Laughlin AFB, Del Rio, Texas. The unit provided ground support equipment for the T-33 and T-37. In 1963 SAC and ATC (Air Training Command) ground support shops were located in the same building at Laughlin on the northwest side of the runway. The missions of the two organizations were different, but at times each unit helped the other.

My most memorable experiences were when the CIA U-2s (we called them the Black Bandits) came in for a landing. They landed and taxied straight into one of the 4080th hangars. The hangar door closed immediately and the pilot shut down the engine. When those same aircraft departed, the U-2 engine was started inside the hangar, then the hangar door opened and it taxied out to the runway for immediate takeoff. The U-2 went almost straight up and out of sight. The 4080th U-2s were gray in color with USAF markings. The Black Bandits were solid flat black with no markings.

At that time I recall Laughlin had two parallel runways. The AGE shop was responsible for servicing the regular Control Tower. We also serviced the generator on a portable Control Tower that was located about midway between the runways. The portable was used during the day when the student pilot flying was the heaviest. It was set on a built-up, earthen pad and had an open area under the building. A fellow airman and I were in a pickup one evening enroute to service the portable tower. We drove up to the portable tower and our headlights revealed a person on the other side of the

Tower. All we could see were two legs standing beside the tires.

Laughlin AFB was outside Del Rio, Texas on the Mexican border. From time to time illegal aliens gained access to the United States by night via the dark areas of Laughlin's runways. Having seen the legs on the backside of the Tower, and being young and not very bright, I jumped out of the pickup, came around the side of the Tower and crouched down. I was ready to leap upon this illegal alien. Much to my surprise, as I came around the corner in my crouched position, I was eye to eye with the biggest, badest German Shepherd dog I have ever seen. Holding his leash was a very large 4080th Air Policeman with a great big smile. He said, "Good evening, may we help you?" My great adventure and plan to capture an illegal alien came to a sudden halt.

Lyn Fite and his 1951 Cushman motor scooter
in front of his barracks (1963).

AGE Shop in 1962. On the right inside was ATC;
on the left was SAC.

RICHARD KEMP
Canton, Georgia

My four short years in the 4080th SRW were some of the best years of my life. I joined the Wing in the Spring of 1961. My first exciting experience with the U-2 was an engine installation that damned near took my head off. To install the J-57, it was first hung on a track that was bolted to the top of the inside of the fuselage and the roller/hanger bolted to the top of the engine. It was rolled in and out on an engine stand. The clearance between the engine and fuselage was so tight that as it was rolled in, the mechanics had to push the engine from side to side to clear other components. I was tasked to do that job on my very first engine installation. As the engine started to roll inside, I bent over to crawl under the engine. Something in the roller broke and the engine fell about six inches into the fuselage, missing me by inches. Six inches doesn't sound like much but that engine weighed about three tons. Needless to say, it scared the crap out of this then-18-year-old airman.

* * * * *

In early 1962 several other mechanics and I were dispatched by C-123, the noisiest airplane inside ever to fly. We went to Biggs AFB in El Paso, Texas, and recovered a U-2. The aircraft had suffered a flameout enroute to Lockheed Skunk Works in California for overhaul and update. Only members of the 4080th SRW were allowed to work on the U-2s. That made it necessary to send us to Biggs to repair and launch the aircraft on to California. After the repairs were made and preparations were made to launch, someone up the chain decided to pull the pogos and hand launch due to the rough taxiways and runways. A man was stationed on each wingtip to balance the airplane while it taxied and started the takeoff roll. With a very small amount of lift, the pilot could control the balance with the ailerons. It was quite a show for those who have never witnessed this feat. We had large crowds of spectators from the base to observe this maneuver. I remember the Base Commander was a very tall, thin full bird colonel and his response after having seen the hand launch was: "Now by God, boys, I've been in the Air Force for a long time and I have seen airplanes take off every way you can think of, but that's the first time I've ever seen two guys throw one up."

* * * * *

Later that year I was sent TDY to Eielson AFB, Alaska. Since the beginning of time, there have been certain individuals in every military unit who know every secret. In this case it was the base bus drivers at Eielson. At that time, most of the U-2s were bare metal with the insignias painted on. While we were there, our airplanes were being rotated back to the factory and the replacements were arriving with the new all over gray paint scheme. Not long after the arrival of the newly painted U-2s, a bus driver inquired of his 4080th passengers, "How do those things take off silver and come back gray?"

* * * * *

At that time, too, the number of missions we were flying increased. As a result, we were given additional aircraft and more personnel were sent from Laughlin. One such engine mechanic was Phil Champion; forgive me, Phil, if you read this. At that time of the year in Alaska, the sun came up about 4:00 AM and it did not get dark until about 11:00 PM. The transport of choice was the C-124 Globemaster. I swear that thing flew backwards most of the time. Phil's flight arrived around 4:00 PM that day and they were all tired from the long flight. We got them some chow and finally settled in their quarters around 5:30 p.m. Phil had a reputation for always being a little late for work. I explained to him that the Line Chief was very strict and would not tolerate any tardiness. I told him to be sure to get to the flight line by the 8:30 AM for roll call the next day. By 6:30 PM Phil was fast asleep. Two and a half hours later at 9:00 PM a couple of us rushed into Phil's room yelling that the Line Chief was mad as hell and he wanted Phil down on the flight line-NOW. He dragged himself out of bed, looked out the window and saw bright sunlight. He dressed and flew down the hall. Someone asked him where he was going at 10:00 at night. Phil said if he hadn't been so tired after just two hours' sleep, he would have killed me then and there.

Not much was known about us because of the mission we were given and the veil of secrecy we worked under. The members of the 4080th SRW were not getting much recognition. We never felt neglected because we did our jobs with pride and for love of country. God Bless America and Dragons everywhere.

Richard Kemp, right, and Richard Pratt. The two were close friends in West Virginia.

Richard Kemp with his private plane, 2006

HARRY R. MAGILL
Moreno Valley, California

Wife: Dixie

THE GREAT TURKEY RAID

During the Cuban Missile Crisis, most of us guys were restricted to the base, even the married fellows. We stayed in the 4080th A&E dorm located directly across from the Chow Hall where we ate all our meals. I had a front-row seat for what became known as "The Great Turkey Raid."

I'm not sure of the thought pattern of the airman who initiated the raid. He managed to get into the kitchen of the Chow Hall. He confiscated a whole cooked turkey and delivered it across the street to the dorm. There he invited all the residents to join him in the feast. We did have a lot of turkey and enjoyed the great feast.

Sometime later the Base Police arrived and asked if anyone knew how the turkey seemed to "fly" from the Chow Hall to the dorm day room. Most of the guys were mum, but the turkey liberator confessed that he had delivered the turkey to the dorm. The humorless Base Police took custody of the remains of the bird and returned it to the Chow Hall. This marked the turkey liberator as the hero of the downtrodden airman, and to this day he is still one of the Squadron's heroes; just ask anyone who was there that day. Maybe Rooster Robinson can better explain that caper.

SAMUEL R. MCDOWELL, JR.
(Deceased April 28, 2007)

Sam provided the following prior to his death.

In mid-1959 I was sent TDY to Taoyan Air Base, Taiwan for three months as an engine technician to the Republic of China Air Force (ROCAF) for the RB-57D. Sgt. Shelhorne, an autopilot technician, worked with me at Taoyan. We helped the ROCAF maintenance guys with a problem they experienced with one of the aircraft engines. One engine was losing power as the RB-57D (#5643 to be specific) gained altitude. It was over-compensating and reducing too much fuel. I suggested they replace the fuel control; but to my surprise, the problem persisted. The maintenance guys asked what they should do next and I repeated my first suggestion--to change the fuel control. They said they had already changed one fuel control. They were dubious about my firm stand on replacing the fuel control again, but they ordered another one and installed it. To their surprise and my absolute delight the problem was corrected.

We discovered that the first replacement fuel control had the same deficiency unit. I was told that after that episode, they wanted to change the fuel control for every problem. Sadly, that plane was shot down on October 7, 1959 by a PLA SA-2 missile killing the pilot, Capt Ying-Chin Wang.

We worked with Line Chief Chung who spoke English very well as did other members of the maintenance team. The Chinese treated us well; I enjoyed my only maintenance TDY. Concerning any cultural or scientific pursuits I engaged in there, I respectfully take the Fifth.

At Laughlin AFB I was in charge of the Jet Engine Shop and did not have the opportunity to go TDY. Adolph Janosky and Harold Brownback were with me in the Jet Engine Shop. I was in Quality Control for a long time and maintained updated blueprints on the U-2. The engineers referred to these change orders when they experienced an unusual problem.

I had another change of career fields to the PMEL shop. I was only a TSgt. at the time and I was put in charge of the shop over fellows with higher rank as sometimes happens in the Air Force. Nobody complained, least of all me. I just continued to do my job. Guys in my shop were frequently in and out on TDY. Sometimes I had to be creative in order to keep the guys busy. Once I assigned each man to take a tech order and develop a test for everybody else. George Devers was assigned "exiting B-57C precautions." He nearly stumped everyone with his question. I don't recall his question, but the correct answer was: Be sure the seat belt pin is in place.

I worked in several different career fields and I can say I never had a bad assignment. There was something about each one that I enjoyed. I retired April 1, 1971. My career had a lot of events that occurred on April 1. One event was that I was assigned to Laughlin AFB on April 1, 1957. After retirement I moved to Indiana and then to Kentucky where I now reside and own a printing business that produces family histories.

I still reminisce about my tour with the 4080th SRW. It was a high point of my career and I made some great friends in that unit.

MSgt. Samuel Riley McDowell, Jr., 1969

Sam McDowell 2006

ROGER (BIG "O") OWENS
(Deceased June 25, 2002)

The following memories were submitted by Roger's widow, Patricia.

Roger was with the 4080th Civil Engineering Squadron from 1959 to 1961. His group was responsible for maintaining the runways at Laughlin AFB. He told me about the many snakes they had to deal with when they were working on the runways there. The Del Rio area seemed a haven for snakes.

The enlisted guys' pay wasn't very good in those days. However, we wives were resourceful with what we had. A few days before payday when money was very short, several families would get together and share whatever we had in the refrigerator or pantry. We had a big community meal. It wasn't a gourmet feast, but it was just a wonderful time of sharing with our friends.

To this day Roger's TDY bag is still packed as it was when he last used it. He missed his family on those TDYs, but we understood his job came first.

Roger retired after 25 years in the Air Force. For the next eight years he worked as a rural mail carrier around De Leon, Texas.

Roger and I had three children--Roger Jr., Richard, and Peggy. Peggy was born at Laughlin hospital. We have two grandchildren, Allyson and Albert. Albert is carrying on the military tradition; he is in the Army.

Roger (Big O) Owens

ARTHUR A. (ART) REICHERT
(Deceased July 26, 1991)

The following memories were submitted by Art's widow, Martha.

Art was stationed at Barksdale AFB, Louisiana from September 1952 to April 1956. It was during this period that we met and married.

In April 1956 Art was transferred to Turner AFB, Georgia where he began his association with the Black Knights, later known as the "U-2 Project". We relocated to Laughlin AFB in 1957 along with about 500 Air Force families. The nearby small town of Del Rio had many unpaved streets at the time. There was no base housing and the local people were closing in carports and garages and renting them to us. Art and I managed to find a tiny house that consisted of a bedroom, bath, kitchen and living room. It had been purchased from the base as surplus property, and we were grateful to have it. Our landlord and landlady were wonderful people; their name was Hill and they owned Hill Lumber Company.

Soon after our arrival, it began to rain. It was a welcome relief from the town's dry, dusty climate. Having never lived west of my native Louisiana, I finally got acclimated to the area after about a year and a half. The next exciting event was the construction of base housing where we were privileged to live in brand new quarters. Our only child, son Tommy, was born at Laughlin AFB Hospital in May of 1960.

Everything was changing rapidly for the families. Our husbands' work was classified TOP SECRET which meant they could not discuss anything at home. On a regular basis the Base Commander would call for the wives to meet in the base theater. He would explain to us that we shouldn't get upset if our husbands couldn't tell us what they were doing. He thanked us for our support and told us how important we were to the success of this project. Of course, that really made us feel special. It was not unusual to get a telephone call from our husbands saying, "We're on alert and I don't know when I'll be home."

Art was in the 4080th Armament & Electronics. He worked on the cameras for the U-2. Art and I had a close bond with the fellows he worked with as well as their wives and families.

In June 1963, Art and I relocated to Davis Monthan AFB when the 4080th SRW was transferred there. I felt that we had the best of everything; we had Air Force friends and through my work a number of civilian friends. We considered it a pleasant "mix."

Art was transferred to Offutt AFB, Omaha, Nebraska in January 1968 and it was the end of our involvement with the U-2 project. It was also our most difficult assignment. When Art was sent to Thailand for a year, our son and I returned to my hometown in Louisiana to be near family. Art spent the last 14 months of his AF career at England AFB where he retired in 1971.

Sadly, Art was in a fatal motor vehicle accident on July 26, 1991. Prior to his death, Art and I often talked of the time we spent with the U-2 project and the many wonderful people we met.

Art and Martha Reichert

GLENN SIMMONS
Lancaster, Pennsylvania

Wife: Marianne

I supported the U-2 program for four years and it was certainly an interesting time in my life. My assignments were in Administration and Operations of the 4025th SRS and propulsion, ground power and orderly room for the 4080th. I kept the jet engine records that were recognized as the best in 2nd Air Force according to the Inspector General auditors.

My memories of those days include Airman Shelby, Airman Fariar, Chief Warrant Officer Underwood and all the jet engine mechanics.

One of my most memorable experiences was when we received a radiation sample that had to be wrapped in a lead sheet and sent to Isotopes in Nevada. President Eisenhower's visit to the area to dedicate the Amistad Dam was a highlight of my tour there. John Wayne's visit while making the movie "The Alamo" was another memorable event of that time.

Marianne's memories:

I was 17 years old when Glenn and I married. When I had saved enough money, I went to Del Rio to be with Glenn and we found an apartment on Fourth Street. Our first child was born December 25, 1959. If it wasn't for the Air Force, I would not have been serenaded in Mexico, an event I remember to this day. I also enjoyed living in the town of Del Rio and meeting so many friendly people, both in town and on the base.

Glenn, Marianne and Diana Simmons, 1960

RICHARD W. STAATS
(Deceased October 16, 2001)

Memories submitted by Richard's widow, Reiko.

Richard and I met during his tour of duty in Japan in 1952 and were married 48 years when he passed away in 2001.

Richard was assigned to the U-2 maintenance unit first at Turner AFB, Georgia and at Laughlin AFB, Texas. His last station was at Davis-Monthan AFB, Arizona. He supported the U-2 program for a total of 11 years.

Our two children and I were accustomed to Richard's frequent absences. One year the Christmas tree remained up until April when Richard returned and the family celebrated together. During the Cuban Missile Crisis, Richard had 30 minutes to pack and leave on TDY to a destination I had not been told. When President Kennedy announced on television of the tension building in Cuba, I thought then that Richard had gone to Florida. On that particular TDY he was gone more than a month.

Richard had another mysterious foreign destination that I remembered. He was directed to pack a civilian suit, white shirt, tie and dress shoes. Money was always in short supply and Richard did not have a suit. Richard's Commander told him that funds would be arranged for him to have a suit. I thought their destination might be a Communist country but I was not sure.

Richard served in Vietnam for one year and returned in 1973 to Albuquerque, New Mexico. He later went to Virginia and retired in Pennsylvania where I currently live.

MEMORIES OF CYNDI STAATS

I don't really remember much about Del Rio because I was just a baby when my parents were there. However, my mother and father have told many stories of the time they were stationed at Laughlin AFB. My parents' eyes would brighten as they retold tales of how the close-knit community supported each other. I recall that my parents were close with a rancher in Del Rio named Mr. Cox who helped them from time to time. My father told stories of deer hunting on the Cox ranch. To this day, my mother stays in touch with other families she met during that time. Although they are scattered across the country, they write as though they just transferred from their last assignment.

Reiko and Dick Staats

Dick Staats

WILLIAM (TURP) TURPIN
Oceanside, California

Wife: June (Deceased February 2003)

I was known by friends and co-workers as "Turp." From 1956 to 1968 I was part of the 4080th SRW and the 100th SRW at Turner AFB, Laughlin AFB and Davis Monthan AFB. My assignment was with the Field Maintenance Squadron structural repair shop, better known as the Sheet Metal Shop. Our motto became, "You bend, we mend." Our shop made high-pressure hydraulic lines, control cables, fiberglass repairs and all manner of sheet metal repairs. We did some minor and other extensive repairs on the U-2s. I was also with the B-57 program and supported the drones.

A number of names come to my mind of friends and co-workers who shared those times. I had some fun times and hard work with Donald Swann, Lowell Foster, Emanuel Peevy, and "Soup" Campbell.

My most memorable experience was a TDY to Australia. I met many wonderful people there and made a lot of good friends. I missed them when I had to leave; seeing real kangaroos and koalas were a special treat.

The Air Force gave me a great education seeing different parts of the world and experiencing new things. However, with the good times came the bad times of being separated from my family and loved ones for extended periods and missing out on family events.

I especially enjoyed the camaraderie of the Air Force, and I now keep in touch by email with some of the guys.

GORDON E. (JOE) WARNER
Carrollton, Texas

Wife: Jane

I am a proud Iowa farm boy from Ottumwa born and raised not far from Radar O'Riley of television's MASH fame. We lived in the last house on the last road so if we saw a dust cloud approaching, it was either the postman or someone was lost. We had no running water or electricity and I attended eighth grade in a one-room schoolhouse. The day I turned 17, I asked my Dad if I could join the Air Force, and he replied, "Why not?" Now keep in mind that the longest distance I had ever traveled was to the Missouri state line to get fireworks and to Des Moines for the Iowa State Fair. You can imagine the culture shock I experienced with my first airplane ride to Oakland, California, and the 11 weeks basic training with folks from all over the United States.

After basic training, I went on to Aircraft Mechanics Technical School in Amarillo, Texas. I was told I would be working on the F-89 Interceptor. I completed technical school and received orders to report to Albany, Georgia. That is where it all began for me.

In February 1956, after a short visit back home with my folks, I traveled to Albany and presented my orders to the guard at the main gate. He quickly told me that I was in the wrong place because there was no organization by that name on the base. I was totally flabbergasted. Finally everything got sorted out and I found my way to the open bay barracks that was to be my new home.

I learned much later that the master plan for forming the new wing was to take the top graduates from technical school, mix in some three to six-year Korean War veterans, and top it off with some of the meanest "brown shoe" sergeants who ever held a wrench. The "brown shoe" term was applied to those men who were members of the Army Air Force and were issued brown shoes or boots. When the Air Force came into its own in 1947, everyone was issued black boots.

We were an eclectic mixture of humanity thrust together to form one of the most unique squadrons of all time. There was one problem--we had no airplanes. With no "real" work, one of the sergeants' favorite pastimes was to gather all us young guys after roll call and have us sweep the hangar floor while they sat and drank coffee in the break room. After we finished sweeping they came out, looked at the floor, kicked over the trash cans and we started all over again. Some days this went on until noon. We later learned the sergeants were observing attitudes and determining who would be the future crew chiefs.

Some of us were assigned to an inspection dock working on the B-57 aircraft; some of our group just disappeared for a few weeks. In 1957 the new Wing moved to Laughlin AFB at Del Rio, Texas and we started receiving the U-2s from Lockheed.

My first TDY was in the summer of 1958; it was Joint Task Force 7 at Eniwetok Atoll. This was an exciting time for me to be able to witness firsthand the atomic tests. We were about 35 miles from ground zero for most of the shots. We could feel the heat on our backs from the blast. The Atomic Energy Commission had a B-52 that usually took off about 3:30 AM. Since the island was in the shape of a dogleg with our living quarters on the short part of the leg, it seemed as though the plane was coming right through the tent.

The high point of that trip was a shot they referred to as "OAK". Our instructions were to roll up our tent sides and put all our stuff on our bunks. When the shot went off, we had an announcement that a wave action would

308

start in 14 minutes. The time came and went with no action. All of a sudden the nearby lagoon dried up right in front of our eyes. I saw the bottom of the lagoon from at least 100 yards. Then the wave came. It covered the bottom half of the island and then receded after a short time. That was a very exciting experience for this Iowa farm boy!

Our wing operated primarily as a TDY outfit. When we were at home station, it was training, training, training. Everyone pretty much hated that routine. The normal rotation was TDY for three months, seven to nine months home, then back on TDY for three months. That routine did change in later years.

I would be remiss if I did not mention our wives at this point. They were the glue that held the home life together. The wives not only kept the household together, but also made complete relocations to other states while our unit was TDY. I went to Alaska TDY from Del Rio and returned to Tucson. My wife, Jane, took care of closing up and moving everything from Del Rio, went to Tucson and rented a house, and had it all set up when I got back. That's one tough lady.

Then there was the infamous trip to Clark AFB and on to Bien Hoa Air Base, Vietnam. We had only three aircraft with inflight refueling capabilities and we needed them for this run. James (Soup) Campbell was Crew Chief on #707, Donnie Brown had #680 (currently in the Smithsonian) and I was the Crew Chief on #703. The aircraft were designated E models because they had not yet been converted to the J-75 engines.

We had several dry runs before we finally got off. I was in the habit of not unpacking all my clothes after all these false alarms. Sure enough, on what we thought was another practice run, we learned it was the real thing and off we went. The boots I had on were pretty well worn and by the time we got to Vietnam, I was putting paper in the soles. One day a C-130 dropped in and I gave the load master $20 to bring me a new pair of boots on his next trip. I never saw the loadmaster with my new boots and I never saw my $20 again.

When we arrived at Clark, it seemed like we had been flying forever. We were bone tired. Our orders were to get at least two of the U-2s ready to fly as soon as possible for a mission the next day. The U-2 had a very sensitive center of gravity and the weight and balance had to be figured on every mission. There was a lot of math involved. When we were at home, someone with a big calculator did it for us. Our Line Chief gathered Soup, Donnie and me and said we would have to do the weight and balance by hand. We looked at each other and Soup spoke first, "I don't think I can do it." Donnie chimed in too and said, "Me neither." The Line Chief looked at me and said, "I guess that leaves you, Warner." I was still there eight hours later when they came back to do the preflight but we got the job done.

* * * * *

Aircraft #954 was a two-seater used by the CIA. It did not have controls in the rear seat but there was a seat for an observer. In the spring of 1965 we were at Davis Monthan AFB and the Wing was considering a training aircraft; #954 was brought in for evaluation. Another factor was that by now almost all aircraft in the Air Force were tricycle gear configuration as opposed to the bicycle gear on the U-2. The pilots who checked out fastest were either B-47 or C-47 pilots.

Keep in mind that when new pilots checked out in the U-2, they did not have the advantage of back-seat instructors. The new pilot's first flight was just that, and it was solo. I have a whole memory bank of images watching those pilots try to get back on the ground after successfully getting airborne. A lot of times they did not even make the corner when they taxied out and had to be pushed around. I won't go into more details for fear of embarrassing someone, but suffice it to say, that was why a lot of the upper echelon thought a trainer was necessary.

No. 954 was on loan to give the "brass" a ride to evaluate the feasibility of a trainer. I was actually cleaning the wheel wells on my aircraft and got roped into helping with this test. After several flights, the pilot asked Colonel DesPortes if it would be acceptable to take the enlisted guys up for a flight since they had been busting their butts supporting this test. Colonel DesPortes responded with a very supportive "Yes." Unfortunately, the pilot's name is in the dark recess of my memory bank and I cannot recall his name.

The way it went down was so quick it was almost a blur. We tossed some gas in that baby, the pilot took off, did some demonstrations of the aircraft's ability and landed.

We did not have flight suits; I remember I was pretty sweaty and greasy. The enlisted guys shared a helmet and that was about it. My flight was one of the last. We took the runway and the pilot asked what I wanted to see. I replied, "I want to see this thing go straight up. I want to see the gust control operation and the low fuel light come on under "G" loads." Talk about an "E" ticket ride! He did everything I wanted and then some. I have flown a lot of different aircraft, including the Lear Jet Model 31, but nothing, absolutely no other aircraft, comes close to the experience I had that day. The sensation of speeding down the runway about 900 feet, lifting off, transitioning to vertical has to be experienced to be believed. It was amazing to realize that our airspeed was not as fast as I had expected. We had an 11,000-pound aircraft, 18,000 pound thrust engine plus fuel. The math tells it all.

Another awesome sensation was looking out of the canopy and seeing the wing tips well above the aircraft. As we picked up speed in level flight, the amount of flex was almost unbelievable. When the gust system was activated, I was astounded as I watched the wings level out. The gust control system raised the ailerons and flaps a couple of inches to unload the wings and allowed a higher indicated airspeed.

The flight was about 25 minutes. We flew north out of Tucson over Mount Lemon. Just let me comment that the heart rate reported on the astronauts does not even come close to mine that day. My experience was totally indescribable.

I hope some of the other guys who got to ride that day give their impressions for this book. With all the excitement, I do not remember any names except for Ken Folken. The whole experience reinforces the camaraderie and relationships that were so strong between the pilots and the enlisted guys with the 4080th SRW. They could have all gone to the Officers' Club and left us to work on the aircraft. There was certainly no reason for them to go that extra mile--but they did.

* * * * *

In 1969 the Air Force decided it was time for me to leave the Wing for a short hiatus to Vietnam. I remember how "picked on" I felt as I prepared to depart. I left my wife alone with a month old daughter. When I returned from Vietnam, I was sent to Big Spring, Texas to work quality control issues. In the meantime Colonel DesPortes came back to David Monthan as the 12th Division Commander. In May 1971, I was summoned to Base Operations. I had no idea what to expect. There was Colonel DesPortes waiting to see me; what a pleasant surprise. He had flown in on a T-33. In that famous

South Carolina drawl, he said, "Son, how would you like to come back to the Wing?" I was almost speechless, but I readily accepted his offer. It sure did not take us long to pack up and get out of Big Spring. That was the kind of guy DesPortes was--always looking after the troops. When we were on the TDY to Bien Hoa, he personally made a visit to make sure we were getting everything we needed to do the mission. "The Colonel" definitely holds a soft spot in my heart; he was a great man and a great leader.

I was going nowhere on the farm before I joined the Air Force. By spending time in the Wing with all those experienced and professional people, I developed a sense of responsibility and a work ethic that had a profound impact on my career. After I retired from the Air Force in 1976, I felt my military training served me well when I owned my own business and again when I worked in private industry. I had approximately 18 years with the squadron and many, many enjoyable times.

Joe Warner, 1959

OL20 Maintenance Group in front of Joe Warner's U-2 #703, Soup Campbell, fifth from left back arms crossed, Donnie Brown third from left Middle row, Joe Warner, sixth from left middle row, Bob Ingram fifth from right back row

DAN WHITE
Cat Spring, Texas

Dan furnished the attached photographs that hold many wonderful memories for him. Several of his TDYs are identified in the photos.

OL-5 Alaska, Summer 1960

Canal Zone TDY, 1960

316

Canal Zone TDY, 1960

TO LAUNCH A RECON AROUND THE WORLD

Aviation in itself is not inherently dangerous.
But to an even greater degree than the sea,
it is terribly unforgiving of carelessness,
incapacity or neglect.

Anonymous

CUBAN MISSILE CRISIS

October 1962 is a date that is vivid in the collective memories of many Americans, but most especially the men of the 4080th Strategic Reconnaissance Wing. They were charged with flying over the Island of Cuba to photograph the presence of Soviet missile sites. The clarity of the photography taken from their U-2 aircraft made it easy for President Kennedy to determine how to proceed to protect our country.

The Joint Chiefs of Staff (JCS) planned and directed the execution of all Cuban overflights. No flights took off before the JCS briefed the President and he authorized each mission. The SAC Recon Center at Offutt AFB, Nebraska transmitted the approved orders through the chain of command to the local command center.

At the Wing level pilots were designated for the scheduled flights. Support functions, such as Maintenance, Photography and Operations were alerted of the forthcoming events. Physiological Support was notified which pilot was scheduled to fly and the technicians had his gear ready when he reported. The pilots tasked for these missions were:

Major Rudolph Anderson
Major Buddy Brown
Major Steve Heyser
Captain George Bull
Captain Ed Emerling
Captain Roger Herman
Captain Charles Kern
Captain Gerald McIlmoyle
Captain James Qualls
Captain Robert Primrose
Captain Daniel Schmarr.

The camera maintenance personnel had special pride in their work. These missions were what they had trained for and they were ready. It was a favorite saying of the unit, "If the camera doesn't work, there was only a training flight that occurred." The following people were there to support the NEPHO operation at McCoy AFB:

F. M. Shipley	Glenn Chapman
Bob Ingram	Joseph (Rooster) Robinson
Jim Manis	John Bell
Jerry Fogel	Ricky Mickle
Bobbie Black	Jim Combs (Hycon Tech Rep)
Ray Callahan	Tom McClung (Perkin Elmer Tech Rep)
Frank Gault	Jim Lobig
John Washburn	B. C. Fowler
John Farris	

When the pilot returned from his flight, the photography specialists quickly offloaded the film and sent it in a waiting aircraft to Washington, DC for processing.

Cuban Missile Crisis pilots and the commanding officers.
Back row L to R: General Thomas Powers, Commander in Chief,
Strategic Air Command, Captain Edwin Emerling,
Major Buddy L. Brown, Major Steve Heyser, Captain James Qualls,
Captain Roger Herman, Colonel John DesPortes,
Front row L to R: Captain George Bull, Captain Charles Kern, Captain
Gerald McIlmoyle, Captain Robert Primrose, Captain Daniel Schmarr.

BUDDY L. BROWN
Knoxville, Tennessee

CUBAN MISSILE CRISIS OCTOBER 1962

My mission photographing and locating Soviet missiles on the Island of Cuba began October 1962. Prior to the Strategic Air Command (SAC) being assigned the Cuban mission, the CIA had been monitoring the weapons' movement with their own U-2Cs. As a result of the increasing tension between the United States and the Soviet Union, President Kennedy wanted to avoid embarrassment of a clandestine CIA plane being lost over Cuba. The President decided USAF pilots would fly the reconnaissance program. The wheels were put in motion.

There were 11 pilots initially involved in the "Missiles of October" crisis. This is my personal account of my first Cuban mission and the events leading to it. I don't remember how I was notified, but Jerry McIlmoyle and I were flown out to Edwards AFB (North Base) to sit in and listen to the dialog between the SAC brass and the Agency (CIA) brass regarding who should take over and fly the Cuban mission, the CIA or USAF. The meeting was in the evening at the North Base Operations building. Jerry and I were sitting at the back of the small auditorium listening to the dialog between the two agencies' big brass. I thought we were both there to get checked out in the Agency's "C" model if SAC was to be assigned the responsibility for this mission. Rudy Anderson and Steve Heyser had already been qualified in the "C" model. The dialog became heated; in fact, Jerry and I were asked to leave before the discussions continued. I don't know what happened for the remainder of the meeting, but the next day I was flown back to

Laughlin AFB along with our contingency of Laughlin brass. We arrived late in the evening. The next morning, I went down to the 4028TH operations and briefed the boss and mission planners on what I had heard and observed at the meeting at North Base. I was surprised to learn that particular contingency had been planned months earlier and was "on the shelf". There were many secure calls made and our operations and maintenance activity increased dramatically. The end result was that the 4080th SRW had replaced the Agency and had been assigned the reconnaissance program over Cuba.

I was selected, along with several other pilots, to fly the initial recon missions. We all reported to Operations in the early afternoon, and received a quick overview and mission update. We were directed to go home and immediately start our required eight hours of crew rest. We were to report back to Operations at 0100 the next morning. I went home, took a sleeping pill and hit the sack. The next morning, I reported to Operations along with the other primary pilots. We started our final briefings. I looked around and it seemed everyone from our Wing was in the briefing room.

After the briefings, we went to PSD (Physiological Support Division) for our pre-mission meal, modified physical, and mission update. The PSD guys helped us get into our pressure suits. It was raining when we started dressing. During our pre-breathing period, I could tell it was one of those Texas thunderstorms. The rain came down with greater intensity and the winds, lightning and thunder all had increased. The weather was looking bad outside. I thought we would never be cleared to take off in weather like this. The crosswinds were quartering tail wind and were way out of limits. The increased thunderstorms were pounding the area. Much to my surprise, SAC executed the mission. I was transported in our PSD vehicle to my aircraft. The rain was so severe, I could hardly see more than a couple of feet in front of the van. The strong winds were shifting the vehicle as we drove out to the aircraft.

The bird I was to fly had slipper tanks installed which contained electronic intelligence collection equipment. It had been spotted on the apron just off Runway 13 (130 degrees). "Great," I thought, "The winds were blowing from approximately 280 degrees with a quartering tail crosswind, and now were way out of U-2 limits of 25 knots." I got out of the PSD van and walked about 20 feet to the ladder to get into the cockpit. The cockpit looked like it had filled up with water. Not so; it was just raining so hard it seemed that wet. I hoped all that water wouldn't short out any of my electronics.

The Mobile Officer was soaking wet, I was soaking wet and everything around us was soaking wet. The Mobile Officer told me to complete my cockpit check solo so he could close the canopy. I completed my cockpit check and signaled Mobile that I was ready to start my engine. I looked out the left side of the canopy watching the wind blow sheets of rain across the runway. The whole scenario was unbelievable, and the Mobile Officer was going to launch me into that? Say your prayers, Buddy Boy.

This was a radio-silent mission, so only light signals were used to start, taxi and clear for takeoff. I led my bird and followed the light wand for the 50 or so feet I had to taxi to the active runway. Just sitting in the aircraft, I could feel the wind buffet my aircraft. The rain was still incredible after all this time. I got a green light, gave the bird full power, released brakes and started my takeoff roll. All during the takeoff roll the aircraft was buffeting. "I hope my pogos drop freely," I thought to myself. As soon as I lifted off and established my climb, I set my controls to the Gust position, slowed to turbulent air penetration speed, and turned every light in the cockpit to "High."

The lightning lit up the sky like daylight, and all the while I was being bounced around. This roller coaster ride lasted until about 50,000 feet when I finally broke out into a clear night sky. What a relief. I hoped everyone made it okay. I continued to climb to cruise altitude, went from Gust to Fair position, locked in the autopilot after reaching cruise altitude and settled in to start my celestial shots. I think there were about six of us that took off that night, and all would return to Laughlin AFB after completing our Cuban missions. I was designated to recover at McCoy AFB, Florida. I crossed the Gulf and after a few hours, I picked up my initial coast in point in the western part of Cuba around Pinar Del Rio.

About 15 minutes before entry, I powered up my B configuration camera, set the mode and checked all the aircraft systems. I crossed over into the Cuban land mass; all my camera equipment was on and operating normally. All my targets were in the western part of Cuba. The weather in Cuba that day was cooperating and my areas were clear. Tracking and staying on course was a snap; I used the driftsight; there were many checkpoints to verify my exact position. After flying my programmed recon track, it was time to head back to McCoy AFB. I exited Cuba and headed north to Florida. Everything was still "radio silent." Before I started the descent into McCoy AFB, I was authorized to make my first radio call and requested landing instructions.

The weather at McCoy was great. I entered traffic from the downwind side, turned base onto final and made a full stop landing. My pogos were inserted, and Mobile cleared me to taxi and led me to my parking spot. As I was taxiing in, I observed a lot of activity at the ramp. Several vehicles converged on my bird as I completed my engine shutdown. The ladder was rolled up to the cockpit and the Operations Officer on the ladder turned out to be Major General Compton, the SAC Director of Operations. What a surprise that was! He welcomed me back and we exchanged a few words while my "B" configuration camera was being downloaded. I had completed my first Cuban mission.

Several more U-2s arrived at McCoy within the next couple of days. The initial cadre of U-2 pilots there with me included Rudy Anderson, Steve Heyser, Jim Qualls, George Bull, Charlie Kern, Jerry McIlmoyle, Pinkie Primrose, Danny Schmarr, Roger Herman, and Ed Emerling. Up to this point I had not been checked out in the Agency's "C" model; however, a few days later, Jim Barnes, a CIA pilot and friend from other bases, flew in a "C" model and gave me my checkout.

To this day, I don't know how we took off from Laughlin on that historic night with no hung pogos and no aborts. Without a doubt, Someone was watching over the 4080th Wing that night.

On what would be forever known as "Black Saturday," October 27, 1962, I was assigned as the primary pilot for my target area in and around western Cuba. The secondary target area pilot was Rudy Anderson. If my target area was forecasted to be weathered in and the secondary target area was open, the secondary pilot would fly. As it turned out, my area was clobbered so Rudy flew his target area. He was shot down that day by a SAM and became the only pilot to be lost during the Cuban Missile Crisis. I remember that day. Some of us were out on the golf course because we could only fly every other day. From the golf course, we could see any U-2 entering the traffic pattern for a full stop landing. I was talking to "Chopper" Kern as we approached the green that was a high point on the course. I looked at Chopper and said, "I don't know what happened, but Rudy should have been back by now."

Later that day we were all summoned to report to Operations. We were briefed on the loss of our fellow pilot, Rudy and his U-2. It was sad to lose one of our own. We had all flown our scheduled missions knowing that it could have been our last. But those thoughts never entered my mind; I had a job to do and I did it.

RICHARD HENRY
Venice, Florida

There were 13 days of the most dramatic world events of my lifetime and I had a front-row seat. Even as President Kennedy and Premier Krushchev frantically looked for ways to pull their countries back from the edge of disaster, they found it difficult to control their own military machines, let alone the rapid pace of outside events. Kennedy ordered saturation reconnaissance of Cuba to keep track of the Soviet missiles located there.

Every single U-2 pilot who was not on duty in Alaska or stationed elsewhere overseas was called into service. My squadron flew as many as six missions a day over Cuba. We observed launch pads recognizable by their peculiar slash marks; also observed were fueling and checkout vehicles, communication lines and prefabricated storage bunkers. The USAF was so intent on carrying out Kennedy's orders that it ignored normal safety precautions. In the predawn hours of October 17, 1962, four U-2s took off from Laughlin AFB at Del Rio, Texas at 10-minute intervals in a blinding thunderstorm that would normally have grounded such a flimsy aircraft. The wingtip of the U-2 piloted by Major James Qualls barely missed the runway because of strong crosswinds. Qualls recalled, "We were just about mapping the entire island." Colonel DesPortes, Commander of the 4080th Strategic Reconnaissance Wing at Laughlin joked that he didn't have many left in the Wing to fly over Cuba.

At McCoy AFB, Florida, tensions were simmering between the Air Force "blue suiters" and the CIA support personnel who were responsible for servicing the U-2s and taking charge of the intelligence materials, such as the photographic film. The Agency people were still smarting from what they perceived as a power play by the Air Force in persuading Kennedy to deprive them of the mission over Cuba. "They were very resentful and made no bones about hiding it," said Anthony Martinez, Operations Officer for the AF U-2 squadron.

According to U-2 pilot Gerald McIlmoyle, CIA personnel "looked for fault in everything we did". Jerry recalled that a CIA officer reported him to Washington for allegedly displaying signs of nervousness by urinating beside his U-2 shortly before takeoff. McIlmoyle had a good defense: He wanted to spare himself the laborious task of relieving himself aboard the aircraft when he was trying to focus on taking pictures of Soviet missile sites.

On October 25, McIlmoyle returned from an overflight of Cuba with an alarming story about being targeted by an SA-2 missile site near the town of Banes on the northeast coast of Cuba. The CIA's U-2s had a device for detecting when they were being observed by enemy radar. When a radar system painted the plane, a yellow light appeared in the cockpit. When a missile locked onto the plane, the light turned red.

The yellow light had already appeared by the time McIlmoyle made a scheduled turn over Banes. As he gently banked his aircraft, he saw two contrails zip up from beneath him and explode in the sky above. They looked like SA-2s. There was still no red light in his cockpit. McIlmoyle figured that either his detection system was not working properly or the operators of the SA-2 had fired the missiles blind, without engaging the guidance mechanism, in order to deprive him of the usual warning.

Higher-ups were skeptical of McIlmoyle's story. A three-star AF general who reviewed the electronic intelligence told him bluntly, "You weren't fired at." McIlmoyle, a Captain who later rose to the rank of

Brigadier General in charge of the President's nuclear codes, believes to this day he was targeted.

If Rudy Anderson was concerned about McIlmoyle's report, he kept his worries to himself. According to colleagues, Anderson was determined to fly more missions than anyone else, which meant somehow leaping in front of Richard Heyser who was ahead in the rotation. Operations Officer Martinez recalled, "Rudy was in high gear all the time. He was very compulsive, patriotic and very, very dedicated. He was an absolute perfectionist."

According to Heyser, Anderson came to him at one point to ask if he could take a mission that Heyser had been scheduled to fly. Since Heyser had already racked up a large number of special missions, he was less concerned than Anderson about cramming in as much flying time as possible. Heyser remembers telling Anderson to check with Lt. Col. Martinez who was responsible for drawing up the roster. Heyser said, "If it's okay with him, it's okay with me. As a result, Martinez scratched my name out and put his name on the roster."

Exactly when this incident took place is unclear. Heyser says it happened on October 26, the day before Anderson's fatal flight. But flight records show that Anderson had already caught up with Heyser in number of missions by that point, which suggests that the incident may have taken place earlier.

McIlmoyle also recalled Anderson going to Martinez on the evening of October 26, expressing an eagerness to fly, and asked to be put on standby the following day. Martinez could not recall this particular episode, although he said it is "plausible," given Anderson's sometimes "intense" personality.

The following morning, at least three other missions were scrubbed at the last minute, making Anderson the next pilot in rotation. Capt. Roger Herman had the job of clearing Anderson for takeoff. He followed him up the ladder to the aircraft and ran through a checklist of 30 or 40 items. He made sure that Anderson's oxygen supply was connected properly. Maps and TOP SECRET target folder were neatly stacked by the side of the ejection seat. A final preparation, called "press to test," supplied a surge of oxygen that briefly inflated Anderson's partial pressure suit and filled the cockpit. When he was certain everything was in order, Herman slapped Anderson on the shoulder. "Okay, Rudy," Herman said, "Here we go, have a good trip, see you when you get back." Anderson gave a thumbs-up sign as Herman closed the canopy.

Minutes later, Anderson's U-2 roared down the runway and headed toward Cuba. "Target number 33 destroyed. Target number 33 destroyed."

JOE GLENN HYDE, JR
Deceased November 20, 1963

The following story appeared in Southwest Texas LIVE, October 17, 2006. It was written by Joe Glenn Hyde III and the article is submitted here with his permission.

THE SKY STILL BURNS IN YOUR MEMORY

On November 20, 1963, from Barksdale AFB, near Shreveport, Louisiana, a USAF U-2C took off on a reconnaissance sortie just after 6:00 AM to take photographs of the Island of Cuba.

One year and one month after the end of the Cuban Missile Crisis, Strategic Air Command (SAC) U-2s from the famed 4080th Strategic Reconnaissance Wing were tasked with continued overflights of Cuba to ensure that the Soviet Union would not redeploy its offensive, medium-range nuclear missiles only 90 miles from Florida. Barksdale AFB was the temporary duty location for the U-2s performing these missions.

The pilot wasn't new to the Cuba mission. He had been flying U-2 missions for over three years. Nor were sorties over Cuba just routine. At the end of the Cuban Missile Crisis, the Soviet Union had removed their nuclear missiles trained on the US homeland. However, the Soviets left Cuban President Fidel Castro with a gift of brand new SA-2 surface-to-air missiles like the one that shot down another U-2 pilot, Francis Gary "Frank" Powers, over Moscow in 1960. Castro was also given a squadron of state-of-the-art MiG 21 fighter aircraft that were clumsy at high altitude, but still considered a formidable threat.

During a previous deployment of support for the Cuban mission that year, this U-2 pilot was awarded the Distinguished Flying Cross (DFC) for out-maneuvering a MiG 21 that attempted to meet it head-on. In all, during his short tour as a U-2 pilot, in addition to earning the prestigious DFC, he was about to pin on his fifth Oak Leaf Cluster to an Air Medal, meaning it was his sixth Air Medal. Even by today's standards, with frequent deployments to war zones of Iraq and Afghanistan, earning six Air Medals within three years is the exception, not the rule. The pilot had an "aw shucks" attitude about the medals. He said that everyone in his unit got them just for doing their job.

By 11:00 AM, the pilot completed the zigzag flight plan over hostile territory taking classified pictures of the areas assigned his mission. He was approaching Key West, with the coast of Florida looming larger in the mid-morning sun. Earlier in the mission, in a required radio position report back to SAC command post, the pilot indicated that his autopilot had failed.

Flying the U-2 was hard enough with the aid of an autopilot. Flying the U-2 without an autopilot was dangerous, especially at high altitude where the air is extremely thin. The airspeed indicator allowed for only three knots (about 5mph) of deviation. If flown too slow, the U-2 stalled and lost altitude quickly. If flown too fast, the U-2 entered a regime called "mach tuck" where the aircraft will exceed the speed of sound and probably break apart. This regime was known among the U-2 pilots as the "coffin corner."

The U-2C flown that November day was a former "Agency" bird, a term used to describe U-2 airframes that were once inventoried by the Central Intelligence Agency (CIA), but transferred to SAC when the USAF assumed more of the high altitude reconnaissance missions in the early 1960s. The U-2C rather than the U-2A was the preferred airframe to use for the dangerous Cuban overflights. It had a more powerful engine and a better suite of threat detection instrumentation that informed the pilot when he was under attack by enemy surface-to-air missiles or other aircraft.

Agency birds, because of their origin in the clandestine world, were modified on occasion to improve mission effectiveness, sometimes at the expense of safety. In this case, the U-2C flying that day had previously had its "stall strips" removed to improve range and maneuverability. Stall strips were installed on the wings of most U-2s then to create a more noticeable stall warning by creating more turbulence over the wings that would warn the pilot of an impending stall. Without the strips, inadvertent stalls were more likely.

With no stall strips, no functioning autopilot, and an airspeed tolerance of only three knots, even a small deviation in temperature or turbulence can quickly put the U-2C in an out-of control situation. With those conditions present that morning 40 miles south of Key West, ground radar following the mission watched in horror as the U-2C plunged almost vertically and disappeared from radar. Within eight minutes, search and rescue aircraft spotted an oil slick at the location the plane disappeared from radar. Ten days of extensive search continued, and the wreckage was salvaged beneath 100 feet of water in the Gulf of Mexico. Hope remained alive for a long time because the survival gear was found, and it appeared that the pilot had departed the aircraft. Maybe, just maybe, the pilot would be found floating, alive, in the water somewhere. With each ticking hour, then days, hope diminished until the search had to be terminated. The body of the pilot was never found.

The pilot of that U-2C was my father, Captain Joe Glenn Hyde, Jr. He was only 33 years old when he died.

My father earned his pilot license at the age of 15. For three years at his high school in Georgia, he was an all-state tackle and in college, a star guard for the University of Georgia Bulldogs in 1948 and 1949. After a nose injury threatened to prevent his dream of a career as an Air Force pilot, he became a capable assistance coach for the Bulldogs in his junior and senior years in college. He accepted an ROTC commission and eventually earned his pilot wings at Greenville AFB, Mississippi.

His first assignment was as an instructor pilot at Greenville AFB. In modern terms, he was what is now called a "First Assignment Instructor Pilot," or FAIP. It was during this tour that he met my mother, Marianne. After his FAIP assignment, he was sent to Korea to fly the F-86. A year later he was assigned to Laughlin AFB as a T-33 IP.

It was a dreadful assignment. No fighter pilot would choose to return to a trainer airplane after a tour flying the F-86. But Dad had a wonderful personality, demeanor and competence for being an IP. His USAF flying records indicate that with volumes of letters of recommendation from senior officers hailing his instructing abilities. SAC needed a strong cadre of IPs at Laughlin to maintain flying skills of the pilots in the recently assigned and secretive U-2 program. The U-2 mission did not afford the pilot much opportunity to practice instrument approaches or landings so the T-33, or T-Bird, was used as a companion trainer.

One story related to me about my father was of a check ride he endured in the T-33 upon arrival at Laughlin. On short final to Laughlin's Runway 13 for final landing, the evaluator pilot deliberately shut off the fuel switches causing the engine to flame out just before touchdown. My father landed safely and allowed the aircraft to coast to a stop. After both pilots exited the aircraft, the evaluator smiled and admitted that he had deliberately shut off the fuel in order to evaluate how my father would handle the situation. Not amused by this illegal and dangerous act, my Dad, who had arms of steel forged from years of football, cold-cocked the evaluator pilot right then and there.

The pilots of the classified U-2 program were some of the most highly regarded pilots in the USAF. "If I am going to be in this business, I want to be on the first team," he told my Mother. After a year of knocking on doors at Laughlin, he was accepted into the U-2 program in 1960. Now he was on the "first team." By flying the U-2, he felt completely fulfilled with his new assignment in Del Rio.

The U-2 community has always seemed like part of my family. During the 4080th SRW reunion in Del Rio in 1993, I learned the details of Dad's accident from some of the pilots who participated in the safety investigation. Although no one knew for sure, the theory was that Dad's U-2 stalled and entered a flat spin. The theory was that he attempted multiple spin recovery maneuvers as the aircraft plunged from 70,000 feet altitude. At 10,000 feet, and according to procedures at that time, he attempted to eject. However, the sink rate and centrifugal G-forces of the spin during the long fall exceeded the operational capabilities of the ejection seat. They doubted his parachute ever deployed.

Some 24 years later in 1987, I learned all about spins in the T-37B as a student pilot at Vance AFB in Oklahoma. On training sorties, students were trained to deliberately place the aircraft into a spin and apply spin recovery techniques. The words for the spin recovery, in shortened phrases still ring in my head to this day-- "Idle, neutral, aft, left spin, left needle, right rudder, BOOM! Stick abruptly full forward after one turn. After spinning stops, recover from dive." The enhanced spin training in place today is probably a result of multiple mishaps involving spins during my Dad's day in the cockpit. In current procedure manuals for all aircraft I have flown in the USAF, there is the warning—should aircraft control be lost at any altitude, an ejection above 15,000 feet offers the best chance of survival. They added 5,000 just for Dad.

I elected to stay in the Air Force and served primarily as an instructor pilot in the T-38 at Laughlin and as a B-52H instructor pilot at Barksdale. I retired from the 96th Flying Training Squadron (Reserves) in August 2006, ending 20 years of service with an assignment as a reserve T-38C instructor pilot at Laughlin, flying the same skies that Dad had enjoyed for a majority of his own flying career.

In the Memorial Student Center at my alma mater, Texas A&M University, there is a Bible verse inscribed in stone that reads, "Greater love hath no man than this, that a man lay down his life for his friends. John 15:13." That is the identical verse read at the memorial service for my Father held on December 7, 1963 in his hometown of La Grange, Georgia.

The most moving tribute to my father was read by his commander, Colonel John DesPortes. It reads as follows:

JOE GLENN HYDE, JR., Captain, United States Air Force
As an officer – Dedicated, dependable, one of the finest.
As a combat crew of the Strategic Air Command – Competent, reliable, eager.
As an individual – Gentleman, great physical and moral stature.
As a citizen - A great representative of his state, his alma mater, and his country.
As a man – Honest, confident, proud of his heritage, a pillar of strength.
As a friend – Loyal, inspirational, sincere.
As an American – Who could rank higher than Joe Glenn Hyde, Jr. who gave his life for all in the cause of freedom?

Young Americans elect to fly for the US Air Force for a variety of reasons today, but it still remains true that service and dedication to our country are foremost on the minds of many of the sharp, young men and women I instructed at Laughlin AFB over the years. In today's political climate of two concurrent "hot wars" in two different countries, the stakes are higher for them than they were for me, yet many continue to volunteer for service.

Every time a new pilot graduates from Laughlin AFB, they are fulfilling the legacy of those who blazed the path before them. The line of preserved airplanes on static display that greet visitors at the entrance of Laughlin AFB should remind all of us of those heroes. Each plane carries its own story and the story of the heroes who flew them into history.

The U-2 community has a poem that is read as a tribute to comrades who died while flying that dangerous aircraft. The poem is as follows:

They were born of the Sun,
They flew for a short while towards the Sun,
And left the sky burning in their memory.

The skies above Laughlin AFB burn in the memory of Joe Glenn Hyde, Jr. and all who have slipped through the clear, blue sky above the Southwestern Texas sagebrush while serving this country on the "first team," as aviators who were summoned to defend this wonderful land and the freedoms we cherish. I hope we never forget that.

I'm sure my Dad would have it that way, too.

USAFA cadets receive a briefing on Lockheed U-2 by Captain Joe Hyde of the 4028th SRWS in June 1962. Left to right: Cadet Gary Yates Dickinson, USAFA '64, Captain Hyde, Cadet Roger Korenberg, USAFA '63.

Photo courtesy of Gary Dickinson and LHF Museum Archives.

WARD GRAHAM
(Deceased May 8, 2004)

The following was submitted by Ward prior to his death.

TERRIFYING DAYS AFTER THE CRISIS

In the Spring of 1964, I was one of several U-2 pilots assigned to fly recon missions over Cuba from Barksdale AFB, Louisiana. Our squadron had been maintaining surveillance of Cuba since October 1962. The "authorities" had determined there was no longer a need to continue these flights. Most of the pilots and airplanes were returned to Davis Monthan AFB, Arizona for reassignment to other missions.

Don Webster, a tech rep, and I were the last pilots left at OL-19 with our commander, Lt. Col. Joe King. One evening in April, Don, the navigator and I were in Colonel King's quarters celebrating the demise of OL-19. We were in the midst of heavily imbibing what Rush Limbaugh calls "adult beverages" when Colonel King's phone rang. It seemed to us that when Colonel King answered, he snapped to attention. What we heard on his side of the conversation were statements like, "Two pilots and airplanes, sir. How soon to launch? Well, sir, both pilots have been drinking, so it would be about 11:00 tomorrow, 12 hours from bottle to throttle, you know, sir. What's that? Waive the regulation? Yes sir, then we can be there by 20 degrees sun angle tomorrow."

Joe flipped a coin and Webster lost the toss. He went to bed to sleep for a few hours. The navigator and I received and planned a route for him to fly over Cuba. Later, we rolled Webster out of bed, got him some breakfast and plenty of hot coffee. The sun peeked over

341

the horizon, and a half-inebriated Don Webster staggered off into the murky dawn. He probably wondered why he was flying to Cuba when the mission had supposedly been shut down.

Don was airborne and making his check-in calls. We listened to the radio and learned that Fidel Castro, Cuba's dictator, had made a bold statement that he would shoot down the next U-2 that violated his airspace. We were all shocked. We knew that with his 24 SA-2 surface-to-air missile sites he could easily bring down a U-2. In 1962 his SAMs had killed one of our squadron mates, Major Rudolph Anderson. We were on pins and needles until Don called his "coast out" message. He had not been fired upon.

While Don was airborne, a classified message came into OL-19 Operations laying on a mission for the next day. Tomorrow would be my turn. The next morning, I made my way south over Sarasota VOR to Key West. I was very apprehensive. I had flown a few missions over Cuba in the past, but it was with the understanding that Castro's dogs were on a short leash and would not track or fire upon us. That day the 90 miles from Key West VOR to the coast of Cuba seemed like an eternity. The island shape began to loom on the horizon. To this pilot it had the appearance of Darth Vader.

Castro continued to echo his threat and Don and I alternated days flying over Cuba. We each flew two or three missions a week for two weeks. Why didn't Castro fire on us? Some months later word reached us that then-President Johnson had called Castro's bluff with something like this: "You may have my U-2, but it will cost you your island!" With the stakes that high, Castro backed down. No aide in the White House elected to pass that message to the two pilots who assumed they were facing death on every mission.

It was during these two weeks that God got my attention and I began asking questions of myself like, "Is there a God? Is He knowable? What would happen to me if I died?" I even tried to get into the Barksdale Chapel one night to find answers to these perplexing questions, thinking that if I "showed up," God, if He existed, would reveal His program to me.

About two months later I was in Panama on another U-2 detachment and God answered my questions through another U-2 pilot, Major Clair McCombs. Backed with biblical references, McCombs showed me how I could know God personally through Jesus Christ, have my sins forgiven and be given the guarantee of eternal life. I would gladly fly those Cuban missions for such an outcome!

CHARLES KERN
San Antonio, Texas

Wife: Nancy

DRAGON LADY COMES OF AGE

From the time that the U-2 entered service with the USAF, it was, with some few notable exceptions, assigned mostly routine missions including air sampling and domestic photography. The month of October 1962 saw an abrupt change to missions and brought the Dragon Lady to the attention of the world.

Steve Heyser, Rudolph Anderson and Jerry McIlmoyle had slipped out of sight for several days. Steve and Rudy flew the first missions over Cuba in "borrowed" CIA U-2s. The "take" (photography) from these early October flights wrote their names in the history books. The US had confirmation of Soviet Medium Range Ballistic Missiles (MRBM) in Cuba.

I first got involved in this action October 16, 1962. Steve and Rudy were already on location and the rest of us pilots were getting involved. We were still at Laughlin AFB when the mission FRAGORD, slang for supplemental Operations Order, arrived and the mission planning area was under heavy security. U-2 launch times were set for 4:00 AM to 5:00 AM in order to reach the photographic targets over Cuba at the best angle of the sun for film exposure. Five aircraft were to be flown. I was on Mobile Control. Rain was falling heavily while I preflighted each aircraft during pilot hookup and checkout. I don't recall which pilot I launched. The Houdah, an umbrella like apparatus used to shield the pilot from sun and rain, could not begin to keep out all that pouring rain. A series of Texas-sized thunderstorms were passing over the Laughlin area so we were all thoroughly soaked. That must have been an omen of the events that were to come.

After the pilot came on board, I checked on his oxygen and pressure suit connections and meticulously ran the aircraft checklist using our challenge-response method. I completed all the tasks so we could close the canopy and get the pilot out of the rain. The canopy lid was lowered and after checking intakes clear, I gave the pilot the start signal, index finger pointing up and rotating. We operated in complete radio silence. With power unit and air starter running, the pilot signaled inward with thumb to ground crew. Whoosh! The air blasted into the turbine starter and in seconds, the low whine of the engine was heard in its starting stages.

Pounding rain, such as I had never seen, lashed us unrelentingly. I put the headlights of the Mobile vehicle directly on the aircraft to aid the ground crew in pulling the pins and chocks. I signaled thumbs up to the pilot, clearing him to taxi. The pilot taxied the few feet to the runway and the maintenance crew pulled the pogos to ensure none hung up on takeoff.

I sat in my chase vehicle. The dark, helmeted shape in the cockpit turned in my direction. My vehicle was off his right wing with the dome light on. The wind and rain continued their driving intensity.

Ten seconds to brake release and the engine speed increased. In seven more seconds, the pilot rammed the throttle forward and disappeared instantly in a cloud of spray, steam, vapor and darkness. I knew he had made it okay when the engine sound, heavily muffled by the continuing downpour, faded evenly and quickly.

I returned to PSD (Physiological Support Division), the team who shoehorned the pilots into the pressure suits. Other launch officers, like me, were deep in thought and envied those who had been selected to fly the first missions. None of us had any idea of the unique significance of what was developing in the Caribbean or that we, too, would be packing within hours to join the team at OL-X, the classified designation for McCoy AFB, Florida.

The order came that night and we loaded ground crews, operations officers, mission planning navigators, the Mobile Control station wagon and all the remaining pilots on the giant C-124 Globemaster and launched for McCoy. The day finally arrived for this unique aircraft to show what it, and those flying and supporting the aircraft, could do for the Air Force and for our country. After years of training and uninteresting missions, the Shady Lady, a term of endearment for the bird, was on her way to the adventures for which she had been designed. She would have a permanent place in aviation and diplomatic history. What a thrilling time to be part of Shady Lady's metamorphosis.

After arrival at McCoy AFB (OL-X), the team was immediately involved in mission planning and flying. There were certainly enough missions to go around with 11 pilots and 10 aircraft. I don't remember specifically what we did; however, I'm almost certain whatever we did probably included "hoisting a few" at the over-crowded Officers' Club. Rudy Anderson was a very serious guy and didn't participate in much of the partying like many of the rest of us. He was scheduled as the standby pilot and as Mobile Control Officer the next day. Two other pilots and I were scheduled to fly photographic collection missions over Cuba. Up to this point, there had not been much apprehension over flying these missions. That attitude changed swiftly and violently.

Early in the morning of October 27, 1962, four of us followed the normal preflight routine: briefing, physical exam, breakfast of steak and eggs. We suited up with the help of the PSD techs. While pre-breathing 100 percent oxygen for one hour prior to takeoff, we studied the target folder, and one more time rechecked the "Green Card." The Green Card displayed the navigation log on the front with oxygen consumption predictions and fuel consumption log on the reverse side.

Thirty minutes before takeoff, the PSD team shoe-horned us into the pressure suits. The outer garment protected the pressure suit laces from catching on the various switches, knobs and handles in the cockpit. I then strapped on my shoulder holster with my long-time companion, the .357 Magnum. For years I had carried this same gun on missions.

I took a deep breath and held it so no ambient air could enter my lungs. I changed the walk-around oxygen bottle for a full one. The air-conditioned van was carrying the pilots, headed for the waiting and already pre-flighted U-2.

We were met at the aircraft ladder by a calm, softly smiling Rudy Anderson. I climbed up the ladder and into the "office", as the cockpit was known. The PSD guys were doing their thing, snapping and connecting everything. PSD switched me to the aircraft oxygen system. I held my breath while they performed the QD (quick disconnect) and safety clipped it. I checked with a firm pull on the connection to ensure it was latched. The lap belt and shoulder harness fastened over the pressure suit and oxygen hoses. We certainly didn't want those hoses in the way during seat separation and ejection. PSD performed a "press to test" and a surge of oxygen inflated all the pressure suit capstans and breathing bladders. Suddenly it was very crowded in that small cockpit. The final check of the face seal determined it was properly seated and securely fastened. Finally, a pat on the helmet indicated "all okay" by another great technician of PSD and then he turned it over to Rudy. "Click", Rudy connects his headset and mike and switched us to "hot mike" so we could talk while running the checklist. The sharply amplified sounds of my breathing were heard in the headset. Rudy was Chief of U-2 Flight Standardization and since I was an FNG (fairly new guy), I didn't joke around. Besides, I had to concentrate on the immediate task of getting ready for engine start and launch. We went through the entire checklist, and then went through the last chance recheck of crucial oxygen system and every connection. Rudy untied the string on the TOP SECRET folder and laid out in the proper places the maps, green card, pencils, dividers and plotter. One final scan of the cockpit and Rudy gave another pat on the helmet and "click." With the hot mike off, he descended the ladder and I waited for clearance to start. I waited and waited and waited.

After an interminably long period, I finally got the signal. The signal was not to start but to get out of the cockpit and stay on oxygen. Somebody "up the line" was trying to decide whether we went or not. PSD came back up the ladder with a walk-around bottle and unhooked me from the aircraft system. I got out of the cockpit and climbed down the ladder to the ramp. After a while, I was told that Washington scrubbed the mission. We were informed to leave one airplane and one pilot ready to go if clearance was received.

In a situation like that our unwritten rule was that the Mobile Control Officer was always the spare pilot and would normally be the next to fly. When the mission was scrubbed, I would not fly if there was a reschedule. With that mission cancelled, Rudy automatically became the next pilot. Some of us mildly protested, but Rudy prevailed. He reminded us of the unwritten rule and jokingly, that he was also the senior guy.

After changing out of the pressure suit and back into a normal flying suit, I went back to the visiting family quarters where we were housed. It was only a short while when Rudy and the new Mobile Control Officer, Ed Emerling, got the call to return to the flight line for what was to be Rudy's final mission.

For lack of something better to do, a few of us headed for the on-base golf course. My golf game was lousy and I wasn't enjoying it at all. But it did beat sitting around waiting for tomorrow. When I arrived back at the house a couple hours later, I learned that Rudy was missing. The Mobile Officer went back to his position at the flight line just in case Rudy might return. Perhaps, we thought, the aircraft had radio failure or some other problem. The Mobile Officer waited until the time that fuel would have been exhausted, then gave up and came back to the house. It was an evening of somber, if not sober, watching TV news.

We didn't fly for a couple of days and we in the detachment didn't have any idea what was going on regarding our participation in the momentous events unfolding on daylong TV news. We got word the Commander in Chief, Strategic Air Command, General Thomas Powers, was flying into McCoy to talk with us pilots. Wow! Must be something really big for "The Man" to come down.

We speculated that Washington would order surgical air strikes to at least take out the SAM site that bagged Rudy and maybe activate protective ECM (Electronic Countermeasures) to jam the other sites so they couldn't pick us up on their radars. Wrong on both counts. We would begin overflights again but without ECM. Our leaders were not about to compromise the ECM equipment that would have to protect our strategic strike force bombers in case we went to nuclear war. An event like that appeared more likely with each passing moment.

We flew exposed and vulnerable as hell. The next day we went in force, five aircraft flying parallel courses about 20 miles apart, staggered with five-minute separation. Our flight plan carried us directly up the island from the east tip to the west, bending 15 to 20 degrees to follow the curvature of the island. This time we did take off and launch in radio silence. I was third in the order and therefore, in the middle flight track. Things went well, and to my left Guantanamo slipped quietly by. The weather was great and I felt good, regardless of my uncertainties about the intentions of the enemy below. We felt sure President Kennedy had sent word to Fidel to lay off the U-2s, but we were not at all confident that the directive had taken place.

Suddenly, over the radio in clear text came an alarmed voice: "Green Arrow! Green Arrow! Green Arrow! I repeat. Green Arrow! Green Arrow!" I said out loud to myself, "Damn! That sonofabitch is after another one of us." That was the recall signal from the RC-121 monitoring our flight. I racked the airplane into a hard left turn, heading for the nearest shoreline. The airplane shuddered and I eased up a bit, and turned 90 degrees. For a few seconds I turned to the right and then back to the left toward open water. Five or six very long minutes went by and I was out of range of the SAMs. Turning off the cameras, I flew east until clear of Cuba and headed for McCoy.

The mission was terminated for that day by the recall. From that point on, the missions ceased being a really fun thing to do. Although this particular mission ended in a recall, there were many more that went textbook.

Our equipment improved, and we became more knowledgeable about the intentions of the enemy. The shrieking of warning systems and the red signal, known as Oscar Sierra, alerted the pilot that the SAM was in the guidance mode. Following its launch it was then locked on to the aircraft. We referred to the OS signal as the "Oh, Sh**" light on the right canopy rail. If that signal went on, we were in deep you know what. Now, there's black humor at its best! That signal was definitely not something anyone wanted to hear at 70,000 feet.

The sweat brought about by trepidation of this nature is uniquely different from normal sweat caused by exertion or uncomfortable heat. Trepidation sweat has a singular pungent quality of its own, a particular scent that is unmistakable. It has been many years since my last combat mission over North Vietnam, but the leather pressure suit gloves I wore over Cuba and Vietnam have retained that distinctive scent to this day. Yes, I still have those gloves…somewhere.

GERALD E. (JERRY) MCILMOYLE
Venice, Florida

MY PARTICIPATION IN THE CUBAN MISSILE CRISIS

The Cuban Missile Crisis began for Rudy Anderson, Steve Heyser, Buddy Brown and me on October 11, 1962. Our Wing Commander, Colonel John DesPortes, came to each of our homes at Laughlin AFB. When he made a house call, we knew something was going on and it was extremely urgent. The Colonel told us to pack our bags. We were headed to Edwards AFB, California. The plan was for us to take over the CIA's three U-2s.

Major General K. K. Compton, Strategic Air Command Director of Operations, was on the aircraft that transported us to Edwards. Enroute to Edwards he informed us that President Kennedy had directed the CIA U-2s be turned over to the Air Force. The USAF was to conduct photographic reconnaissance over Cuba. General Compton also told us that the President was still unhappy with the CIA's failure of the Bay of Pigs Operation the year before and he wanted the military to take over the Cuban mission.

CIA pilots instructed us in the differences between the Air Force and CIA U-2s. The next day CIA pilots Barry Baker and James Barnes conducted the ground school at Edwards AFB North Base. Both Barnes and Baker had been in my squadron at Great Falls, Montana before joining the CIA. They were obviously unhappy about being directed to give up their planes to us.

One major difference of the CIA U-2 and the AF version was the J-75 engine which enabled the CIA pilots to fly about 2,000 feet higher than the AF with their J-57 engine. Their birds also had a strobe display about the size of tennis ball on top of the instrument panel. The strobe display indicated direction and distance of any Cuban radar in operation. Lethal range of the SA-2 surface to air missile was 25 miles from the launch site.

The CIA planes also had an aural signal in the headset that would sound a warning when a surface to air missile went into its final radio guidance mode. It was a fluttery sound, called a fan song after the metallic sound of a paper hand fan used by women in the non-airconditioned church of my youth. The sound was soft but menacing. If the signal was heard, the pilot was to initiate a 30-degree bank turn and do an "S" maneuver back to the flight path and by then out of range of the missile launch site. The SA-2 could not turn with the U-2 at altitudes of 70,000 to 75,000 feet, the altitude we maintained enroute to Cuba. To fly at that altitude, we flew short fuel and film loads. Each pound of fuel equals one foot in altitude. If we carried 300 or fewer gallons of fuel we could increase altitude by 2,000 feet. Another nice feature of the CIA U-2s was the thrust diffuser to spread and shield the jet engine exhaust from infrared homing sensors and prevent a heat-seeking device to guide a missile into the aircraft.

On October 14, Steve Heyser took off from Edwards and flew the first overflight of Cuba. He landed at McCoy AFB, Florida. Steve's film was immediately flown to Washington, DC for processing. President Kennedy was briefed on the photographic evidence of Soviet Medium Range Nuclear missiles installed in Cuba. The remaining two CIA U-2s were ferried to McCoy by the CIA pilots. Rudy deployed to McCoy and Buddy and I▸returned to Laughlin from where we flew our first overflights of Cuba. Buddy and I recovered at McCoy. By October 17, 1962, we had 11 U-2 pilots and 10 U-2 aircraft at McCoy. During those first days, we flew about five overflights of Cuba each day.

On October 25, the Soviets made their first attempt to shoot down my U-2 with two SA-2 missiles launched near Banes, Cuba. I received no signal from any of the warning systems. I wasn't even aware that I had been fired at until I saw the missile contrails in my rear view mirror. It was a gorgeous clear day with dark blue sky above and a blue-green sea below—those contrails were quite a contrast. I was in my turn north. I looked back over my left wing, and I saw the missile condensation trails went all the way back to the ground pointing to the Banes SA-2 site. I continued my turn to set up the cameras to record the contrails and burst clouds from the missile. I turned back to the right so the left wing was raised and the cameras began to record. For the next couple minutes, I continued taking pictures of the whole scene.

Two days later, our Operations Officer, Tony Martinez, held a pilots' meeting to discuss the SAM and MIG-21 threats and our tactics to evade them. It was real to us alright. We all knew the Soviet threat we faced and we realized we probably would not receive any warning of intercept attempts. Tony also stated the need to have a pilot standing by each day in case we were directed to fly more overflights than were scheduled. The increase in overflights had occurred several times previously. Rudy volunteered for the standby alert pilot duty for the next day. From then on we were directed to rotate the duty through our cadre.

We had three overflights scheduled for October 27 with Rudy as standby alert pilot. The three flights had taken off earlier in order to be over the target with the sun at the best angle for good photography. It was a bright clear day and the sky was a beautiful dark blue. Steve Heyser and I had not been scheduled to fly so we went out to play golf. Golf was our recreation as we could not fly for two days before another flight.

354

At about 11:00 AM, Steve and I heard the unique sound of a U-2 taking off. We turned to see the aircraft climbing out at a steep angle. The plane was silhouetted against the blue sky, and we watched until it was out of sight. We both knew that it was Rudy going on a special mission and we silently prayed he would be safe.

Rudy's mission covered the area near Banes, Cuba, a known location of the almost finished Medium Range Ballistic Missile (MRBM) launch complex with a defending SAM site. The US radar site at Guantanamo Bay, Cuba reported they lost their track of Rudy at a time and location when he should have been on his photographic run over the target.

We never knew exactly what happened but I believe that Rudy had no system warning of the intercept. He was known to fly with intense concentration and dedication; I believe he was totally focused on flying the most stable platform in order to gather the best possible photographic intelligence.

On that date, October 27, 1962, after Rudy's shootdown, the Soviets capitulated and agreed to remove their nuclear tipped MRBMs from Cuba and cease construction of their associated launch sites. The crisis was over.

PERSPECTIVE OF COLONEL ANTHONY MARTINEZ

On the evening of October 13, 1962, Major General K. K. Compton and Brigadier General Robert Smith, SAC Deputy Chief of Staff Intelligence, arrived at Laughlin AFB in General Powers' own VC-97. The purpose of their arrival was to transport Colonel DesPortes and those of us on the recovery team (Operations, Maintenance and Physiological Support) for Steve's arrival the next day at McCoy. Upon arrival at McCoy, we took over the CIA's operation of all pilot facilities except the Communications

355

Room. It was obvious that we were not welcome there, but we were there to do our job and we managed to do that.

We learned later that Mr. Cunningham, the CIA Operations Supervisor, had been sending communications to his boss. His messages were full of negative information indicating the Air Force people were not doing the job properly. He reported that we were forgetting to remove the covers from the camera windows, our pilots were sweaty and showed fear as they were being suited up. All allegations were completely false. It was definitely a sporty few days there.

ALASKA, NORTH POLE AND VIETNAM FLIGHTS

Flight might not be all plain sailing,
but the fun of it is worth the price.

Amelia Earhart

BUDDY L. BROWN
Knoxville, Tennessee

MY BUSIEST U-2 MISSION

I say this was my busiest mission, but it would be more correct to say this was "one" of the busiest missions. There were a couple of northern missions out of Eielson AFB, Alaska using celestial grid navigation that also got my attention. The worst thing about flying north and using grid navigation was the need to out guess the gyro precession rate and in which direction. Would they precess in the direction forecasted for the next rating period? Also, remember, once over the extreme northern latitudes, every direction is south. The gyro should indicate the correct south longitude heading for the next flight route segment, not one headed south. This happened to Chuck Maultsby, but that is another story.

Jim Qualls would also remember our 100-plus days on Okinawa where we flew only System IV night missions into the northern reaches of the Sea of Japan. Landing the next morning, we would have red, blood-shot eyes. For any non-technical folks reading this, in the mid-1950s, the U-2s had no high tech navigation systems. Our primary navigation tool was simply the sextant.

Now a little explanation for those same non-technical folks, the System IV was a signals intelligence electronic detection system or SIGINT. It consisted of a large number of antennas to cover frequencies the Soviet Union used for command and control, missile tracking, aircraft control, radar frequencies, etc. Information collected was stored onboard the U-2 and later analyzed to determine how far the Soviets had advanced their electronic technology.

Okay, back to my original story. I forget the exact date Jerry McIlmoyle and I flew these particular missions, but I vividly remember it was winter. The purpose of the mission was to collect SIGINT into the Bering Sea in order to map the Soviet radar order of battle. The equipment bay of the U-2 was loaded with a specially designed System IV-A SIGINT package that expanded the frequency spectrum. I think the project code name was "Venice Lake II." I vividly remember the mission planning for it was rather complicated. It got complicated because it was a coordinated mission with a C-121 radar aircraft to monitor us and ensure that we did not deviate outside a very narrow corridor. The C-121 was originally a Lockheed Constellation converted to a Navy aircraft with Airborne Early Warning (AEW) capability. During our pre-mission briefings, several local SAC permanent staff personnel sat in and made useless suggestions that had nothing to do with these missions.

However, the C-121 would be monitoring our collection leg once we were in the target area in the Bering Sea off the Kamchatka Peninsula. In the briefing, it was determined that the C-121 would send coded messages consisting of a bunch of numbers. We had to write down the numbers and evaluate whether we were north or south of our track, left or right of course and how far in either direction. So at each celestial plot, in addition to taking three star fixes and plotting the position based on celestial information, we now had to write a bunch of numbers from the sextant and evaluate whether to throw out the celestial information and use the C-121 plot or vice versa. As if that wasn't enough to do, we had to copy all of the Fox Trot "do not answer" high frequency transmissions. A Fox Trot message was a coded SAC Headquarters communication to control a particular mission using a series of numbers transmitted at high frequency. Using a translation device in the cockpit, the numbers were converted into a coherent message. The Fox Trot message would give instructions to continue the mission, to abort the mission and land at a designated recovery base, to be alert for Soviet fighters being scrambled, etc. Response to Fox Trot message commands did not require an answer, just compliance. It also kept electronic transmissions to a minimum to avoid giving away the aircraft's position. The C-121 monitored our position via radar tracking to maintain the designated course, thus the comparison between our celestial and the C-121 plot.

I remember Jerry McIlmoyle and I sat in the briefing room and listened to the dialog between the C-121 jocks and the permanent SAC staff; we were shaking our heads. At one point, one of the SAC guys said, "I don't know how you're going to do all this stuff." Those were my thoughts exactly.

Well, the briefing was finally over and I was scheduled to fly the first mission; I think Jerry flew in the C-121 to monitor my mission as it progressed. Looking at my map boards, I had little pieces of paper stuck all over my route with the numbers the C-121 may or may not transmit while I was in the sensitive area.

My takeoff time was about 10:00 PM in the dead of winter in Alaska, so it was an all night mission. The U-2 had a specially designed System IV installed. Marshall Hughes was a civilian electronic whiz employed by Ramo Wooldridge, the company that built the System IV. Hughes had designed an array of new antennas to collect some special intelligence from the Kamchatka Peninsula. Kamchatka, located west of Alaska bordering the Bering Sea on the east and the Sea of Okhotsk on the west, was the location of most all of the Soviet ICBM experimental test facilities and several fighter bases. To operate the System IV wasn't too difficult; when flying north, turn the antenna switch to the left. When flying south, turn the switch to the right. Heck, even I can remember that one.

From the briefing, we headed for the BOQ to begin our crew rest period. The next evening after the pre-mission briefing which included a weather update and C-121 procedures, call signs, etc., I was fitted into my pressure suit and transported out to the bird. It had just been pulled out of the hangar and was ready for my arrival. The winter temperatures in Alaska remained at about minus 30 degrees to minus 50 degrees so the U-2 was kept inside the hangar until just before the pilot arrived. Once in the cockpit, I was hooked up, completed the cockpit check, replied to the challenge response, started engines and taxied out to the active runway. I received the "cleared for takeoff" signal, advanced the throttle and was on my way.

The mission was to fly from Eielson down the Aleutian chain to Shemya, then make a right turn in the northern direction into the Bering Sea and on into the corridor-collection area. The C-121 had taken off from Eielson hours before me in order to be in position to monitor my progress. I received one "Fox Trot" message from the C-121 that they were in position. The navigator/mission planner pre-computed all my fixes to be three-star fixes. It made for extra work but I was using the Rudd Star Finder (Computer RADAR AID, Type R-1) to plot my fixes so it cut down on time to plot and evaluate my position. (By the way, I still have that plotter.) We were told that "higher authority" directed us to stay within the corridor.

For the next three plus hours, I was constantly writing down the C-121 transmitted numbers; evaluating their position information, taking three-star fixes, and evaluating one or the other for my position. (Remember, this was in the dark of night and I was in a constrictive pressure suit.) Fortunately, the altitude winds were as forecasted and I had a stable platform for my celestial. As far as I knew, I copied all the Fox Trot messages designated for me. When the mission was completed, I returned to Shemya and back to Eielson AFB. When I started my descent for landing at Eielson, the weather was near minimums with heavy ice fog. I wasn't too concerned about flying a final approach at 80 knots, I couldn't get into too much trouble. I was cleared to start my approach and landing when GCA reported, "The field is now below minimums. Do you want to continue with your approach or proceed to your alternate?" I responded, "Continue approach." I told the GCA final, "It's just you and me now anyway." I was only going 80 knots, and by the time I got to the runway, it might be above minimums. I continued my approach and it seemed to take forever. I was really bushed, but I drank my last pint of orange juice just prior to my penetration so I could remain alert before I started my descent. Finally, the centerline strobes started filling my windscreen; the field was still zero-zero. As the strobes continued, GCA called out, "You're passing over the end of the runway." I then put my head back against the headrest using my peripheral vision to keep the runway lights even on my left and right sides of the canopy. I continued my descent until I touched down on the runway. After the first skip, I held the aircraft off until it settled into the runway. I couldn't see much past the nose of my bird, but the mobile folks walked in front of me with their wands guiding me to the taxiway and back to the hangar.

When the next mission was flown, Jerry was primary pilot and I flew in the C-121 as observer. I remember the C-121 was an interesting flight, but it lasted about 10-12 hours. I sat in the back and watched the radar screen as Jerry's mission progressed; I could relate to what he was going through and how he would return to Eielson with blood-shot eyes. I believe the intelligence community got what they were looking for with these missions, but I don't think the C-121 monitoring was really necessary.

Buddy Brown suited up.

BILL E. BYE
Prescott, Arizona

Wife: Janet

I was assigned to the 4080th SRW in October 1961. My first recollection was standing in the Navigation Planning Room asking Bob Yates, "Where do we go from here?" I was thinking about career progression. Bob replied, "You have arrived." Apparently I was the first officer assigned through normal channels. I recalled frequenting the flight line snack shop with Ed Schug; we both enjoyed miniature cigars.

My first TDY was to Eielson AFB, Alaska with John Wall and Buddy Brown. They were part owners of an older Chevrolet they named "Simone." They had purchased the vehicle for local transportation there and had invested many hours of tender loving care restoring it. I wonder whatever became of Simone? One of those memorable events at Eielson was planning Don Webster's flight to the North Pole.

While on TDY at Bien Hoa, South Vietnam, Meteorologist Freddie Haman forwarded the high altitude wind information to me on scraps of paper. My thoughts were, "Here we are using low tech communications for this high tech operation."

Those were some of my best days in the Air Force; I just didn't realize it at the time.

EDWARD B. DIXON
Vero Beach, Florida

MY TICKSI RUN

In 1960, pilots Dick Leavitt, Jim Bedford, John McElveen and I with our navigator Charlie Brown, were chosen for a special mission. Our U-2s were modified with a 15 nautical mile notch under the viewfinder handle. We each flew a practice mission along the Gulf Coast of Texas maintaining 15 nautical miles off the coast with the help of the viewfinder notch.

In February we TDY'd to Operating Location 5 at Eielson AFB near Fairbanks, Alaska. Joe Jackson was our Detachment Commander. There were also 30 very important support crew members who took part in the mission. The mission was to fly 15 nautical miles off the coast of USSR to Petropavlovsk on the south to Tiksi Air Base on the North Coast.

The missions were divided into about eight segments. Each end mission was 3,650 nautical miles which was a stretch for sure. The U-2 Handbook said it could fly 4,000 nautical miles to air flameout. In the Arctic, the temperature at U-2 altitude is about 20 degrees warmer than over the US. The U-2 would level off about 2,000 feet lower and use more fuel. After each of us had flown a mission, we were promoted to Spot Major. We were in "high cotton" because Dick Leavitt was already a Spot Major.

In the Arctic, the ocean was frozen and covered with snow. We observed the ocean had a light gray tinge probably due to the salt content of the water. The terrain had only grass, no trees. Three rivers flowed north out of the USSR and they were fresh water, no gray tinge. Just where was the coast?

Dick Leavitt was chosen to fly the Tiksi mission. Unfortunately, he became disoriented and over flew Soviet territory; luckily he was not spotted by the Soviets. We ceased flying special missions off the coast of the USSR while the fellows in the corner office thought about it. We didn't seem to have cause for an international incident. Meanwhile, we flew nuclear debris collection missions over the Pacific Ocean looking for a reported Soviet nuclear bomb detonation residue at high altitudes. Then word came down that we were going to resume flying special missions and now it was my turn to try for Tiksi.

I knew #953 to be a great, reliable bird. It was well trimmed, would fly straight and had a fine autopilot and Mach sensor. I asked our commander, Joe Jackson, if I could use it and he readily agreed.

The weather was satisfactory so the mission was on. I took off at 0800 and coasted over Wainwright Beacon at 62,000 feet altitude. The weather was clear with unlimited visibility. My celestial lines of position were at an angle to my flight path. So, I had neither a speed line nor flight line information.

I recognized a landmark about an hour from Wainwright near Fairbanks, Alaska. The frozen ocean was criss-crossed with many vehicle trails. My aircraft shadow was visible in a circle halo of ice crystals below me to the right. I patted old #953 on the dash and told her that she was doing a great job.

On my fourth celestial shot I looked up and saw land. I was flying faster than planned; therefore, correcting to the left made me coast in too soon. I turned to the right, turned on my camera and headed for the 28-nautical mile channel between the Soviet mainland and the New Siberian Islands. I could see the Tiksi Bay ahead. The

366

camera gently rocked the aircraft as it went through its repositioning cycle.

I flew west past the bay at Tiksi, turned 90 degrees left so it was on my right. I passed Tiksi Airfield, waited for two more cycles of the camera. With the autopilot off, I turned 180 degrees to the left, as steeply as I dared to get out of there. I exited through the channel between the islands and headed for home.

As I entered the Alaskan ADIZ (Air Defense Identification Zone), I called Wainwright and gave them my estimated time of arrival. I was ahead of schedule by about 20 minutes. They gave me a challenge and asked me to fly the maneuver code. The Maneuver Code is in a numbered sealed envelope that each pilot picks up at Operations when the flight plan is filed. I reported that I was light on fuel and asked to read them the code. They concurred. Flying the code would have used up an additional 5 minutes of fuel. Since I had been airborne for seven hours, I'm glad they felt sympathetic.

As I neared Eielson, I began to let down and requested an approach time. Control gave me a 20-minute approach time delay. The low fuel level light came on and I had 40 gallons remaining. I put old #953 in gust control. It reduced wing loading by raising the flaps a few degrees and was a safeguard in turbulent air. I cancelled my Instrument Flight Rules clearance and spiraled down over the runway under visual and landed. On the runway as the crew installed the pogos, I had 22 gallons remaining of the 1,335 I had started with. Now that is what I call cutting it close! Old #953 got another pat on the dash.

ROGER HERMAN
Fort Worth, Texas

TROUBLE OVER THE ARTIC

One of the 4080th SRW's major U-2 projects of the early days was completed by 1960. Project Crow Flight, a High Altitude Sampling Program (HASP) for the Armed Forces Special Weapons Project (AFSWP), had done its job of providing the Agency with a background of radiation levels at altitudes from 40,000 feet to the U-2's maximum altitude. The two-year project of long north-south flights from Plattsburg AFB, New York, Ramey AFB, Puerto Rico and Ezeisa International Airport, Argentina had shown a decline in radiation during that period. Apparently, it was due to the voluntary test ban then in effect.

Our sampling program was reduced to two six-week projects each year from three locations. This reduced our TDYs considerably and the flights were shorter. One of the locations was Eielson AFB, just outside Fairbanks, Alaska. I was scheduled for the Fall deployment in 1961. It was projected to last from September to November, not a bad time to be in Alaska.

As often happens in the military, we listen for words like "Standby for change!" I returned home from a shopping trip with my wife on Saturday of Labor Day weekend at Laughlin AFB. I received a call from the Command Post directing me to "Pack up, we're moving out." The Russians had broken the Test Ban Agreement. Three of the pilots were flown to Palmdale Airport in California to pick up newly modified U-2s to fly to Eielson AFB. Our easy six-weeks deployment was now an indefinite deployment. The Russians were testing on

368

Novaya Zemlya, an island in the Arctic Ocean just north of Siberia. AFSWP was going to have us sampling all over the area--north, west, south of Alaska and even long flights straight across Canada.

During this testing period, the Russians announced they would detonate a 100-megaton device. They did detonate a large device. It was estimated to be only in the 50-megaton range, but still a large explosion. The detonation occurred late at night, Alaska Time. I went to the weather station for a briefing the next morning, and the meteorologists indicated they had observed a slight rise in atmospheric pressure. It spread across the Arctic and had resulted in a rise in pressure at Eielson.

At the end of October, with days becoming shorter and colder, AFSWP found a favorite route that we flew almost daily. We proceeded northeast from Eielson to a point on the northwest Canadian coast, and then almost due north to the north coast of Banks Island. We descended to 40,000 feet and flew northeast to Ellesmere Island, a point approximately 250 miles north of Thule, Greenland. We reversed course and returned to Banks Island, still at 40,000 feet. For our return to Eielson, we climbed back to normal cruise altitude. I don't know why the "higher ups" picked islands to overfly since we were flying in pitch dark and couldn't see them anyway. This route went directly over the magnetic North Pole and, required Grid Navigation. We didn't follow the SAC procedure used by the bomber crews. We neared the magnetic pole and the aircraft went into a slight bank to hold heading due to rapid changes in variation. Rather than upset the gyro, we went to free run on the slaved gyrocompass and used that heading as our reference. It was surprising how little precession we experienced when we didn't mess with the gyro. The sun was now setting around 3:30 PM. Our takeoffs were planned around 7:00 AM so we could land in daylight and tail in on the ice-covered runways and taxiways. We relied on the sextant for navigation, so at the start we hoped for a good shot of a well-known body. The sun would make a very brief appearance in the southeast as we flew to the northeast. The navigators computed a celestial shot for us. Most notably, the sun was normally around a minus six degrees elevation for a few moments before disappearing again. .

On my day of fun, I proceeded to the descent point. I leveled at 40,000 feet and encountered one of the J-57 engine's quirks. It was not unusual to encounter those quirks sometimes on maintenance test flights. We were required to level off for a short period at 40,000 feet to run a few checks, and continue the climb to max altitude. We added power for the continued climb as the engine would chug or compressor stall. It might take several tries to get it through that range. Since we were going to max power, once we got it through that range, we could continue flying with no further problems. In my experience flying over the Arctic, I wasn't going to max power. I needed an intermediate power setting for cruise at 40,000 feet. I could ease it through the stall range but the power at that point was too high for my cruise at 40,000 feet. Four or five times I tried to ease it back to my cruise power setting, and each time it would revert to chugging. I couldn't complete the assigned mission at a non-chug power setting, in pitch dark and with surface temperatures of minus 55 degrees. I didn't feel this was the time or place to fool with a balky engine.

The mission was aborted. I reversed course and started a climb back to normal cruise altitude. Although I couldn't complete the assigned mission, everything was now pretty well under control. I no longer had celestial for grid navigation; I merely had to fly a reverse course on my free-run gyro. Within 20 to 30 minutes, I should pick up a radio beacon on the north coast of Canada.

Now the fun started! Once established in the climb and back on course, I made a call to the SAC Command Post at Eielson asking them to advise our detachment of my situation. Everything was under control; I gave a rough estimated time of my arrival back at Eielson. If I had known what was about to happen, I would have claimed radio reception problems.

The 15th Air Force Command Post at March AFB, Riverside, California heard my call to Eielson. Since Eielson is under their command, 15th AF wanted to get into the act. Bombers must have a two- or three-page emergency checklist to report any unusual situation. The Command Post probably has to log all this information just as a CYA (Cover Your Ass) procedure. So 15th Air Force Command Post started asking me questions. For example: How many crewmembers were aboard and where were they located; how much fuel and where was it located; etc, etc? When 15th finished, the Command Post at Laughlin AFB back in Texas started calling. The 15th AF Command Post then told Laughlin to get off the radio because they (15th AF) had an emergency in progress. Laughlin, being part of 2nd AF and not familiar to 15th AF controllers, advised 15th AF that the aircraft in question belonged to 2nd AF and by golly, they would talk to it. Sometimes, people on the ground can be a bigger problem than the airborne problem.

I reported another successful conclusion to a fun day in the U-2. We finally packed up and went home prior to Thanksgiving. The Russians took a break for the Winter. The next year, as the Russians resumed testing, AFSWP decided to fly directly to the North Pole; there was nothing to navigate by on the surface. But that another year and another crew.

371

U-2 ENTRY INTO VIETNAM

The 4080th SRW became involved in Vietnam operations quite suddenly in February 1964. Much like our entry in the Cuban Missile Crisis, the "Powers That Be" decided it was time for the military to become involved in the reconnaissance of Southeast Asia (SEA). You could say that we stole this mission from the Agency (CIA) just as we had done with the Cuban operations a year and a half earlier.

This operation started for me as my involvement in the Cuban operation had begun in 1962 from Laughlin AFB. Now we were comfortably situated at Davis Monthan AFB, Tucson, Arizona. I was scheduled for a Monday night celestial training mission. I received my weather briefing and presented my clearance to the dispatcher at Base Operations. He informed me that my training mission had been cancelled and I was advised to return to the Squadron.

The Squadron people were somewhat evasive, but they told me to go home on crew rest. They told me I would be called when it was time for briefing, between 12:00 midnight and 1:00 AM. I was told to pack for an indefinite stay in a tropical climate.

The plan was to deploy three U-2s to Clark AB, Philippines and become operational in minimum time. The plan was for three aircraft to be ferried to Hickam AFB, Hawaii. The aircraft were to be refueled and regenerated and ferried on to Clark with inflight refueling over Wake Island. Flight time from Hawaii to Clark was approximately 13 ½ hours. Two KC-135s supported the group for logistics and IFR (Instrument Flight Rules). The first support aircraft departed Davis Monthan early. They were to be in Hawaii for the arrival of the U-2s. This allowed the pilots for the second leg to crew rest enroute prior to their demanding air-refueling leg. Pilots aboard the first support aircraft were Steve Heyser and Jerry McIlmoyle; C. B. Stratton would fly the second leg. Jim Qualls, our Detachment Operations Officer, flew the first operational mission the morning after his arrival at Clark.

Early on the morning of Tuesday, February 14, 1964, I departed Davis-Monthan enroute to Hawaii; Jim Rogers and Bob Spencer followed. We flew three U-2Es (J-57 powered, IFR capable). Before daylight I crossed the Southern California Coast; it was a very uneventful, if somewhat boring, flight to Hawaii. Shortly after sunup, as I was descending towards Hawaii and within radio range, I was contacted by the Hickam Command Post. They reported that the first support aircraft had encountered extreme headwinds and would be 50 minutes behind me. The normal light winds at our altitude allowed the three U-2Es to pass the KC-135 enroute to Hickam. We spent quite some time circling the area and getting an early morning aerial tour of the Islands.

We finally landed, and everybody hit the ground running. All three aircraft were in good shape. The three of us pilots completed our debriefing, and we became Mobile Control Officers for the continuation leg. The first KC-135 spent minimum ground time before departing for Clark. Jim Qualls again left with the first support aircraft. It was time for the "Ball Buster" U-2 flights.

Our timing was critical for the second support aircraft because we had to do some of the refueling over Wake Island. The second KC-135 was readied and parked at the end of the runway, with engines running. I was Mobile Control Officer for C. B. Stratton in the last U-2 to depart. The minute Stratton was airborne, a jeep rushed me to the crew ladder of the KC-135. The aircraft began moving towards takeoff position before I was strapped in my seat.

I watched the inflight refueling of the U-2s over the KC-135 boom operator's shoulder. I didn't envy those three guys—the U-2 pilot, the KC-135 pilot and the boom operator. Wake Island was about one-third of the way to Clark. The U-2 pilots displayed immense stamina and deserved a lot of admiration for what they accomplished. They were awarded a well-deserved Distinguished Flying Cross (DFC) for their flight.

The second KC-135 had to stop at Andersen AFB, Guam to refuel before proceeding to Clark. The reason was two-fold—there was a delay in the refueling area; some of the KC-135's fuel tanks were used for the special fuel for the U-2s. A little trivia—we missed Ash Wednesday. We departed Tucson early on Shrove Tuesday, landed and departed Hawaii before noon on Tuesday. Enroute to Guam we crossed the International Date Line putting us into Ash Wednesday. We spent a few hours on the ground to refuel at Andersen late in the evening before departing for Clark where we arrived early on Thursday morning.

Most of us were up late after arrival at Clark. Those of us not recovering from an exhausting U-2 flight were present for the launch of our first operational mission over Vietnam flown by Jim Qualls. The target was a small inlet in the southern part of North Vietnam (NVM). We were searching for a NVM gunboat. This was a prelude to the infamous Gulf of Tonkin Incident. Jim encountered solid cloud cover over the entire area and was unable to do any filming. I flew the second mission on Friday, same target, same result. Jim Rogers flew the third mission. His target was the same, but he was directed to remain in the area. Rogers waited and waited for any breaks in cloud cover; still no luck.

Things started falling apart. Jim returned and just after lunch, a number of us decided to hit the golf course. It was a warm, bright sunny day, and we needed a way to kill some time. While on the golf course, a clubhouse employee caught up with our group and told Steve Heyser he had a phone call. Colonel DesPortes was enroute to Guam and we were to go to Guam, too. The US Embassy said we didn't have diplomatic clearance to bring U-2s into the Philippines. For years the Agency had operated their U-2s from the US Naval Air Station just west of Clark. The Agency had a large presence in the Embassy and it sounded like retaliation for the Air Force taking over one of their missions. Whatever!

We had to move the airplanes immediately. We left Clark on February 18, 1964 and relocated to Andersen Air Base, Guam. Jim Rogers, Bob Spencer and I ferried the U-2s to Guam after a late departure from Clark. I wasn't feeling well after golfing so long. My pressure suit seal across the back of my neck and the helmet frame across my forehead were uncomfortable. That late at night, there were no radio stations broadcasting and the only one I could pick up was Voice of America. The broadcast was in a foreign language, but they did have music. Every 15 minutes they would play a few bars of "Columbia, The Gem of The Ocean." The music and a celestial shot every 30 minutes were the only things to break the monotony. Flying against the clock, we arrived in Guam early on February 19. There we cooled our heels until March 4.

In wintertime Guam is an ideal vacation spot. However, we didn't execute a max effort deployment to sit around for days waiting to complete our mission. Boredom and frustration became strong emotions to us. During those two weeks, things became routine. On base there was a tight, nine-hole golf course that had been hacked out of the jungle. Golf was good recreation, but we broke the evening routine by going to the open air theater to watch thrillers like Errol Flynn in his swash-buckling movies. We had to remember to carry our raincoats because in the middle of the movies there always seemed to be a shower. That was normal tropical weather in Guam. After sunset the air rises over the warm landmass dragging in moist air from the ocean producing showers. The brief showers cool the landmass stopping the whole process for a short period. The good news was the movies were free!

On March 3, 1964, we received orders to bypass Clark and proceed directly to South Vietnam. Our detachment was located at the Vietnamese Air Force (VNAF) Base located at Bien Hoa, some 30 miles northeast of Saigon. The base had a beautiful, new 10,000-foot concrete runway, ramp and taxiway but no hangar space. The rest of the base was rather primitive. Bien Hoa was a widespread piece of real estate that housed not only VNAF operations but also a number of small stores, residences and a club.

Before our departure for Vietnam, every one of us was required to receive the necessary inoculations—plague, cholera, etc. Again our threesome, Jim Rogers, Bob Spencer and I, flew the U-2s into Bien Hoa AB on the morning of March 4. Because of our scheduled flights the next morning, we couldn't receive inoculations before leaving Guam. When we landed at Bien Hoa, the local USAF Flight Surgeon was waiting for us. As soon as we got our arms out of the sleeves of our flight suits, we were hit with the needle.

The USAF at Bien Hoa flew B-26s and the A-1Es, a multi-place ex-Navy attack aircraft. The B-26 had been grounded for some time due to a wing problem. This boded well for us because the only air-conditioned quarters were the B-26 pilots' alert trailers. They were located near the flight line which was quite a hike from the US cantonment area where the mess hall, operations, club, etc. were located. At first, we thought we had hot showers and flush toilets in the trailers, but it was not to be. We were told the water was potable, drinking water only. Back to the open-air showers.

The flight line operations were constricted and primitive. Remember, we were not yet at war and the US was there only in an advisory capacity. US military dependents still lived in Saigon. We had to share crowded flight line facilities with the USAF A-1s. Their ramp and maintenance area consisted of a wide patch of asphalt with a lane along the edge reserved for a taxiway with a number of rows of A-1s parked perpendicular to the taxiway. A sort of nose dock building ran the length of the parking area behind the aircraft. It was more of a "lean-to" and just deep enough for the nose of an aircraft. The U-2s couldn't park in line with the A-1s. The A-1s had propellers and when they cranked up, their propellers shot off dust and rocks that would have damaged the fragile skin of the U-2s. We commandeered three of the nose dock spaces. The U-2s had to be pushed into the nose dock between the rows of A-1s. The rows of A-1s were not quite far enough apart for the U-2 wingspan. One U-2 wingtip would just miss the tails of the A-1s on the left while the other wingtip went under the nose of the A-1s on the right. The large, four-bladed prop on the A-1s had to be rotated as the U-2 wingtip parked under the nose. We did not bring our Mobile Control to Vietnam so another primitive aspect of our flight operations was the WWII weapons carrier truck. It was equipped with a UHF radio that we borrowed from the Vietnamese for our Mobile Control chase vehicle.

We got off to a good start after our arrival in Vietnam. The weather cooperated and on the third or fourth day, under perfect weather conditions, we launched two aircraft to photomap the entire country of South Vietnam and several missions over NVM and Laos.

Colonel DesPortes summoned me with a message indicating that I was to return home as soon as possible. I learned that Lockheed was ready to evaluate the second of two new autopilots built specifically for the U-2. These autopilots were installed in one of the Agency's U-2Cs. I had been selected for the first evaluation the previous December. I had just returned from Barksdale AFB and the Cuban operation where we flew U-2Cs borrowed from the Agency. Lockheed wanted the same three pilots who flew the original evaluation to fly the second for comparison purposes. I jumped on a T-39 that same evening that was transporting our exposed film from that day to the photo lab at Clark. I caught a military charter flight from Clark to Travis AFB, California where I was picked up by one of our Wing's C-123s for a late night arrival back at Davis-Monthan.

When I arrived at Edwards AFB North Base for the evaluation, I learned I was the only one of the original three pilots returning for the second evaluation. I came back from halfway around the world for this evaluation. The other agencies, the CIA and Systems Command, didn't think it was important enough to send their pilots.

I hadn't finished my original tour in Vietnam, so I returned for a 90-day tour in late July 1964. The detachment had been reduced to a two-aircraft operation. Two of us incoming pilots ferried two "A" models into Bien Hoa and the two remaining "E" models were ferried by rotating pilots back to Davis Monthan.

Things had changed a lot since I left the detachment in March. We now had a Ford station wagon as one of our regular Mobile Control units. General Thomas Powers, Commander-in-Chief of SAC, had sent some surplus property from the deactivated Bomber Wing at Biggs AFB, El Paso, Texas. The alert facility at Biggs included several air-conditioned, three-bedroom house trailers. They were flown to Bien Hoa on a C-130 and installed adjacent to the US cantonment area. The trailers were connected to the area electricity, water and sewer systems.

Two of the trailers were used for crew quarters and one for Operations. The fourth slightly smaller trailer was designated for Physiological Support equipment and quarters for our detachment Flight Surgeon. Compared to what we had when I left, this was almost like a country club.

Flight line security was provided by the Vietnamese military prior to the Gulf of Tonkin Incident in August 1964. We armed our own personnel to provide security for our flight line operations. There had been a report that a Viet Cong infiltrator was on base for the express purpose of sabotaging the U-2s. As a result of that information, security procedures at Bien Hoa changed drastically.

A squadron of B-57s from Clark was deployed to Bien Hoa. The squadron required night weather formation penetration. One plane crashed in a mid-air collision. The next morning an F-100 squadron was deployed from Clark. The weather still required an instrument approach. After one of the F-100's broke out on final approach, he was shot down. The large, concrete ramp was now pretty well congested. I wrote to my wife that I felt the safest while flying; the approach to landing was the harriest part of the flight.

With these recent events, SAC determined a three aircraft operation was in order. Bob Powell arrived a few days later with the third aircraft. During his debriefing, he said he felt sorry for one guy who transmitted several times that he was under missile attack. Later, Ed Perdue returned from his mission into the Hanoi-Haiphong area of North Vietnam. From Ed's debriefing, he heard about Bob's comments. Ed yelled, "You SOBs. That was me!" Ed had started a turn when missiles came at him, and he saw two "telephone poles" go by and detonate above him.

After my return to Davis Monthan in late October 1964, the Command Post asked me if I remembered the combination to the safe in Operations at Bien Hoa. When I was at Bien Hoa, Operations was manned 24 hours a day and there had been no need to ever lock the safe.

Consequently, the combination was never passed on. A while later the base came under mortar attack. Everybody hit the trenches and the safe was locked for what was probably the first time. The Navigator was the only casualty during that attack; a piece of shrapnel caught him in the derriere.

MICHAEL (MIKE) HOROCHIVSKY
Lompoc, California

Wife: Machi

I was a member of the 4080th SRW from May 1963 to November 1964 and was assigned to the Wing Laboratory Branch. In June 1963 I was assigned to the 2nd RTS Photo Lab at Barksdale AFB, Louisiana in support of precision processing of the photos taken over Cuba. In February 1964 I was assigned as Chief, Wing Laboratory Branch and went TDY to Tan Son Nhut Air Base, Saigon, Vietnam to support Operation "Dragon Lady."

As a symbol of our high *esprit de corps* at the Photographic Processing Center (PPC), all PPC members had obtained modified "Aussie slouch hats," also known as "Gung Ho hats," embellished with a red, white and blue ribbon, the 4080th SRW emblem patch, the Vietnam and Tan Son Nhut patches. After about two weeks in country, the PPC Commander, Lt. Col. Jacobs, called a meeting. I recalled his face was quite pale as he informed us that the Viet Cong had placed bounties on all members of the 4080th SRW, $10,000 for officers and $5,000 for enlisted personnel, dead or alive. That was a sobering thought, so we put away our "Gung Ho Hats" and anything that referred to our unit. Apparently, our mission had made quite an impact on Viet Cong operations.

The US Navy provided military buses as transportation for all military in the Saigon area. The buses had meshed steel bars over the windows as protection from periodic shelling from the Viet Cong. The photographic personnel from the PPC were allowed to sleep in air-conditioned hotels in Saigon. It was necessary because of their long working hours and primarily to always be alert in their precision photo processing activities. It rained almost every day while I was there; when it was not raining, it was very hot and humid. The buses would pick up our personnel either at their hotel or at specific locations within Saigon. After work, buses returned our personnel to their hotels.

We had a long bridge to cross over a river whenever traveling between Saigon and Tan Son Nhut AB. Vietnamese National police dressed in white uniforms guarded the entrance of the bridge at each end, 24 hours a day. The GIs labeled these police as "White Mice" because they "always happened to be missing" if something was about to happen there. This would be primarily during the dark hours when most incidents occurred. There was a common expression at that time: "Vietnamese in the day time, Viet Cong at night." Several times at night the "White Mice" were missing; when the bus crossed the bridge, everybody was sweating, and it was not due to the weather.

About a week after my arrival at the PPC, I noticed 42 AR-15 rifles in one of the closets. It appeared as if nobody took care of them. The firing mechanisms in some of them were frozen. I asked the commander why these weapons were in the closet. He said they were for our protection. After informing the commander of the condition of the rifles, I was assigned to clean and maintain them. It took about two weeks for our lab personnel to clean the rifles in their "spare time." I then asked the base Security Police where the firing range was located and they told me on the northeast perimeter of the base. My immediate response was, "Wait a minute. Isn't that the same location where we hear the "boom boom" sounds of Viet Cong mortars firing every evening?" The reply from the Security Police was, "Yes, we secure it during the day and the Viet Cong operate there at night!" I went back to the PPC Commander and informed him that we would not fire the AR-15s at the firing range after all.

Occasionally, the Viet Cong used powerful plastic explosive bombs to destroy buildings in Saigon. I remember two such incidents. The first one occurred in May 1964 before I arrived at the PPC. The PPC operated out of the same building as the permanent party Reconnaissance Technical Laboratory. In fact, some photographic equipment was shared between both units. An American captain, a photo interpreter, was assigned to the permanent party laboratory. He worked along with a Vietnamese major who was an intelligence officer. All during the captain's one-year tour, the Vietnamese major offered to show the captain some of Saigon. The American captain was skeptical about going into Saigon at all, especially at night. Finally, a couple weeks before his scheduled return to the States, the major talked the captain into going into Saigon. Their destination was a small nightclub. That night the Viet Cong blew up the nightclub with a plastic explosive bomb. Four people were killed immediately and another 16 were wounded. The American captain was evacuated to the Philippines for surgery to remove a piece of shrapnel in his wrist. The Vietnamese major lost one of his legs and died a couple of days later.

The second incident involved the plastic explosive bombing of the third-story cafeteria in a seven-story hotel that housed American military and civilian personnel. Our PPC Commander, Lt. Col. Jacobs, had just finished eating lunch there and had exited the building when the entire third story was completely demolished by a plastic explosive bomb. It was about 1:00 PM with a light rain settling on the area. I was a couple of blocks away at a bus stop, waiting to catch the Navy bus to go to Tan Son Nhut. I heard a loud explosion somewhere off base. Lt. Col. Jacobs arrived at the bus stop and we sat together on the ride to the base. I noticed that Colonel Jacobs was extremely pale and shaking, and I asked him if he was sick. He then told me about the explosion and that he had just two weeks remaining before rotation to the States. His quarters were at Tan Son Nhut and he said he would never again go into Saigon. He was one very nervous individual during his last two weeks at the PPC.

Shortly before Lt. Col. Jacobs' departure, Lt. Col. Daniel R. Orlitzki arrived from the States to assume command of the PPC. I knew him when we were assigned to the 8th RTS at Westover AFB from 1959 to 1961. Because of our previous acquaintance, I was selected to meet him with a staff car upon his arrival at Base Operations. After he briefly met with Colonel Jacobs at the PPC, he decided to go to a hotel in Saigon. I urged that he consider remaining on base. There had been angry, political, mob demonstrations in Saigon for the past three days. All American personnel working at Tan Son Nhut were advised to stay on base until these demonstrations were over. Despite the warnings, Colonel Orlitzki insisted on going into Saigon. Both of us sat in the rear seat of the staff car and I placed an AR-15 rifle on the floor. The weather was hot and muggy and the car had no air conditioning so we opened the windows. After we crossed the bridge into Saigon, we were immediately surrounded by an angry mob. We quickly rolled up the windows and started to perspire profusely. I mentioned to all in the car not to look anyone in the eye, so we kind of looked down and occasionally peeked out the windows. I felt that it was likely the mob would break the windows and attack us. They shouted and shook our car. Four hours later, we finally arrived at Colonel Orlitzki's hotel, a trip that would normally take 30 minutes. I returned to the base by another route, but it still took three more hours. Lt. Col. Orlitzki came to work the next day with all his luggage; he had decided to stay on base until the demonstrations ceased five days later.

For anyone who has ever been in Southeast Asia or near the equator, the taste of "swamp" water is a unique experience. We were fortunate at the PPC. We had to manufacture distilled, pure water at the lab for precision photo processing. Soon the word was out and many people on base learned about our water. They would come at specified times with gallon containers and we would provide them with "the best water in Vietnam." I filled a gallon jug with this water every day and froze it at the lab. Then I took it back to my quarters and drank it as it thawed out. Every morning I drank two glasses of water mixed with orange Tang. After two months, I swore off Tang forever.

During my entire tour of duty at Tan Son Nhut, I only went into Saigon three times. The good hotels built by the French also served outstanding French cuisine. The one meal I remember was a filet mignon dinner. It started with a large shrimp cocktail followed by a filet mignon about five inches in diameter, three inches thick surrounded by bacon covered with a tasty mushroom sauce. The steak was served on a hot, sizzling metal plate embedded in a wooden plate with French fries, enough to serve four people and a fresh vegetable salad with French dressing. The dinner was accompanied with a large bottle of "Ba-Mui-Ba" beer (Vietnamese for 33). What did that delicious feast cost? It was a mere 95 cents!

I purposely did not include any stories about work at the photo lab. However, I would be remiss if I did not mention that all the photographic personnel did an outstanding job. On average, they worked 12 hours per day. There were days, however, when the team worked non-stop for 24 to 40 hours. It was a pleasure to work with such dedicated men.

Gung Ho hat worn by Michael Horochivsky briefly in Vietnam.

COZIER KLINE
Pottsboro, Texas

Wife: Jan

ROGER COOPER'S EMERGENCY LANDING
ON A FROZEN LAKE IN CANADA

During my four years of flying the U-2, I never had anything happen that was unusual. However, I was flying on that winter day when Roger Cooper lost power over the middle of Canada. Roger called me over the radio the minute he flamed out. We had previously talked about such an occurrence. At that time we agreed we would enter into a circle flight to glide down so that in case of a failed air start we would have a pretty accurate position. I made a notation on my mission planning green card of the exact time he called me with the flameout.

After 35 minutes, when I thought he should have had his first chance for attempted air start, I began calling on the SSB radio to the SC-54 flying behind us. I was exactly one hour in flight behind Roger, so I decided to start a flight circle over our route exactly one hour after he called me.

Meanwhile, I finally got a response from Barksdale SAC Command Post on the SSB radio; no one else would answer. I asked Barksdale to call the Laughlin AFB Command Post and start a relay between us to see if they could contact the SC-54 rescue aircraft; Barksdale complied. I passed on the exact time of Roger's flameout and my best estimate of the coordinates of his position as Roger and I were flying the same routes. By going ahead exactly one hour on my flight plan, I could help him.

I arrived at my estimate of Roger's position and started circling. By my calculations I would have about 15 minutes flying time left when I got back to Minot AFB. About 30 minutes after circling, I was able to talk to the SC-54 on SSB radio and told them when Roger flamed out. The SC-54 needed to go to full military power on their aircraft and get down to Roger's location. The SC-54 said they had received a radio call on SSB radio and were already "balls to the wall" headed to where they thought Roger would be. The SAC command posts were already on the ball at getting the Canadian people involved. It turned out the Canadians had a helicopter that supplied the information of who might be near Roger's projected location. The helicopter located and rescued Roger.

I was entering the landing pattern at Minot AFB when the Tower called and said there was a Colonel from SAC Headquarters who wanted to talk to me. I told the Tower to tell him I was too damn busy right then and I was flying on fumes. I told the Tower I would call him back after I had landed. The Colonel only wanted to ask me about everything we had in our survival pack, in the seat pack and a bunch of other stupid questions.

The final chapter to this story was that Ray Haupt flew to the frozen lake. He took Roger's U-2 off on a bulldozed short runway on the frozen lake, and flew 300 miles to the nearest Royal Canadian AFB. There further checks were made on Roger's U-2. Ray flew it back to Minot and we put Cooper's plane in the hangar. About 2:00 AM the next morning, we got a call at the BOQ that one of the U-2s had smoke coming out of it. We all rushed down and towed it out of the hangar for the fire trucks to extinguish the fire. There were some wire bundles that had chaffed bare and that may have been the source of Roger's problem.

RAY LODIN
Glendale, Arizona

Wife: Sandra

I spent seven years supporting the U-2 program. I would have continued to serve the Air Force but I was forced into retirement in December 1964.

During my time with the U-2 program, I was assigned to Mission Planning in Flight Operations. My job was to assist the pilots in planning their missions, such as determining time and distance to their destination. I enjoyed the interaction with the pilots: Jim Black, Ajack Moon, Buzz Curry, Buddy Brown, Pat Halloran, Jerry McIlmoyle, Mike Pierce, Joe Jackson, Ray Haupt, Roger Herman and many others.

While TDY in Australia, a lady friend took me down to the ocean to watch the small penguins return to their nesting spots. It was a fascinating experience. The beach was crowded with people watching them as we were. The penguins were so focused that they just walked among the people and headed for their nests. It was during the TDY to Australia that we learned President Kennedy had been killed. It was a sad ending to an otherwise pleasant TDY experience.

I enjoyed the TDYs and took advantage of new experiences. In addition to Australia, I was able to go to Puerto Rico, Alaska and Hawaii. In Saigon, Vietnam, I flew in, went to a French restaurant and witnessed the bullets across the river falling like fireworks.

During the Cuban crisis, I went to Florida to plan the pilots' missions and coordinate time over the target for the best photos. Weather conditions were a big consideration in planning these missions due to the angle of the sun.

Ray Lodin, 1964, Bien Hoa Air Base, Vietnam

CHARLES "CHUCK" MAULTSBY
(Deceased August 14, 1998)

The following is an episode from a manuscript edited by Chuck's widow, Jeanne.

ACCIDENTAL OVERFLIGHT OF THE SOVIET UNION

The latter part of September 1962 I was notified that I had been tapped for my second tour in Alaska. I didn't look forward to going back that time of the year because, unlike summer months when it is daylight 24 hours a day, the winter months are bitter cold and dark almost the entire day. I would much rather have been flying missions out of our Operating Location in Australia. It is summer there during our winter months in the US.

Off I went on a KC-135 back to Eielson AFB, Fairbanks, Alaska. Lt. Col. Forrest "Whip" Wilson was the Detachment Commander. Captains Don Webster, "Wee" Willie Lawson and I were the U-2 "drivers" and the three navigators who did our flight planning were Captains Billie Bye, Bob Yates and First Lieutenant Fred Okimoto.

The missions being flown were the same High Altitude Sampling Program (HASP) missions I had flown during my previous tour, with one exception. Don Webster was the first U-2 pilot to fly to the North Pole and back. He covered a distance of 3,000 miles. It was celestial navigation all the way, using the stars for a fix. The only radio beacon used was located at Barter Island, located off the north coast of Alaska. From there, the Pole was nothing but ice caps and polar bears.

"Wee" Willie Lawson was the next U-2 driver to fly to the North Pole. My turn would come later. I sat in on all the flight planning and briefings to be prepared for my own flight. Unlike the other HASP flights, this one was to be accompanied by a Duck Butt flight as far as Barter Island where they would orbit and wait for the U-2s return. Duck Butt was a search and rescue team flying a Douglas DC-4. If we were forced to bail out between Barter Island and the North Pole, they would make every effort to locate us. We understood the chances of a successful Duck Butt rescue were slim.

The team said if a pilot bailed out over the North Pole, they could make one orbit before heading for the nearest landfall. It was no use having the para-rescuer suffer the same fate. I asked one of the jumpers what he would do if he had to bail out over the Pole. He said, "I wouldn't pull the ripcord." I was sorry I asked. With that in mind, I wasn't sure why the rescue guys tagged along after I heard that response. They couldn't land on those jagged ice caps. Even if they were lucky enough to find the pilot, by the time a ground party could reach him, he would either be frozen solid or decomposing in the belly of a polar bear.

"Wee" Willie didn't have to worry about either of the two prospects. His flight went according to plan and he returned with some of the most radioactive material collected to date. The Russians must have popped some mighty potent caps.

On October 25, 1962 Billie Bye, Fred Okimoto, Bob Yates and I planned my flight to the Pole for the following day. The same Duck Butt team sat in on the briefing that followed the flight planning, but I didn't ask them any questions. I already knew their answers and once was enough.

Since my takeoff was scheduled for midnight on October 26, I tried to get plenty of sleep during the day. It was next to impossible. Throughout the day, people were tromping in and out of the BOQ in their heavy snow boots. The harder I tried to sleep, the more awake I became. I finally gave up and went down to our Operations building and sacked out on a cot. No one would show up until three hours before my takeoff time.

I woke around 8:00 PM and went to the Officers' Mess for a breakfast of steak and eggs. Bob, Billie and Fred were there. They didn't get much sleep either.

The preflight preparations were completed. I took off on time and proceeded directly to Barter Island. Duck Butt gave me a call on a prebriefed frequency and said we both should arrive at the same time over Barter Island. They wished me luck and said they would keep a "light in the window" for me.

Over the Barter Island radio beacon, I set course for the Pole and prepared to take the first fix. Right on the button. Those navigators were masters of their craft. All went according to plan until I was about halfway between Barter Island and the Pole. Streaks of light started dancing through the sky making it difficult to take a fix on the star I was shooting. This was my first experience with "Aurora Borealis" or Northern Lights. It couldn't have occurred at a worse time. The further north I went, the more intense the lights became. I held my heading and hoped the star I thought I saw was the right one.

The last few fixes before reaching the Pole, if in fact I did reach it, were highly suspect. I had no reason to believe I was off course, despite the suspect fixes. I decided to go ahead and do a 90-270 degree left turn that would put me over the Pole. It was: 90-270 degrees turn, then left turn for 90 degrees, then immediately reverse the turn for 270 degrees until heading back along the same track, only in the opposite direction. This new track should have headed me straight for Barter Island. I was out of radio range with Duck Butt. There was not anything they could do, but I would have felt comfortable hearing a friendly voice now and then.

I had never flown over a landmass that had not a single light from horizon to horizon. Of course, there were no lights on the ice caps, but didn't the Duck Butt crew say they would "leave a light in the window" for me? The first two fixes I took after leaving the Pole were wishful hoping and I realized something was terribly wrong. I began calling in the clear, hoping somebody out there might hear me and steer me in the right direction. I thought I was on the right track for Barter Island, but the ETA (Estimated Time of Arrival) was some time away.

It wasn't until I was out from under the Aurora Borealis force that I knew for sure I was off course, but which direction? I didn't bother to attempt to take any more fixes; I would just fly time and distance and hope for the best. I was approximately 300 to 400 miles north of Barter Island, or I thought I was, when the first radio contact with Duck Butt was accomplished. I even heard someone in our command post at Eielson calling over the single side band radio, but they couldn't receive my call. Surely I was in range of the radio beacon on Barter Island, but I couldn't pick it up. Had it shut down or what?

As the ETA for Barter Island wound down to 30 or 40 minutes, Duck Butt called and said they would start firing flares every five minutes. They started immediately. Duck Butt orbited over Barter Island and reported the radio beacon was operating okay. They received a transmission loud and clear. I didn't see any flare and asked them to fire another one. By this time I should have been over Barter Island and I should have been able to see the flare. They fired another flare. Again I saw nothing. It was all I could do to fight off a panic attack. I was either many miles east or west of Barter Island, but which?

The navigator aboard the Duck Butt called and asked me if I could identify a star. I told him I had the Belt of Orion constellation about 15 degrees left of the nose of the aircraft. Several minutes later the navigator called and told me to steer 10 degrees left. Immediately, I received another call from an unknown source, using my call sign, telling me to turn 30 degrees right. What the hell was going on? The navigator in Duck Butt didn't hear the latest call, so I was certain I was miles west of Barter Island. I received a call again from the unknown source with a definite Western-sounding voice telling me to turn right 35 degrees. I challenged him, using a code only a legitimate operator would know, but I received no response.

Duck Butt called and asked me if I could see a glow to the east on the horizon. I replied, "Negative." Transmissions from Duck Butt were getting weaker by the minute and the last one I heard was, "Turn left 15 degrees." The transmissions from the unknown source were loud and clear, but I ignored them. I selected the emergency channel broadcast and yelled "MAYDAY! MAYDAY! MAYDAY!" as loud as I could. I had about 30 minutes of fuel left, with no prospect of landing back at Eielson or anywhere else for that matter. The U-2 carries enough fuel for nine hours and forty minutes of flight and I had already been airborne nine hours and ten minutes.

Suddenly I picked up a radio station directly off the nose of the aircraft; it sounded like Russian music. It came in loud and clear. Now I knew where I was! The suppressed panic was now real and seized my lungs. I heard my own pulse pound in my ears. Through my panic, I knew for sure I wasn't going to be another Gary Powers and spend time in a Russian prison.

With what little fuel I had left, I decided to get as far away as possible from that radio station. I turned left until it was directly behind me and I kept calling "MAYDAY" until I became hoarse. "Why bother," I thought, "There's nothing anyone can do, so I may as well save my breath."

Twelve minutes of fuel left now. I made a call in the clear, to let anyone who might be listening, know that I was going off the air. A sense of despair overwhelmed me. I shut the engine down. Here I was just above 75,000 feet over God-knows-where, encased in a pressure suit which had inflated to keep my blood from boiling and all I could think of was, "This is a fine mess you got yourself into, Charlie."

When the suit inflated, I neglected to pull the lanyard to keep the helmet from rising. I had a hell of a time seeing the instrument panel until I finally got my helmet back into position. The windshield fogged up immediately and the helmet face shield fogged up too.

I wanted to conserve the battery so I could make one call before I punched out. I thought for a moment the altimeter was stuck. At least 10 minutes went by before the aircraft started to descend. With my face close to the faceplate, I could lick the condensation off. Now all I had to do was keep the wings level, maintain a rate of descent for maximum range and hope my Guardian Angel wasn't taking a nap. The silence was deafening. I could only hear my own labored breathing.

Up to now Mother Nature hadn't extended an invitation to relieve my bladder, but wouldn't you know, she makes a call at the most inopportune time. I wasn't about to unzip the pressure suit and have my "winky" pinched off during ejection. Besides, I didn't think I could find my "winky" under all the winter gear I was wearing. I felt like a 40-pound robin. I wandered off the heading I had established. That it would not have mattered that much, but I still wanted to feel I was in control of an impossible situation.

Twenty minutes passed since flameout. Damned if I didn't see a faint glow on the horizon directly in front of me. I thought I'd hold this heading and rate of descent until I reached 20,000 feet. If I'm in an overcast condition, I'd better punch out. I didn't want to meet up with a mountain, if one was in my flight path. If there aren't any clouds, I would descend to 15,000 feet and take it from there. I descended through 25,000 feet. There wasn't any cloud cover and my pressure suit started deflating. I thanked God. Now I could look around because it was light enough to see the terrain, which was blanketed in snow.

There were no mountains in sight, but what I did see was breathtaking to me. There were two F-102s, one on each of my wings. They were both flying near stall speed and their angle of attack looked dangerously steep. I activated the battery switch and gave them a call on the emergency frequency. They welcomed me home and said they had been following me for the past 15 minutes. They also said I had just passed over a little airstrip about 20 miles back. I told the F-102 driver off my left wing that I was going to make a left turn, so he'd better move off. He said, "No sweat, come on."

When I turned into him, he stalled out and disappeared under my wing. He said, "While I'm down here, I'll look for that little airstrip." As I passed through 10,000 feet altitude, I decided to attempt an engine restart. I was still gliding at 160 knots indicated airspeed and didn't have quite the engine RMP for a restart but I tried anyway. Was I ever relieved to hear the J-57 engine come to life!

I descended below 5,000 feet. The F-102 drivers were getting nervous. They were used to setting up a flameout pattern with a high key of 10,000 feet, but they weren't flying a glider. I reached 1,000 feet flying over a truck. I could not detect any crosswind, which was one less thing to worry about. I started a left turn out to sea and the F-102 drivers came unglued. "Bail out! Bail out!" they screamed. I continued my turn on around to low key, lowered the flaps and decided I was getting too much thrust out of the idling J-57. I shut it down. Everything looked good so far. I was coming up on the truck now with more airspeed than I wanted.

As I passed over the truck at about 15 feet, I deployed the drag chute and kicked the rudder back and forth. That took care of the excessive airspeed. The U-2 still didn't seem to want to stop, even without an engine.

Call it luck or the help of that Guardian Angel, I think I made the best touchdown ever. I hardly felt a thing as both landing gears settled in one foot of snow. When the U-2 came to a complete stop, I just sat there staring straight ahead. I was physically and emotionally drained.

I don't remember how long I sat there, but a knock on the canopy startled me. I turned to face a bearded giant who was grinning from ear to ear. He reminded me of the television character, Grizzly Adams. I breathed a sigh of relief; he wore a parka that I recognized as US Government Issue.

Before I opened the canopy, I unbuckled the seat belt and shoulder harness, made sure all switches were off and stowed the maps that had been useless to me. I took off the faceplate and I sucked in a breath of real air. I opened the canopy and the bearded giant said, "Welcome to Kotzebue." I replied, "You don't know how glad I am to be here." It was bitter cold as I tried to climb out of the cockpit with all my heavy flight gear. My legs were numb and I didn't think they would support my weight. My new-found friend sensed the difficulty I was having, so he put his hands under my armpits and gently lifted me out of the cockpit and put me on the snow as if I was a rag doll. He wasn't even standing on a ladder or box!

There were several more personnel from the radar station that gathered around, plus a half dozen Eskimos who came from the shacks I saw while airborne. Grizzly gave me a hand taking off the helmet and had someone place it in the vehicle the rescuers drove. The two F-102s buzzed us rocking their wings, then headed east. I thought, "I have to thank them somehow for making this landing possible."

My bladder was about to burst so I excused myself and shuffled to the other side of the U-2. The Eskimos followed me, but when they saw what I was about to do, they politely turned their heads. More people showed up to look at the strange bird until there were about 20 or so gathered to see and hear the ruckus. I never before in my life had such a large audience to watch me tinkle.

The radar site commander let me use a secure phone in his office and brought me a mug of hot coffee to sip on. I finally got hold of "Whip" Wilson. He had been standing by the radio since I took off. I told him the aircraft was okay, no damage done, but the fuel tanks were dry. He said a C-47 was loading up now with drums of fuel and maintenance people. Whip said he would be along to fly the U-2 back to Eielson. I asked if anyone had notified Jeanne, my wife, that I was overdue and he said no one had. Good. At least she wouldn't know a thing until I told her. Whip let me know that my little excursion over Russia sure had the White House and SAC Headquarters shook up. I thought, "I'll bet."

It took several hours before the C-47 landed at Kotzebue. I had time to unwind and get acquainted with the radar site personnel. The site commander asked if I would like to see where I had been. He took me to a room with the largest plotting screen I had ever seen. There was a map about 15 feet square of the polar region including Alaska and Siberia overlaid with plexiglass. He flipped a switch and a battery of lights illuminated the entire screen. There was my entire flight from start to finish, indicated by little tick marks made with a yellow grease pencil. The tick marks traced a path from Eielson

AFB direct to Barter Island, then to the North Pole. A 90 degree turn over the Pole was indicated, but instead of a 270 degree turn in the opposite direction, it looked like I turned 300 or 310 degrees before rolling out and heading for Siberia. At this point, I was beginning to understand my flight path. I followed the tick marks where the Duck Butt navigator told me to steer 10 degrees left and later 15 degrees left. The tick marks made a sharp left turn and headed for Kotzebue. I was about to slug the radar site commander and ask him, "Why in hell hadn't I been given a steer when all along you knew where I was," but my attention was directed to six little tick marks on either side of my flight path as I changed course to Kotzebue.

I asked the commander, "What are those little curly cues?" He replied, "Six MIGs were nipping up trying to shoot you down." Well, that got my attention and I thought, "Shit! I'm glad I didn't know it at the time. Whew!"

I stumbled over to a chair and took the weight off. I feared my legs were about to give out. He pulled up a chair alongside mine and said, "I know what you are thinking and I don't blame you. There is a good reason why we couldn't help you. I can't tell you, but maybe someone higher up will." I said, "Gee thanks. I hope the reason justifies throwing away an aircraft and crew."

I was still digesting all that I learned when the phone rang and someone in another room said it was for the U-2 pilot. The call was from one of the F-102 pilots stationed at Galena AFB who escorted me to Kotzebue. He said he was glad to see that I had made it down safely and apologized for yelling, "Bail out" when I turned out to sea at 1,000 feet. He had never seen a U-2 before and couldn't believe one could glide like that. I invited him to come visit us at Eielson and we would give him a "cook's tour."

The C-47 finally arrived from Eielson with Lieutenant Colonel "Whip" Wilson, several maintenance personnel and enough fuel to get the U-2 back to Eielson. When Wilson checked the aircraft forms, he noticed I neglected to fill out my takeoff and landing times. I remembered my takeoff time at midnight but couldn't remember when I landed. The radar site had me logged down at 10:25. That was 10 hours and 25 minutes of flight time. The U-2 had only nine hours and 40 minutes of fuel; that meant I had 45 minutes of glide time. There was that Guardian Angel again.

Wilson took off in the U-2, and I climbed aboard the C-47 with the maintenance crew for the long haul back to Eielson. "Wee" Willie met the C-47 and told me I had 30 minutes to pack all my gear because there was a KC-135 waiting to fly me to SAC Headquarters at Offutt AFB in Omaha, Nebraska. I was to brief my flight to the Commander in Chief of the Strategic Air Command, General Thomas Powers and his staff, especially the part over Russia. He also told me that Major Rudolph Anderson had been shot down over Cuba that day by a SA-2 surface-to-air missile. That was depressing news on top of everything else I had recently experienced. Everyone that knew Rudy would sorely miss him, myself included.

I don't remember how long the flight to Offutt AFB took, but it couldn't have taken long enough to suit me. I wasn't anxious to meet General Powers. I was the only passenger aboard the KC-135 and that made me extremely anxious about the briefing I was to give at SAC Headquarters. General Powers must have deemed it crucial to learn the circumstances surrounding my overflight of Russia. He must know all the details by now, but I supposed he wanted to hear it directly from me.

The KC-135 flight crew was curious to learn why they were flying me to SAC Headquarters, but they never came right out and asked. They had probably been briefed not to discuss the reason for this flight with anyone, especially me. They did provide that hot meal I was hoping for so long ago back in Eielson.

We landed at Offutt and a staff car took me to the SAC Headquarters building. A full colonel met me and escorted me to the underground Command Post. The room was a beehive of activity. People were actually running from place to place, as if their lives depended on it. Adjacent to the Command Post was a briefing room with a table that could seat at least 20 people. At the head of the table was an easel with an aeronautical chart on which my flight was plotted to the North Pole. A sheet of paper covered the portion of my flight after leaving the Pole. A colonel told me to take a seat and General Powers would be with us in a few minutes. General Powers entered the room and eight other generals followed. Those ranking generals looked as if they hadn't been out of their uniforms for days. Their eyes were bloodshot and some hadn't seen a razor in the past 24 or more hours. I stood at attention while they were all seated. General Powers sat directly across the table from me. He looked extremely tired, but he was clean-shaven and wore a fresh uniform.

As soon as everyone was seated, with all eyes riveted on me, General Powers said, "Captain Maultsby, how about briefing us on your flight yesterday." I stood at the easel while describing the type mission I had flown. I used the pointer to indicate the route I had flown from Eielson to the North Pole. I mentioned the difficulty I had taking fixes because of the Aurora Borealis.

Until I pointed to the North Pole, no one stopped me to ask questions. General Powers then asked, "Captain Maultsby, do you know where you went after leaving the

Pole?" I said, "Yes, sir." The other generals squirmed in their seats as if they were sitting on tacks. General Powers said, "Show us, please." I took the pointer and lifted the paper that had covered my flight path after leaving the Pole. The other generals really became excited now, but General Powers only smiled. He asked, "How did you know?" I told him that I saw my flight path plotted at the radar site at Kotzebue. General Powers turned and looked to each of the other generals and asked, "Gentlemen, do you have any more questions?" They all nodded negatively. He turned back to me and said, "Too bad you weren't configured with a system to gather electromagnetic radiation. The Russians probably had every radar and ICBM site on maximum alert."

General Powers thanked me for the briefing, told me not to discuss my overflight with anyone and left the room. The other generals followed in order of rank, and the last to leave the room was a brigadier general. He stopped in front of me and said, "You are a lucky little devil. I've seen General Powers chew up and spit out pilots for a hellava lot less."

The colonel who escorted me into the Command Post asked me if I'd like to wait in his office; he said there was a U-3A flying up from Laughlin AFB to pick me up. It wasn't due for another hour or so. I thought now would be a good time to find out why I wasn't given a steer when every Tom, Dick and Harry had my flight path plotted. The colonel wouldn't tell me why, but he did say that my overflight came close to starting World War III. If it hadn't been for my "MAYDAY" calls, the Russians may have pulled the trigger. He told me that when President Kennedy was informed about my overflight, he simply said, "There's always some son of a bitch who doesn't get the word." Well, if I had gotten "the word", I wouldn't be sitting here now. Just one steer would have prevented all this commotion.

403

A phone call from Base Operations announced the arrival of a U-3A from Laughlin. I thanked the colonel for his hospitality and left the underground Command Post still wondering why I wasn't given a steer. It bugged me for years before I learned the reason.

Captain Ed Purdue was waiting for me in the flight planning room in Base Operations. He said everyone back at Laughlin had been sweating me out. Ed didn't think anyone had told Jeanne and I was thankful. He was anxious to hear all about my fiasco, but when I told him General Powers told me not to discuss the flight with anyone, he didn't pursue the issue.

Ed said that he flew through some pretty nasty weather on his way up and hoped it had cleared for the flight back. The weather station forecast wasn't optimistic. Just north of Enid, Oklahoma we ran into icing conditions and couldn't maintain altitude. We called Vance AFB near Enid, told them we were icing up and requested immediate landing instructions. To make matters worse, one engine was losing power which increased our rate of descent. We requested a straight in GCA (Ground Control Approach) and declared an emergency. When GCA picked us up, we were already below the glide path and still descending. I thought, "What a way to go and after all I'd been through in the past two days." GCA was screaming for us to level off; we were way below the glide path. I could see the ground now through light fog and was certain we wouldn't make it up to the runway. I swear Ed was trying to hold the airplane up by pulling up on the yoke. It worked because we touched down in the overrun 50 feet from the runway.

I arrived back at Laughlin and I recited the same briefing for my Wing Commander, General DesPortes. Not one word was spoken throughout the entire briefing, except for an occasional muttered, "Oh, shit," when I described the six MIGs after my fanny, no one asked a question until I finished. Everyone seemed more interested in the thoughts that went through my mind during the ordeal rather than the cause of the overflight. They all were glad not to have been in my place. General DesPortes thanked me and said, "Now get back to Jeanne and the boys and take the next two days off."

Jeanne met me at the door with a "cool one" and said, "After you change your clothes, I'm dying to know what all the commotion is about. Just tell me one thing with a quick "yes" or "no"; does it have anything to do with Rudy Anderson being shot down?" I replied that it did not, "However, if the boys come in, I'll have to wait to fill you in on my latest escapade."

Jeanne sat attentively, her huge eyes looking larger as I went through the events of the past three days. "Well, that's it. Now you know what all the commotion was about." She just shook her head and said, "I let you out of my sight and you try to start World War III!" Before she could say another word, Chuckie and Shawn came bursting through the door shouting, "What did you bring me?" I felt like saying, "I brought your Daddy's ass home in one piece."

SAC Headquarters sent a team of navigators down to Laughlin to get a look at the article known as the U-2. Some had never seen a U-2 much less the navigation aids it carried including a periscope sextant and coffee grinder. The team was led by a full colonel, who when introduced to me, said he remembered my name associated with another incident but couldn't put his finger on it. I was chosen to escort the team because they were aware of my overflight. I let them sit in the cockpit of the U-2 and explained what the instruments were and how they were used. I could tell they were disappointed in what they saw. They were expecting all sorts of sophisticated equipment. After they observed the flight planning for several days and results of the local flights, they all agreed that a U-2 pilot certainly earned his flight pay.

Many years later at Davis Monthan AFB, Tucson, Arizona I received a call from a major inquiring if I was the same Maultsby who landed a U-2 at Kotzebue back in 1962. I told him that I was, and I invited him to visit the squadron first chance he got. I didn't really expect him to accept.

Weeks went by before the major showed up at the door of my office. We spent about an hour recalling the events that took place in those infamous days, October 26 and 27, 1962. He wasn't the radar site commander at Kotzebue back then, but I certainly did remember meeting him. Just as a lark, I thought I'd ask him why I wasn't given a steer, since my flight path had been plotted from start to finish. He was surprised that no one ever told me although I had made several inquiries. He didn't go into detail how my positions were relayed to the radar site, but he did mention some satellite station off the coast of Siberia on an island that could relay the information without giving their position away. Apparently Uncle Sam regarded the satellite stations more important to our national defense than one lost U-2 aircraft and pilot.

That explanation never satisfied me. Kotzebue could have contacted Duck Butt and they could have given me a steer before I wandered out of radio range.

ADDENDUM BY COLONEL (RET.) CHARLES KERN

Anyone who has flown missions around the Iron Curtain is most certainly aware of the hazards. The Soviets transmitted false signals on radio and navigational aids under their control. They would try to get Allied aircraft to navigate on them, leading our pilots into Soviet or East German airspace. It was called "MEACONING." There were specific procedures in the Enroute

Supplement for reporting such contacts. I had one reportable incident in four years of flying around Iron Curtain countries. It sounded like the real thing to me, except it was coming from a place I didn't think it should have been.

ADDENDUM BY COLONEL (RET.) ANTHONY MARTINEZ

I have talked with Leon Schmutz, the F-102 pilot who was the wingman of Captain Dean Rands. It was Rands who intercepted and escorted Chuck Maultsby to Kotzebue on October 27, 1962. Schmutz said he and Rands were on alert at Galena with their Deuces (F-102s) and armed with only air-to-air missiles. They were scrambled to the west to intercept the U-2 that had been tracked over Soviet territory. The Deuces were controlled by "CAMPION," the Early Warning Radar site near Galena, Alaska. About 30 to 40 minutes after their takeoff, they were vectored to the U-2 target. The U-2 was intercepted at an altitude of 45,000 to 50,000 feet altitude. Rands, the flight leader, made radio contact with the U-2 pilot. They continued to escort him toward Alaska, but it was slow going. They had to do some turning to stay with him. All this time they were under control of CAMPION. Rands said he and Schmutz were not aware that MIGs were airborne and were attempting to intercept. He said he did not know exactly where they were when they intercepted Maultsby's U-2. But if you measure 40 minutes flying time at 400 to 500 knots west of Galena, it places you over or near the Siberian land mass. Kotzebue is on the north end of the Alaskan Baldwin Peninsula and there is nothing west of that but open water of the Chukchi Sea. Chuck was blessed by many fortunate events that happened that day leading up to his successful landing.

GERALD E. (JERRY) MCILMOYLE
Venice, Florida

U-2 ENTRY INTO THE VIETNAM WAR

In 1963 the 4080th Strategic Reconnaissance Wing had moved from Laughlin AFB in Del Rio, Texas to Davis Monthan AFB in Tucson, Arizona. The tempo of U-2 operations had increased and it seemed like we were meeting ourselves coming and going. We were going on temporary duty assignments and flying the U-2 all over the world. I had returned from two months in Alaska and was looking forward to a long stint at home. It was February 1964 and the Tucson weather was fantastic and great for flying the U-2.

I had just returned home from the flight line when there was a knock at our door. There stood our Wing Commander, Colonel John DesPortes. Twice before I had answered a knock on the door and he had been standing there—smiling. The first word out of his mouth was "Maaj," that was his Alabama drawl for Major. I knew Colonel DesPortes' visit did not portend well. The first of his previous appearances signified the start of the Cuban Missile Crisis; the second was when he asked me to accompany him to break the news to a wife of a fellow U-2 pilot who had died in a crash in California. Colonel DesPortes instructed me to pack my bags and be at Base Operations for departure on a KC-135. He said Steve Heyser, Chuck Stratton and I were going to deadhead (fly and sleep) that night enroute to Hickam AFB, Hawaii. Three other U-2 pilots were preparing to fly three U-2Rs, the mid-air refueling model, to Hickam. Steve, Chuck and I were all qualified in the U-2 mid-air refueling. In the morning we would fly those U-2s to Clark Air Base in the Philippines. DesPortes said we were to plan on an extended stay.

I was the last to arrive at Base Operations. I guess I took too much time saying goodbye to my wife, Patty, and our kids, Patrick and Ruthie. The entire navigation section was there gathering maps for our flights from Hickam. The navigation crew was even gathering all the maps they could find of North and South Vietnam.

I remembered that at the end of the Korean War President Eisenhower had emphatically stated publicly he would never involve the United States in a land war in Asia. At that point in time we had advisors stationed in South Vietnam but no independent military units. We got airborne out of Davis Monthan AFB, for Hickam AFB, Hawaii with our navigation, maintenance and PSD teams on board the KC-135. Steve, Chuck and I were told to get as much sleep as we could because we had a long flight ahead of us. I took a Seconal and went right to sleep. We were each to fly a U-2 the next day from Hickam AFB, to Clark Air Base, Philippines with one mid-air refueling near Guam.

At Hickam Steve, Chuck and I were advised that the Strategic Air Command (SAC) Advanced Team (ADVON) had already set us up with office space and a place to sleep. The Navigation Team started planning our flights for the next day with takeoff schedule for 6:00 AM. Our maintenance crews did not get much sleep either; they recovered the U-2s being flown in from Tucson, servicing them with fuel, oil and oxygen. They fixed any maintenance problems identified on the U-2 flights to Hickam from Tucson. We were directed to start flying reconnaissance over North Vietnam (NVN) as soon as possible. The PSD guys worked all night getting our pressure suits ready to wear for the next morning's scheduled launch. The three of us were to fly over Wake Island and Guam and conduct our inflight refueling; we would continue on to Clark Air Base. A total of 15 hours was scheduled to elapse from the time we put on our pressure suits at Hickam until we removed them at Clark. Someone dragged us from bed and drove us to the flight line to go through our pre-flight ritual of getting a medical check and eating a steak and egg meal (high protein, low residue). We would also pre-breathe oxygen to eliminate 75 percent of the nitrogen from our bodies to prevent the bends. Fifteen minutes before each takeoff the PSD technicians strapped us into our aircraft. They hooked up the connections, checked our pressure suit and oxygen connections and tested everything to ensure it all functioned properly. Steve was scheduled to take off first, with me and then Chuck following at 30-minute intervals. Steve was strapped into his U-2, ready and waiting, radio on, ready to copy his authentication of the execution order from SAC Headquarters. The Navigation Team planned his celestial navigation calculations for a 6:00 AM takeoff. The execution order didn't come. We waited and waited and waited. Thirty minutes went by, the limit upon which preplanned celestial readings were considered useable. They gave Steve my charts and planned celestial as it was for 30 minutes later in the day. The domino affect took place. Having given my charts to Steve, they then appropriated and gave me Chuck's charts and started re-planning Chuck's flight. And like most bad dreams, every 30 minutes of delay in the execution order our charts were shuffled forward. Old military descriptions of this three-ring circus comes to mind, "hurry up and wait," "situation normal all ____ up", etc. We went through the total cycle twice and were arguing over whether to start a third cycle at 10:00 AM.

I let our Operations Officer know that we had now been on the flight line for almost six hours. I thought combining the delay with our planned flight time would mean that we would exceed SAC regulation crew rest

410

requirements. I suggested we notify SAC Headquarters we were aborting for crew rest. Little consideration was being given to the Navigation, PSD and Maintenance teams that had been on duty in excess of 24 hours.

I was sitting in a lounge chair in the PSD van when I saw our Operations, Maintenance and PSD guys milling around the three U-2s lined up on the flight line. What was going on? Wouldn't you know, the execution order came right when we were ready to pack up our bags and go to Waikiki Beach.

I tried to tell the Detachment Commander saying, "It's too late." But by then this gaggle had its own momentum and it was going to grind on no matter what. I was informed in plain language that regulations are only a guide to the Commander, not the inviolable law. So, Steve launched without celestial charts. Thirty minutes later I followed Steve, also minus the celestial charts. Steve, Chuck and I dead reckoned our way across the beautiful blue Pacific Ocean. It was a clear day with no clouds, no haze and no fog. Were we ever glad to see Wake Island over our plane's nose about 250 nautical miles ahead. We experienced a big boost to our confidence in our flight planning based upon the forecast of high altitude winds.

The earth is supposed to be mostly surrounded of water. We saw a lot of water that day. Four hours out of Hawaii, Steve radioed me he had picked up the Wake radio beacon and it was right on the target. Steve could not talk to Chuck, the third and last guy behind us; the two of them were separated by 425 nautical miles. I was in the middle and could talk to either of them so I relayed messages for the three of us. Steve reported he had passed Wake Island. I could make out the speck of black in the ocean on the horizon 200 plus miles away. It was indeed Wake Island. I passed Wake and radioed both Steve and Chuck that we were all about five hours out of

Hickam. We had eight more hours to go to reach Clark AB. Chuck radioed back to me, "Keep your comments to yourself, thank you very much." We were three tired and bored U-2 pilots and had eight hours to go.

Three hours later, Steve communicated to me that he had turned on his radio beacon to allow the KC-135 refueling tanker to home in and rendezvous with him. His next report was that he was in radio contact with the tanker and was starting his letdown for mid-air refueling. The procedure was to descend to 25,000 feet and put on the U-2 "Gust Control." That action raised the flaps and ailerons up a couple of inches and reduced the wing and tail loading. It provided greater safety in rough air. It also allowed the maximum indicated airspeed (IAS) limit to be increased from 160 knots to 220 knots IAS. I heard Steve report to the tanker that he was at 25,000 feet and holding 200 knots IAS. That was good news.

I heard the tanker report they had Steve in sight and were coming up on his left side. They would advise him when their airspeed and altitude were stable for him to slide over for refueling. The minimum airspeed of 200 knots IAS was required for the KC-135 to maintain a stable platform at 25,000 feet altitude to conduct midair refueling. It was also a major safety factor during refueling for the U-2. I heard the tanker crewman report he was ready and the boom operator said his boom was engaged in Steve's aircraft; the refueling process began. About two minutes later I heard the boom operator report that Steve had a full fuel load. Steve was instructed to reset his aircraft's fuel counter. Steve disconnected from the tanker and thanked them for their service. He was over Guam and heading for Clark AB.

We planned the refueling to end over Guam. In that case we would need fuel and could land at Andersen AFB on Guam and get fuel there. The tanker called me and instructed me to turn on my radio beacon. The tanker was coming toward me at a closing rate of over 800 MPH for rendezvous and refueling. After letdown from 70,000 to 25,000 feet, the tanker looked beautiful as it pulled up close to me just off my left wing. I slid into position for refueling and reminded myself of the tanker bow wave. That bow wave was not visible but it was there. It is similar to the upheaval of water behind a speeding power boat only in my case there was upheaval of air behind the tanker. When my U-2 slid in behind the tanker it acted like a surfboard; it first catches a wave and then is riding it. I had to throttle back almost to idle as the U-2 caught the tanker's wave. We used our speed brakes while refueling as that would give us better aircraft control. During refueling, the pressure from the tanker boom and the flow of fuel helped keep the U-2 from over-running the tanker. The U-2, in my mind, felt like it wanted to do just that.

It seemed like only a second later the tanker boomer radioed me that I had a full load. The tanker pilot eased his aircraft to my left, wished me well and turned back to refuel Chuck. The refueling for Chuck went without any problems. Following Chuck's refueling, the tanker turned toward Clark AB. The tanker had our ground support crew on board and they had to get to Clark before Steve to prepare for his arrival. It was not to be. Steve, Chuck and I encountered a tail wind of about 30 knots that gave us ground speed of 450 knots. The tanker had about a 100-knot head wind. We would arrive at Clark AB and land before the tanker and our support guys.

I could see the sunset reflecting off the cloud cover below us. On arrival at Clark radio beacon at 20,000 feet altitude, I initiated an approach pattern letdown. I was going to position myself for a Ground Control Approach (GCA) pickup on their radar and their guidance to Clark. They lined me up and set me up for landing. I broke through the overcast at about 1,000 feet above the ground.

I could see the Clark runway directly in front of me and followed the GCA instructions to the landing threshold. When I crossed the runway threshold, GCA released me and I landed visually. To me, it was more of a controlled crash than a landing. There was a nice breeze down the runway so I was able to fly the wings and keep them level throughout my landing rollout. I was fortunate that I continued to be able to fly the aircraft through the turnoff to the runway and onto the taxiway with the wings still level.

In my entire life I do not believe I have ever been that tired and that dehydrated. The Clark transient ground crew was there to help me get out of the aircraft and into the staff car that had been sent for me. I felt as if I was in a fog. The staff car delivered me to a crowded and dimly lit room; someone handed me a beer. That was the last thing I remembered.

The next day we were tasked for our first overflight of North Vietnam. The detachment commander, navigators and maintenance teams arrived the same night in the KC-135, the same aircraft that refueled our flight of three U-2s over Guam. Those were long reconnaissance flights— the flight from Clark AB to North Vietnam and back to Clark. The flight included three hours deadhead time to NVN two hours over the target area and then another three hours deadhead time back to Clark. We flew these missions over NVN over a period of about four days. The Philippine Government then became aware we were flying out of their territory and ousted us and our U-2s. We were declared "Persona-non-grata;" they gave us four hours to get off their sovereign territory, another political crisis in the making.

We made our Philippine imposed four-hour deadline and flew the three U-2s, support personnel and all our equipment back to Andersen AFB, Guam. There was no space in the Bachelor Officers' Quarters (BOQ) so the officers in our detachment were installed in two vacant four-bedroom family houses. Andersen had space in its Non-Commissioned Officers' (NCO) quarters for all our maintenance, PSD and other support personnel. It seemed like we stayed there forever but it was only about a week or 10 days. One significant occurrence came to me during that time. Cassius Clay beat Sonny Liston for the World Heavyweight Boxing Title. The reason I remembered that was because I bet Steve Heyser $5 that Clay would win. We gathered around the radio that night to hear the fight broadcast over Armed Forces Radio. I collected my huge winnings from Steve!

In a couple of days we received an execution order to move the detachment to Bien Hoa Air Base in the Republic of South Vietnam. Steve, Chuck and I ferried the birds to Bien Hoa which was about 20 miles north of Saigon. It was a clear day with light winds as we flew over the Bien Hoa radio beacon for approach and landing. Several times from my plane I called "Ben Ho" on the radio but received no answer. An English-speaking voice finally came on the radio and said, "Try 'Ben Waa'." I called "Ben Waa" exactly like that and right away a voice on the radio answered in English. I never understood why they didn't answer to "Ben Ho." I guess it was a French thing; if you don't say it to their liking, they don't answer.

A week after we arrived in Vietnam several members of the detachment were invited to meet at the embassy to meet the US Ambassador in Saigon. The Ambassador informed us that there were about 15,000 military personnel in South Vietnam. They were in an advisory capacity throughout the country. He told us we were the only independent unit there made up entirely of Americans. We were warned to be careful of what we said and what we did. He said we must be armed at all times and travel only in groups of two or three. We should never get into a position where we would be vulnerable to attack; we should never allow ourselves to be isolated from our unit. The Ambassador said they had found that the entire cadre of barbers on Tan Son Nhut Air Base was Viet Cong at night and friendly barbers during the day.

I drew a .45 caliber pistol because I had qualified expert with it. Chuck, being the hunter among us, had a carbine. Bob Spencer wanted something heavier and drew a Thompson submachine gun. We joked with him saying, "We didn't need to carry our weapons as long as you and your Tommy were with us."

The next day we started flying U-2 photographic reconnaissance missions over all of North Vietnam right up to the borders of China, Laos, Cambodia, Thailand and South Vietnam. Within a month we had mapped most of Southeast Asia (SEA).

Our Intelligence Briefer informed us the Viet Cong were everywhere around our airfield. To avoid ground fire on our landing approaches, we adjusted our landing patterns so we would arrive over the field at 3,000 feet or higher above the ground and then spiraled down so our ground track was within the perimeter of the base. We planned the touchdown point at the first taxiway down the runway, approximately 2,000 feet from the end. Every so often while I was there, the Viet Cong would lob a mortar shell onto the base but nothing was ever hit.

The U-2 pilots were quartered in Vietnam in two bedroom trailers with two men to a bedroom. The trailers were located close to the base Control Tower. I was always apprehensive about that because I thought the highly visible Control Tower would make a good target for mortars. That was where we lived, though. After I had rotated back to Davis Monthan AFB the Viet Cong destroyed several B-57s sitting on the ramp not too far from our U-2s and trailers. Everyone ate in the same mess hall in a barbed wire fenced compound. Our

Officers' Club was primitive with only a bar, a few lounge chairs and a chessboard. We did receive first-run movies though; a new movie was shown every night at no charge. Jim Qualls and I played chess and drank MIG-5s (a drink consisting of two shots of Scotch and one of Drambouie) until we didn't care who won. Jim usually won. With a few MIG-5s under my belt I didn't care.

Going to church was a unique experience. There was no chapel in the compound so we walked about a mile to a church in a small village. I worried at first about walking out in the boondocks to go to church. Our Intelligence Briefer informed us that almost all hostilities were suspended on Sundays. I gave him a little smile and asked him if the Viet Cong knew we do not fight on Sundays. I never understood the attitude of the Viet Cong. Supposedly they were Communists and by definition did not believe in God. Why was Sunday any different kind of day to them? I guess everyone needs a day off occasionally, even the Communists.

VICTOR L. "VIC" MILAM
Del Rio, Texas

Wife: Louene

MY SCARIEST U-2 FLIGHT

I was returning to Bien Hoa Air Base, Vietnam after a flight over North Vietnam. Everything was normal until about four and a half hours into the flight. I was still North of DaNang Air Base headed south at about 70,000 feet altitude. With no warning, I suddenly lost all pitot static instruments. Airspeed went to zero; vertical speed indicator dropped to the bottom of the dial and stayed there. The attitude indicator tended to float. I immediately disengaged the autopilot knowing that it functions with information from the pitot static system. My dilemma was to let down, keeping my airspeed within what we called the "chimney".

At the cruise altitude of the U-2, the difference between stalling the bird and exceeding its limiting Mach was about eight knots indicated airspeed. I was trying to stay between the stall buffet on low side and high speed Mach buffet on the other with no instruments to help, only the feel of the aircraft. My only option was to start descending. I was most thankful then that I was just North of DaNang rather than over North Vietnam where I had just been for the previous couple of hours.

It was almost impossible to avoid looking at the instruments in my situation in order to fly the airplane. But looking at them was somewhat less than productive since they were totally useless. I knew I had to ride the Mach buffet because getting my bird into a stall buffet would probably be disastrous. If the U-2 stalls at those

418

altitudes, recovery is unlikely before the tail comes off the airplane. The airplane is unstable at these altitudes and tends to continue further into the Mach buffet or stall attitude buffet if it should get into either one.

Trying to maintain a Mach buffet was a real "seat of the pants" pilotage challenge for me. A little too much nose down meant to pull back on the yoke which caused more buffet. Then coming out of that into no buffet, I had to nose down again or risk a stall. I had retarded the throttle but could not risk lowering the gear or going into the gust position. It would add too much turbulence and hamper my feel for how the airplane was flying. I had to get lower first and I was sweating bullets as it was. After what to me was an agonizingly long time, I was able to descend to a more favorable altitude. I then lowered the gear and extended the gust to give myself a larger airspeed envelope in which to fly. Still no instruments, but I could tell by the rush of air noise and feel of the airplane that I was within a safe flying airspeed.

This condition continued until at 17,000 feet when everything suddenly jerked back to proper indications. I continued to Bien Hoa Air Base and made a normal landing.

There was really nothing to write up for post flight. In talking with Maintenance personnel, it was decided that somehow moisture had formed in the pitot static system. The moisture then had moved into a position to freeze, thereby causing me to lose pitot static instruments. I had never had that happen before or since.

Of the Air Medals and two Distinguished Flying Crosses I received for being at the right place at the right time, I thought this incident was more deserving that any other was. However, it was not reported and I was just thankful to get the bird and myself down safely.

Victor Milam, center, with crew chiefs, preparing for a flight.

Victor L. Milam, 1968

FAMILY AND COMMUNITY

One of the greatest gifts that life can give to
anyone is the very
special love that families share.

Craig S. Tunks

MILITARY WIVES

It was just another harried Wednesday afternoon trip to the commissary (grocery store on military bases). My husband was off teaching young men to fly. My daughters were going about their daily activities knowing I would return to them at the appointed time, bearing among other things, their favorite fruit snacks, frozen pizza, and all the little extras that never had to be written down on a grocery list. My grocery list was in my 16-month-old daughter's mouth, and I was lamenting the fact that the next four aisles of needed items would have to wait. I was extracting the last of my list from my daughter's mouth, when I ran my grocery cart over an old man.

This man had no appreciation for the fact that I had 45 minutes left to finish the grocery shopping, pick up my 4-year old from tumbling class and get to school, where my 12-year old and her carpool mates would be waiting.

I knew men didn't belong in a commissary, and this old fellow was no exception. He stood staring blankly in front of the soap selection, as if he'd never had to choose a bar of soap in his life. I was ready to bark an order at him when I realized there was a tear on his face.

Instantly this grocery aisle roadblock transformed me into a human. "Can I help you find something?" I asked. He hesitated, and then told me he was looking for soap.

"Any one in particular?" I continued.

He said he was trying to find his wife's brand of soap. I started to loan him my cell phone to call her when he said, "She died a year ago, and I just want to smell her again."

Chills ran down my spine. I don't think the 22,000-pound Mother of all Bombs could have had the same impact on me. Tears welled up in my eyes, and my half-eaten grocery list didn't seem so important; neither did fruit snacks or frozen pizza.

I spent the remainder of my time in the commissary listening to a man tell the story of how important his wife was to him: He told me how she took care of their children while he served our country. He was a retired, decorated World War II pilot who flew missions to protect Americans. He still needed the protection of a woman who served him at home.

My life was forever changed that day. Every time my husband works too late or leaves before the crack of dawn, I try to remember that sense of importance I felt that day in the commissary.

Sometimes the monotony of laundry, housecleaning, grocery shopping and taxi driving leaves military wives feeling empty; that kind of emptiness is rarely fulfilled when our husbands come home and don't want to or can't talk about work. We need to be reminded at times of the important role we fill for our family and for our country. Over the years, I've talked to a lot of military spouses about how special they are and the price they pay for freedom, too. The funny thing is that most military spouses don't consider themselves different from other spouses. They do what they have to do, bound together not by blood or merely friendship, but with a shared spirit whose origin is in the very essence of what love truly is. Is there a difference? I think there is. You decide for yourself.

Civilian spouses get married and look forward to building equity in a home and putting down family roots. Military wives get married and know they'll live in base housing or rent some place. Their roots must be short so they can be transplanted frequently.

Civilian spouses decorate a home with flair and personality that will last a lifetime. Military wives

425

decorate a home tempered with the knowledge that no two base houses have the same size windows or same size rooms. Curtain sizes have to be flexible and multiple sets are a plus; furniture must fit like puzzle pieces.

Other spouses have living rooms that are immaculate and seldom used. Military wives have immaculate living room/dining room combos. The coffee table has a scratch or a broken leg in the move from Germany, but it still looks pretty good.

Other spouses say goodbye to their husbands as they leave for a business trip and know they won't see them for a week. They are lonely, but can survive. Military wives say goodbye to their deploying spouse and know they won't see them for months, or a year, or longer. They are lonely, but will survive.

Some spouses, when a washer hose blows off, call Maytag and then write a check for having the hose reconnected. Military wives have to cut the water off and fix the hose themselves.

Spouses get used to saying "hello" to friends they see all the time. Military wives get used to saying "goodbye" to friends made the last two years.

Other spouses worry about whether their child will be class president next year. Military wives worry about whether their child will be accepted in yet another school next year and whether that school will be the worst in the city...again.

Other spouses can count on their husbands' participation in special events, such as birthdays, anniversaries, concerts, football games, graduation and even the birth of a child. Only military wives count on each other because they realize that the flag has to come first if freedom is to survive. It has to be that way.

Certain spouses put up yellow ribbons when the troops are imperiled across the globe and take them down when the troops come home. Military wives wear yellow ribbons around their hearts and they never go away.

A lot of spouses worry about being late for Mom's Thanksgiving dinner. Military wives worry about getting back from Japan for Dad's funeral.

Other spouses get emotional watching the television program showing an elderly lady putting a card down in front of a long, black wall etched with many names. The card simply says, "Happy Birthday, Sweetheart. You would have been sixty today." A military wife is the lady with the card, and the wall is the Vietnam Memorial.

I would NEVER say military wives are better than other spouses, but I will say there is a difference. I will say without hesitation, that military wives pay just as high a price for freedom as do their active duty husbands. Perhaps the price they pay is even higher. Dying in service to our country isn't nearly as hard as loving someone who has died in service to our country and having to live without them.

God bless our military wives for all they freely give.

--Author Unknown

BUDDY L. BROWN
Knoxville, Tennessee

OILDALE SECRET

The first orders for the U-2 came from the CIA for 20 aircraft. Building 82 at Lockheed in Burbank, California was straining with an order for 29 more U-2s pending. The Air Force needed a larger and more secure assembly building. There was nothing in Burbank suitable or available. A former potato warehouse in Oildale, my hometown, was available for lease. It was almost new, windowless and adaptable to assembly work. The warehouse also had the advantage of direct access to the Bakersfield Airport for delivery via an Air Force C-124.

Like all Skunk Works projects, it required the utmost in security precautions. The new Oildale facility would be called Unit 80 and would have no signs to identify its ownership. All parts were fabricated in Building 82 in Burbank and trucked to Unit 80 in Oildale.

The first five or six U-2s were assembled at Burbank and flown by C-124 to the Nevada test site. Thereafter, Unit 80 assembled and delivered some 50 U-2s via C-124 to Bakersfield Airport. The C-124s arrived in the dark of night and taxied to a revetment in a remote corner of the airport.

Production began in the spring of 1956, and ended by September 1957 with a peak production of eight aircraft per month.

Security at Unit 80 was never breached and in late 1957, everything was transferred back to Burbank. Neither the Air Force nor the Agency nor Lockheed ever admitted knowledge of activity at Unit 80. However, in 2002 an Oildale TV station reporter and Minter Field Air

Museum representatives dug through piles of records. They made many telephone calls and invoked the Freedom of Information Act to put together the true story about what took place at Unit 80. The story about Unit 80 and the U-2 was broadcast on TV and reported to residents of Bakersfield and Oildale.

A few months after that report, I received a call from Major General Jim Whitehead, himself a former U-2 pilot and a member of the aviation board at the museum in Bakersfield. He explained that he had learned I was from Oildale. To celebrate some events that had been planned in the Bakersfield area, the General invited me to Bakersfield for some interviews and local TV appearances. The highlight of the event for me was the invitation to be the guest speaker at the Founders Banquet. I accepted the invitation and in February 2003 spent five days in Oildale.

I spoke at the banquet given in my honor and began my discussion by saying, "I can't believe, me, a guy from the little town of Oildale, to be honored like this. It is something I'll remember forever." It was a great trip; I met many WWII vets, some old school mates and had a visit with my sisters, one of whom is a retired minister with 27 years in the pulpit. I pointed out now that the secret was out, the people of Bakersfield and Oildale should be proud of their contributions during the Cold War.

Buddy Brown

JOHN HARVEY
(Deceased January 15, 2007))

The following was submitted by John's widow, Lilas.

John received orders for Laughlin AFB, Del Rio, Texas in the summer of 1954. He and I remarked, "Why is it we always seem to get these remote bases?" Before Laughlin, we were at Hunter AFB, Savannah, Georgia with the B-47s. One of our friends in Savannah had a cousin who was a postman in Del Rio. There was no base housing at Laughlin at the time and rentals in town were few and far between. Through our friend's cousin, all the postmen in Del Rio were alerted to be on the lookout for a house for a colonel, his wife and four daughters. We arrived in Del Rio one afternoon at 5:00 PM and stopped for dinner at a café on Main Street. When the waiter took our order, he inquired where we were going. John answered that he was newly assigned to Laughlin AFB. The waiter replied, "You must be the new colonel with your wife and four daughters. All the postmen in the city are trying to find you a house." We thought that was a beautiful way to be introduced to our new assignment.

After a few months, we were assigned to a house on base. We needed some unpainted bedroom furniture— two bunk bed sets for the girls. We were referred to Ricks' Furniture Store on Main Street in Del Rio. With our four daughters in tow, Pam age 10, Leigh age 8, Lindsey 6 and Jane 3, we visited the furniture store. We had finished picking out the furniture when a clerk approached us and asked, "Do you have a little blonde haired girl?" When we replied that we did, the clerk said, "You better come with me." At the front of the store there was a display of children's furniture. Sitting on the potty chair was Jane, waving to the huge crowd outside the store window. The spectators laughed and waved back. The *Del Rio News Herald* reported the following day Colonel John Harvey's arrival at Laughlin and Del Rio was upstaged by his three-year-old daughter, Jane's big splash at Rick's Furniture Store.

* * * * *

The Val Verde County Library in Del Rio conducted a fund raising program and our Officers' Wives' Club offered to participate. Zina Worley, wife of Colonel John Worley, and I volunteered to organize the Wives' Club contribution. We auctioned off some artwork and one of the sergeants at Laughlin, an artist himself, donated some of his work as a gift. The sergeant offered to help with the sale, but at the last minute he had to decline because he had to participate in a GI party. Both Zina and I were outraged that he made the commitment to help us and then said he had to go to a party. Zina and I begged our husbands to try and get him to ditch that party so he could help with our auction. Both husbands said they couldn't help us. Zina learned a few days later that a GI party was really an "all hands on board clean up of the barracks" and no absences were permitted.

* * * * *

One hot 110-degree summer day, our four children joined a group for a 25-mile horseback ride to one of the Del Rio ranches. There were no horses left for the sergeant leading the group, so he rode a donkey. When they all departed, he announced in a loud voice, "There will be no slouching in the saddle and no Coke breaks." I drove alongside for a few miles pretending to take pictures, but it was really to ensure nobody passed out

432

from the heat. They finally arrived at the ranch, and the sergeant prepared a delicious stew for lunch. Of course, no one knew until they finished eating that it was rattlesnake stew.

A sudden rainstorm blew in, typical of those hot summer days. I called John and asked him to get a base bus to rescue all the children. He was very reluctant but he finally gave in. John arrived with the bus and offered the children shelter on the bus, but they were only worried about the horses getting wet!

* * * * *

When we first moved on base, we had one of the temporary duplex houses. Base housing at Laughlin was located in what had been scrub brush fields and home to a variety of wildlife. It wasn't long before we realized we had an invasion of field mice in our attic, behind the walls and occasionally inside the house. Their antics sounded like a non-stop bowling game. We became accustomed to their racing up and down the Venetian blind cords inside the rooms. One day I had a coffee party at our home and some of the women sat on the floor. I noticed something beside the couch that looked like pink bubble gum. On closer inspection, I saw newly birthed mice rolling out from under the couch!

* * * * *

There were a number of stories that surfaced during and after the construction of the base housing. When the fields were cleared prior to construction, a number of rattlesnake nests were disturbed. We had so many rattlesnakes slithering up on the warm sidewalks and roads; we walked with our heads down looking for coiled snakes. We even learned bold techniques such as

433

throwing a rock aimed at their heads. Fortunately, I don't recall ever hearing anyone being bitten by one of those rattlesnakes.

The black widow spiders, too, lost their prime real estate when the field was cleared. They just built new nests over the doors of the houses. We learned to look up prior to entering the door to be sure a spider wasn't swinging down on its web.

* * * * *

The road to the back gate of the base was temporarily opened and I decided to use it one morning. I was in a rush to pick up our maid who lived in town. I use the term "road" loosely here; it had recently been graded out of the scrub fields. I took Jane, our youngest still in her nightgown, with me; I had thrown on some old clothes and had not put on any makeup. In my haste, I did not realize the road was wet from an early morning thunderstorm. Right at the back gate, my car sunk into mud so deep, I couldn't move it. I was totally humiliated to be stuck there and to look so unkempt. It took two cranes to get us out. My John came out and laughed at my predicament. What an embarrassment.

* * * * *

We moved into our new base house, but we had to furnish our own grass. The people of Del Rio generously furnished us with grass from their own yards as well as shrubs and trees. Right after many of us had finished planting the plugs of St. Augustine grass, we had one of those Texas rains. The newly planted grass came loose and went floating down the street. All our neighbors came running out with plastic sacks and wheelbarrows to retrieve the precious grass plugs.

434

* * * * *

Just to give an idea of the intensity of those infamous rainstorms, I was the honoree at the Officers' Wives' Club welcoming coffee party. At the very moment I was trying to get out of the car at the Club, a huge rain cloud burst over the base. It delayed my arrival for a short while. I was told the runway had several inches of water and there were waves with whitecaps on them. This particular storm was captured by a photographer and was filed by the base historian.

* * * * *

In October 1960 movie star John Wayne came to the area to film "The Alamo". He had requested permission from the Base Commander, my John, to use the runway for his own plane. As a "thank you," Wayne invited my John and me to dinner with his wife, Pia, and their children at their temporary home in Brackettville. I was amused at the number of people who knocked on their door while we were having dinner to get a glimpse of the celebrities. The whole family was understanding and gracious about the intrusion. Wayne gave us a pass for our car to come watch the filming of the movie. I filled up our station wagon with at least 12 people and we drove to Brackettville to the movie site on a private ranch. That was certainly an interesting occasion for all of us.

* * * * *

President Dwight Eisenhower visited Laughlin in July 1962 and met with President Lopez Mateos of Mexico. The occasion was a celebration to open the Amistad Dam that spanned the Rio Grande between the two countries at Del Rio. Our house was selected as an emergency

435

location should President Eisenhower suffer any health problem while he was at Laughlin. We were the only ones at the time with a king-size bed; they were so new we couldn't even find a king-size bedspread. I sewed two double bedspreads together to cover our king-size bed. Eisenhower's advanced team arranged for the special red telephone installed on the bedside table with a direct line to the White House.

Considering the entourage that accompanies the President now, it was interesting that President Eisenhower had no aides with him, only a female secretary. The President walked down the stairs of his airplane and was greeted by a great contingent of military and civilian dignitaries. My John followed behind the President and could hear him asking the secretary each time he was introduced, "Who in the hell is this? And this one?"

Our children's horse drill team wanted to greet President Eisenhower riding their horses at a full gallop with flags waving. It required permission from the White House and the President. Eisenhower was so concerned for the children, he did not approve the full gallop because he was afraid someone would be hurt. He did approve of the horse drill team with flags waving, but the horses could only walk.

President Eisenhower met the President of Mexico in the small town of Cuidad Acuna, across the Rio Grande from Del Rio. In preparation for the two presidents' visit, Cuidad Acuna freshly painted all the buildings and paved the entire travel route.

The town of Cuidad Acuna had little industry and depended on tourism for much of its economy. There were few paved streets and utilities, such as electricity and water, were in short supply or non-existent in some areas of Cuidad Acuna. A local dentist, Dr. Ramon Ortiz, offered his large home with a swimming pool for the meeting. Much to our surprise, when a review of the meeting site was conducted, planners discovered there was no water in the pool. Prior to the two presidents' meeting, Laughlin sent water trucks to fill the pool.

* * * * *

My John told me many of his on-the-job stories of those early days at Laughlin. One such story was about shooting the birds in the hangars because their droppings corroded the metal on the airplanes. There were occurrences of the maintenance technicians being the target of occasional droppings as they worked on the airplanes in the hangar. I can only guess that the sound of gunshots must have created quite a show in the hangar.

* * * * *

Joe Kerr, a resident of Del Rio, invited my John to his ranch to observe "real" ranching in action. The action they were watching was cattle roping. John didn't know at the time that "greenhorns" like him were ranchers' entertainment and their kind of ranch humor. Joe and some of the other fellows there chided John into roping a calf. Being a good sport but completely out of his element, John did rope a calf over and over again. After all that "real" ranching, John's clothes were dirty and torn and he was a disheveled mess. With Joe accompanying John to the gate at Laughlin, the guard asked the disheveled occupant for his identification, which he didn't have with him. He said, "I'm Colonel John Harvey, the Base Commander." As you might imagine, the guard didn't believe him and he called his commander to come identify John and his guest. I'm sure the guard never forgot that day and he probably made it an amusing story in the retelling. I know for sure my John never forgot the incident.

John and Lilas Harvey at their farewell party at Laughlin AFB.

Welcoming the first group of Taiwanese student pilots to Laughlin AFB.
L to R: Major Chan Hia, USAF officer, Major Mike Hua, Major Shia, Col. John Harvey, Major Gen Wang, Col. John Desportes, Major Yang, Major Tiger Wang

JAMES S. LONG
Del Rio, Texas

BUT WHAT DOES HE DO?

My sister, Mary Kay Long, was taking her friend, Jane, daughter of Colonel A. J. Bratton, home one afternoon from school to the family residence on Laughlin AFB. They stopped the car at the main gate and a young Air Policeman (AP), noting an unregistered vehicle with two cute girls, stuck his head into the driver's window. He demanded identification. While Mary Kay was retrieving her driver's license, Jane passed her military ID across to the policeman and said, "I think this will help." The AP grasped the ID, scanned it briefly and quickly returned it. He abruptly withdrew his head knocking his hat off. He retrieved his hat, stood at attention and saluted smartly. Mary Kay was very impressed with the attention they received. As they drove off, she asked Jane, "What does your Dad do?" Jane replied, "He's the Wing Commander!" Mary Kay persisted, "I know, but what does he do?"

WETBACKS ON THE RAMP

Shortly after the Lockheed U-2s arrived at Laughlin AFB, my cousin, Warren Long, who was with the Army Corps of Engineers, was assigned to do survey work on the flight ramp. He was accompanied by an escort officer when he worked in close proximity of the classified aircraft. While Warren was occupied with his surveying, the escort officer noticed some individuals crossing the ramp and exclaimed, "Well, I'll be damned! Here we are

440

with the most sensitive aircraft in the Air Force inventory and those illegal aliens are right in the middle of them!"

WHO FIRED THOSE SHOTS?

My father, Stillman Long, and I were returning about dusk from a hunting trip northwest of Brackettville, Texas, approximately 30 miles east of Laughlin. It was during the Christmas holidays. We were driving our Jeep station wagon when we had some engine trouble on US Highway 90 near the end of the Laughlin runways. I volunteered to walk to the gate and call for a mechanic while my Dad remained with the Jeep and our rifles. A carload of kids passed and tossed out some fire crackers setting off a series of loud bangs. I arrived at the main gate of Laughlin, explained our situation to the guard, and he allowed me to call the mechanic in Del Rio, seven miles away. As I was making my call, a sedan arrived at the gate with two men in the rear seat armed with submachine guns. They demanded of the guard, "Who fired the shots?" I volunteered that I had seen that it was only kids with fireworks. The driver then asked the guard, "Who is he?" They seemed satisfied with the answer and drove out the gate to US Highway 90 only to return a short while later.

With my call made and the mechanic on his way, I walked back to the Jeep. I told my Dad about the fireworks incident and the guys with submachine guns. He said, "I guess that's why those guys over there have been watching me with their field glasses." Sure enough I saw the vehicle parked on Laughlin property that my Dad had seen.

PHOTOGRAPHIC SECURITY

As an aviation fan and avid model airplane builder, I had built several of the Hawk Company's Lockheed U-2A models after the full scale aircraft arrived at Laughlin. I was proud to be the first civilian to get one of the new model U-2s. I had the idea to place the models on the sidewalk at our house to simulate the ramp. I hung one from a pecan tree nearby with monofilament fishing line in a flight position. After I took a number of 35mm color slides, I sent them off to Kodak for processing in Dallas where I sent all my film for development. After an unusually long time, the slides were returned with special markings on the box. A special notation showed that it had been examined by Kodak security department. It then occurred to me that the photos had looked realistic enough on first glance for a censor to examine them!

* * * * *

I remember the date and time vividly, June 28, 1957. A high school classmate who lived near the Del Rio Municipal airport called me and hurriedly explained that a jet aircraft was landing, probably a Navy Crusader. I figured he had it all wrong, but I told him I would come pick him up on the way to the airport to catch a look. When we arrived at the airport, we saw a bunch of people running to the northwest part of the airport near Gulick Hill. From where we stood, we could only see a large silver object on the ground. We then drove toward Gulick Road and the hill near what we now understood was a crashed airplane. It appeared to have occurred only moments ago.

We left the car and ran towards the still unidentifiable aircraft just as a USAF H-19 helicopter landed at the site. We crossed the fence and were within 50 to 60 feet of the aircraft when the security force exited the helicopter. They ordered everyone back 50 feet beyond the fence and within a few moments we were told to move back 100 feet. The final order was for everybody to get completely out of the area.

The Laughlin fire truck crossed the runway and started up the slope to the crash site. The fire truck passed a number of people who had slowed to a walk. A puff of black soot escaped the exhaust as the driver accelerated to pass through the fence without slowing.

We jockeyed for position as close to the aircraft as we dared. What we observed that day remained with me even now. The fuselage was upside down and the pilot was still strapped in his seat. We took note of the tail number of the aircraft and my friend remarked, "Do you see anything funny about the tail number? It is all sixes and nines!"

We were still spellbound by the activity, and I saw Mr. Frank Gulick, the owner of the property where the crash occurred. He was taking pictures with his movie camera. I felt certain that his camera, or at least the film, would be taken from him. His niece later confirmed the camera and film had been confiscated.

After we were ordered away from the area by the security force, I took my friend home. I later returned with my Brownie Hawkeye camera and took a photo of the wreckage. The film was processed, but I never showed it to anyone until the early 1990's when I had it enlarged for a 4080th SRW reunion.

James Long is Chairman of the Board, Laughlin Heritage Foundation Museum.

PATRICIA MCILMOYLE
Venice, Florida

MY THOUGHTS

When my husband was flying the U-2 all over the world I never worried about him. I believed he was the best of the best of pilots, I thought! At the end of this story you will understand I feel different. It is never too late to change our hearts and minds.

Did other wives in the Squadron really put jar lids filled with vinegar or some concoction under the crib legs to keep spiders, scorpions or earwigs from getting into our child's crib. I did that! Did military people earn the same salaries in their rank? Was I rich or poor? Wherever else in a same development would we get the same design of housing, a huge commissary, lovely parks, brand new swimming pools, nice ceramic and art classes, all kinds of athletic games? Those perks were exceptional. Weren't mothers all around outside to help monitor their children and the neighbors' children? Our Clubs were the best in food and shows. Didn't some of the men get up with their head covered (so we wouldn't recognize them) as we watched their "button" moving in circles imitating a whistle? The act was called "The Whistling Midgets". I had a ball! What talent we were exposed to. Didn't we have the best of imitators and also the best of dancers, whatever their act might be? In another way, didn't I take my sick children to the doctor; didn't he say to me that the children were okay and that they had the Fifth Disease because they missed their father when he was on TDY? Did I believe that? Was that true?

Were our experiences and adventures not so sophisticated as we have today? Did any other families have picnics underneath the bridges around the base area? We were afraid of the bats that would come flying out at us. Wasn't it like going to a zoo to take our littlest ones to the back gate to watch bunny rabbits bouncing around looking for food? Did you hear of one or more little boys sitting down on the street curb with the sharper edge of a dinner knife in one hand? They were swatting a rattlesnake on the head and they did not get hurt.

Were you there on base when the men were flying over Cuba? I put duct tape all around my windows so nuclear dust would not harm my children. I doubt, when I think about it, that Russia would nuke Del Rio. Who would want two young kids to sleep in her bed when their Dad was on TDYs? I wanted that! Did I ever get drunk at the Club and get sick? I did but it wasn't good for me. We drove back home through the back gate because my spouse did not want the guards to see me "toss my cookies." Did your children get up in the morning when it was still dark? Their father was home from a flight but they wanted breakfast so they went to the frig. The older one poured KoolAid (whatever became of milk?) onto his and his sister's cereal.

Were you one of the women who came to this church meeting that one friend had? A crowd of members in the group came to that insignificant mini-meeting. How did my friend manage to serve homemade pie to so many people? Well, she was an Air Force wife and everyone there had an adequate piece of pie and all the coffee they wanted.

Do some of you remember the singing group at most bases and especially the Women's Chorus we had at Del Rio? Our super director and artistic pianist were the best in talent. Did we have fun? Yes!

Some family, relatives and friends would visit us on-base but were disturbed by sounds of the jets revving up their engines so early in the mornings. Did those jet screams bother you? Not me!

Might you remember one cute Captain's wife who sewed an outfit for herself for the luncheon's fashion show? Showing off her outfit and seeing her bounce around the table were wonderful to me. She was the epitome of a pretty officer's wife. What about those lovely teas we would go to at some hostess' home? I will never forget those times. Whoever would get their children in their new Volkswagen bus and with another family drive clear to Breckenridge Park in San Antonio for a picnic? It was three hours away! I have had that experience.

Well, to get back to what I think of all of us and our husbands' careers, I find that my thoughts are different now. I liked all the events we have had and the good times. But, flying and working in support of that Squadron seems scary to me when I hear or read these stories. My heart tells me that these men were handsome, good husbands, good fathers and superb airmen. But, now I think they also are brave.

I am the wife of...a US Air Force Cold War Reconnaissance Pilot.

CLIFFORD B. (CLIFF) MELTON
(Deceased November 1, 1980)

The following was submitted by Cliff's widow, Virginia.

Cliff was an engineer by education and was assigned to the Field Maintenance Operation of the 4080th SRW.

When Cliff was assigned to Laughlin, we rented a house in Del Rio. Our nextdoor neighbors on one side were Bob and Barbara Ingram; on the other side lived Rudy and Jane Anderson. Bob and Barbara's daughter, Stacy, was about the same age as our daughter, Joyce, and they became friends. Our sons played with Rudy and Jane's boys.

During the time Cliff was with the 4080th SRW at Laughlin, we had three young children, Joyce, Wes and Bill, who was born in Del Rio. Our kids were involved in a variety of activities. I became a volunteer, mostly because I had already driven them to their functions. I was Cub Scout leader with Wes and Bill and a Brownie leader with Joyce. The boys were also into sports and played Little League baseball.

I was a home economics major in college and enjoyed teaching my daughter and the Brownie Troop to sew. One of the Brownie projects was to sew a Barbie dress using a pattern that I made for each girl. They sewed the dresses by hand and later I took their carefully sewn clothes and finished them on the sewing machine so they would not come apart. Shortly after they finished sewing the dresses, we had a Father/Daughter Banquet. The girls brought their Barbie dolls with newly created outfits to the banquet. The dolls were set on the table and held the place cards for the dads.

While we were in Tucson, Joyce's high school cooking class made cookies for the men in Vietnam. We wrapped and sent them to Cliff for distribution to the fellows at his base. Each of the men who received the cookies wrote thank you letters to the girls.

Clifford B. Melton, 1966

WILLIAM T. (RODY) RODENBACH II
Riverside, California

Wife: Barbara

MEMOIRS OF A U-2 PILOT'S WIFE

Charles Dickens said it best in the opening of his book, *A Tale of Two Cities,* "It was the best of times and the worst of times." Rody received transfer orders from the 71st Strategic Reconnaissance Wing at Larson AFB, Moses Lake, Washington in June 1957 to join the 4080th SRW at Laughlin AFB, Del Rio, Texas. That wasn't such bad news. For two years we had enjoyed living at Larson in a nice little house on Doolittle Drive. Many of our friends previously stationed with us in Bitburg, Germany also transferred to Larson. They were the Bedfords, the Mohans, and the Bellingers. The Dixons lived a couple of streets away, which was a safe walk for our daughter, Janie, to play with her best friend, Diane. We all had two or more kids. On a freezing, snowy night our fourth child, Chuck, was born at the Larson AFB Hospital on January 17, 1957. You have heard it all before, I'm sure. It was time to leave for the hospital, labor pains were three minutes apart, but the car would not start. Bill opened the hood and I got behind the wheel to turn the key; we finally got it going. This was the *best of times*, a new baby boy, a new assignment and a new adventure.

We were pleased to hear that many of the Larson AFB families would be with us in Del Rio. It was especially nice for the wives and the children to transfer together, as an extended family, from one location to another. Most of us were many miles from close relatives so these great friends became "family." While living in Washington

State, Rody and I couldn't have been much further from our roots in Connecticut. The children of our Air Force friends were babies in Germany, toddlers in Moses Lake and now they looked forward to attending school together in Texas.

We took our annual leave in the summer to spend time with family. We drove to Connecticut from wherever we were stationed. Our families were overjoyed to learn that the kids and I would be spending the summer with them at the family cottage in Madison, Connecticut, on the shores of Long Island Sound. Rody made a wooden car bed for five-month-old Chuck to ride in the back seat of the car. I painted it blue and made a mattress for the combination bed and playpen. This was many years before secured child seats and seat belts. The children and I took turns riding in the back seat with Chuck and we referred to his bed as "the box." More than once when we stopped for gas or at rest stops, strangers would ask the kids what they had in the box. Our kids innocently replied, "Our baby brother." There were more than a few surprised looks from those same strangers. The box worked well for giving Chuck a safe, comfortable place for sleeping and playing under the watchful eye of his back seat companions.

Rody took on the packing of our household goods at Larson and then endured the white glove treatment of inspection before checking out of base quarters. After clearing the base, he drove the long trip back East to pick us up and move us to Texas.

We had heard that Del Rio was no paradise. However, that wasn't enough to prepare me for the long drive into that part of the country. The children and I had never been to Texas; consequently, it was hard for us to grasp how really big the state was and how long it took to drive through it. The children frequently asked their Dad if they were *still* in Texas. We drove farther south, each

450

day hotter than the previous one. Our car did not have air conditioning and all four kids were cramped, tired and cranky. The rolling hills and tall trees of the eastern landscape were replaced with mesas and numerous species of cacti. The terrain became very flat and barren; tumbleweeds rolled across the road in front of our car. We could see for miles and miles with not a hill nor even curve in the otherwise straight as an arrow road. I felt as though we were driving to the end of the earth and within a few more miles, we were going to fall off.

DEL RIO, TEXAS

Base housing had not been by built the time we arrived at Laughlin. We had to find houses or apartments to rent in town. Many of us found houses in a dated development not far from the base on Kennedy Drive. Some of our Moses Lake group settled nearby and others were scattered around town.

Now to the *worst of times* category. We had barely emptied packing boxes and arranged the furniture when Rody had an appointment at Lackland AFB Hospital in San Antonio, approximately three hours away by car. I had assumed it was a physical exam related to his new flying job. I was not prepared for him to be admitted into the hospital for surgery on both ears. I suddenly felt overwhelmed as he drove off and left us in this unfamiliar place for four weeks and without a car.

While Rody was confined to the Lackland Hospital, the children and I spent those hot August afternoons on the shaded carport catching a slight breeze. We had not even had time to buy an electric fan or plastic wading pool for the kids. I filled the biggest pan I could find from the kitchen and sat little Chuck in it while the three older kids played and sprayed themselves with the garden hose. At night I opened all the windows hoping for some

451

breeze and lower temperatures to cool off the house. In the morning I pulled the shades in hopes of trapping the slightly lower temperature for a while longer.

I was so grateful to have friends like Joe and Ann Nemo who lived three houses down from us on Kennedy Drive; Millie and Buzz Curry lived nearby as well. They were all family. They checked on the kids and me and drove me to the base commissary for groceries. We were all one-car families then; the guys usually car pooled to the base leaving a car for the wives to go to the commissary or to ferry the kids to sports activities. In those days, neighbors helped neighbors.

I laughed when I recently looked at those photos I had taken of our kids posed in front of the Kennedy Drive house. The children were not standing on grass, but instead they stood on sandy soil where prickly things grew and fire ants built hills. Scorpions and huge roaches were also in residence.

CAPEHART BASE HOUSING

All of the Moses Lake families who lived around Kennedy Drive moved a year later into the completed Capehart base housing. What a joy it was to have a brand new house with all new appliances, a lawn landscaped in soft, green grass and new trees and shrubs. The term "tree" was really a misnomer; they were newly planted sticks that would take many years before they grew to provide shade from the Texas sun. Rody and neighbor, Phil Chase, solved that problem by cutting down three big cottonwood trees that grew along a stream out in the desert around Laughlin. Phil said he knew the cottonwoods to be excellent transplanting trees for this location regardless of the fact that they didn't have roots. Cottonwood trees are known to be resilient but horticulture experts recommend transplanting with a rootball. These adult trees were planted along one side of the house and by the patio in back. The next morning base photographers were in our yard taking pictures of this overnight "miracle" on Arantz Drive.

The Wing Commander and two US Senators came to see the new housing area. They asked if we would allow them to tour our house. We were honored to be asked especially when we learned one of the visitors was Senator Capehart, the very man who sponsored the Congressional Bill for construction of the housing on military bases. The visitors were very impressed with our fully leafed out cottonwood trees. These were the only adult trees in the entire housing area.

The other famous visitor to Laughlin was President Dwight Eisenhower, who was driven through our new housing area in his motorcade. I'll always remember seeing him standing in the convertible waving to us. I read that Senator Homer Capehart and President Eisenhower were very good friends.

THE U-2 SPY PLANE

The move to Laughlin didn't seem much different from all the previous ones. Rody was happy in his new job. He was checking out in a new plane, and enjoying the new assignment. The two older children were enrolled in Eastside Elementary School in Del Rio, and the two younger ones were at home with me. I don't remember hearing rumors at Moses Lake about the reason for the transfer to Laughlin, but Rody and the other pilots knew they were going to fly the new U-2 spy plane. The project was called Dragon Lady and everything surrounding it was secret. Wives were not told anything, because as one Colonel put it, "If the women know, it won't be classified for long."

It wasn't long before everyone on base was aware of the mission. Rumors started to fly, and we noticed the black planes with long wingspans parked on the ramp. I had totally forgotten about the day back at Moses Lake when Rody came home for lunch. That was very unusual for him to come home during the day. He usually grabbed a fast lunch at the base cafeteria. That day I asked what brought him home as he hurried to the bedroom; he explained he had to go into town for an appointment. When he came out, he was dressed in civilian clothes. He said he couldn't tell me about it right then, but said, "Don't be concerned. I don't know much about it myself so we'll both know later."

It was long after we moved to Del Rio and after the security was lifted on the U-2 that he told me the two men he met at Moses Lake were from the CIA and they came to talk to him about flying the plane for the Government. He learned the flying job would require him to be away from his family of three and soon to be four children for extended periods of time; he declined the offer.

Laughlin was a well-known training base for pilots. I should have been able to put it all together, but I was never a "had to know everything" military wife. I kept busy with our home, children and my own volunteer projects. As it turned out, Rody was at Laughlin to fly the U-2, not for the CIA, but for the Air Force.

This was becoming *the best of times*. From my point of view we had great housing, convenient shopping at the commissary and base exchange, a hospital and Officers' Club. When I was asked to write what it was like to be the wife of a U-2 pilot during the late 50's and early 60's, I was sure I would have to decline. So many years have passed. However, once I turned the pages of my saved copies of the Laughlin Officers' Wives Club newsletter, known as the *LOW JET*, I recalled such pleasant memories of happy social events I had attended.

454

Both the Officers' and Wives' Clubs were the glue that kept us socially and actively connected. Considering how remotely situated Laughlin was from a city with theaters, a choice of restaurants and cultural opportunities, it was important to have active clubs. I looked forward to the monthly Newcomers Coffee gatherings and luncheons. We socialized and established friendships with many of the women through the club.

Once a month and on special holidays, the club would hold a big theme party. Each squadron would take a turn sponsoring the party, such as Casino Night, Ship Wrecked party and Valentine dinner dance. Anyone with an ounce of talent could count on a full-time non-paying job in the entertainment. One outstanding party at the club was St. Paddy's Night with the talent of John Quinn. He wrote, casted, directed and performed in the show.

Not long after we moved on base, I joined the Laughlin Players, a Little Theater group. I helped the enlisted men and women put on talent shows at the NCO Service Club. I was dancing in a show one time when a local dance studio owner and volunteer, Helen Marie Jones, stopped in. She had just finished writing a Mexican musical called Ole', and she was looking for dancers. She invited me to join her show and I was honored to accept. The show was a success at Laughlin. Helen Marie offered the show for Del Rio and Cuidad Acuna residents at La Macarena. I thought the show was so funny. Imagine a troupe of gringos performing the Mexican Hat Dance and the Flamenco to the Hispanic audience. It was such a success that we were asked to continue the show for two more nights.

Those five years spent at Laughlin were definitely the best of times. It was long enough for us to feel part of the community and a closely knit family on base. In all honesty, the long separations from our guys were the worst of times.

455

Rody left the U-2 program in the summer of 1962 when he was reassigned to Command and Staff School in Montgomery, Alabama and we bid a sad farewell to our many friends at Laughlin.

RODY'S FLAMEOUT

On September 16, 1958, Rody was on a training mission in the U-2 when he experienced an engine flameout at a critical altitude. Following proper emergency procedures, he called "Stargazer" for assistance in fixing his position and informed controlling agencies of his difficulty. His UHF radio would not respond after repeated efforts to contact any ground station.

Rody then turned off all electrical switches and descended to a safe airstart altitude. He had enough to deal with, but the canopy and his faceplace frosted over during the descent. Rody managed to clear a small area in the faceplate by rubbing his nose against the inside and successfully flew the aircraft on instruments.

The first airstart attempt was successful, but he was without hydraulic pressure. He continued on to Laughlin and lowered the landing gear by the emergency system. After penetration a GCA straight-in approach was requested. Three miles out, he realized he could not reduce airspeed. He attempted two more landings trying to reduce the airspeed without drag devices and managed to bring the aircraft down on the final try by lowering the engine RPM past the idle setting. The drag chute deployed and he completed a safe landing.

Investigation revealed a faulty speed brake hydraulic line had failed resulting in complete loss of the hydraulic system.

Rody was named the 4028th SRW Pilot of the Month in October 1958 for his skillful handling of the flight emergency.

MEMORIES OF BILL RODENBACH
(THEN 11 YEARS OLD)

My first rattlesnake roundup was in one of the base hangars. A guy stood inside a big box giving a lecture as a bunch of rattlesnakes slithered around his feet. I listened to his speech the whole time but wondered why the snakes didn't bite him.

Our house on the base was beside the playground and our large side yard was the site of many football games with Eric Chase, Gene Smith, Don Schweikert, Ricky Waters, and Chuck Wilcox. When we played football for Del Rio Junior High, our moms carpooled to pick us up after practice and brought us back to the base.

We caught the school bus down the street from the Colonels' houses. I think it is part of the golf course now. The Del Rio public school bus picked up students along the way and then left the base by way of the back gate.

I mowed yards on the base to earn spending money. One of my customers was the U-2 pilot who was shot down over Cuba. I learned what had happened when I saw the moving van outside his house.

Dad and I drove many of those three-hour trips to San Antonio for me to go to the orthodontist. In the summertime on the way home, we stopped at a river and swam, and then bought a watermelon for 25 cents. What a treat. Our car didn't have air conditioning so we had a canvas bag full of water on the outside of the car to use in case the car overheated and to drink if necessary. The water from the canvas bag didn't taste good and I didn't drink it unless it was absolutely necessary.

MEMORIES OF JANE RODENBACH
(THEN 9 YEARS OLD)

After we moved to Arantz Drive, we heard a lot about rattlesnakes being found around the houses. There was a story that the brand new fence surrounding the housing area was snake proof with a fine mesh on the lower part of the fence. Unfortunately, the housing was built on Rattlesnake Hill and it appeared the snakes were fenced inside!

One Halloween I returned home after Trick or Treating unexpectedly and was surprised to be hosed down in our driveway by Bill and one of his friends. I was dripping in my wet costume. I reached for the screen door and heard the rattle. There was a snake coiled up between the inside door and the screen door. I let out a big scream that got the attention of my brother and his friend and we all went for help.

The best part of being an Air Force dependent, especially at Laughlin, was the freedom to walk by myself to the swimming pool, to the movie theater, to the new library with its wonderful children's section or to visit friends close by. I loved going to the stables for horse riding lessons and trail rides. To me the base was like a safe little village.

JENNIFER RODENBACH
(THEN 5 YEARS OLD)

I don't remember a lot about those days, but I do have a vivid memory of one morning watching my Dad as he got ready for work. To me he looked so patriotic and handsome in his uniform. I watched as he pinned on his rank and wings to his uniform shirt. It needed something more. I ran to my bedroom and brought my little American flag attached to a stick and put it in his back pocket as he walked out the front door. I'm not sure how far he went before the flag was discovered.

CHUCK RODENBACH
(THEN 2 YEARS OLD)

I was the youngest member of the Rodenbach crew at Laughlin and the one who was transported to Texas in "the box." Because I was so young, I remember very little of those days. I liked riding my bike in our driveway, the only place I was allowed to ride. One day I felt adventurous and went a little farther and got lost. All the houses looked alike. I was so happy to see Mom coming for me on the back of a neighbor's motor bike.

William T. (Rody) Rodenbach II

**Barbara Rodenbach and dance partner
in the production of Ole.**

REPUBLIC OF CHINA AIR FORCE U-2 PILOTS

REPUBLIC OF CHINA
AIR FORCE U-2 PILOTS

Through an agreement between the Republic of China and the United States, the USAF trained ROCAF pilots to fly the U-2 reconnaissance aircraft. Laughlin AFB at Del Rio, Texas and Davis Monthan AFB at Tucson, Arizona trained the Chinese pilots. The training experience for the Chinese pilots was a combination of exposure to a new aircraft, new culture and for some most significantly, a new language. The U-2 was a difficult aircraft for the best of pilots to master and for an added challenge, all training material was in English. Due to the ROCAF pilots' culture to present a positive appearance, they would often reply "yes" when asked by their USAF instructors if they understood the material.

A local school principal in Del Rio met weekly with the Chinese pilots to help improve their English skills and their understanding of American slang. The Chinese pilots were told that local citizens thought they were Hawaiian. USAF families "adopted" many of the ROCAF pilots and introduced them to American traditions and customs.

The following ROCAF pilots trained in the U-2 aircraft and returned to Taiwan where they flew missions for their own country.

Shi Chu (Gimo) Yang
Huai Sheng Chen
Chung Kuei Hsu
Tai Yu (Tiger) Wang
Chih Yao Hua
His Chun (Mike) Hua
Chang-di (Robin) Yeh

462

Lee Nan (Terry) Ping
Liang Teh Pei
Li Yi (Jack) Chang
Hui Chia Yang
Chen Wen (Pete) Wang
Shih Hi (Steve) Sheng
Tse Shi (Charlie) Wu
Chuang (Terry) Liu
Ching Chang (Mickey) Yu
Jen Liang (Spike) Chuang
Ling Pei (Tom) Hwang
Chung Li (Johnny) Shen
Tao (Tom) Wang
Peo Wei (David) Lee
Denny Huang
Chen Wei
Chu Chien
Hung Ti (Andy) Fan
Hseih (Billy) Chang
Erh Ping Yang
Mory Tsai

REPUBLIC OF CHINA
AIR FORCE U-2 PILOTS

ROCAF T-33 Squadron
Top row – far right, Robin Yeh

Gen Lee Po Wei (David)

**Maj Gen Jude BK Pao,
with P-51 Mustang**

Black Cat Squadron, left to right: Simon Chien, Chris I,
Bob Birkett, Tom Wang, Mike Chu, Joe Wei, Mory Tsai

Andy Fan

Mory Tsai with U-2

Robin Yeh with General Chiang Kai Shek

Left to right: Johnny Shen, Chih Yao Hua, Tom Wang, David Lee, Andy Fan

Tom Wang

Mike Chu

Simon Chien

Andy Fan

471

BLACK CATS

Left to right: Johnny Shen, Tom Wang, Gimo Yang, unknown pilot, Tiger Wang, Andy Fan, last two pilots unknown

Left to right, standing: David Lee, unknown, Johnny Shen, Mike Chu, unknown, Seated: Tech Rep, Andy Fan, Bob Ericson, Tiger Wang

General I Fu-En with Mory Tsai

Left to right: Gimo Yang, Chiang Ko Kung, Mrs. Yang

Left to right: unknown, Jack, David, Robin and Mory

1990 ROCAF Reunion for Robin and Jack
Seated in middle row: Gimo Yang, center, in dark jacket

2005 4080th SRW Reunion
Mory, Jack, Robin and Andy

2005 4080th SRW Reunion,

Left to right: Robin Yeh, Jack Chang, Margaret Hua, Mike Hua, Chris I, Keiko Yeh, Mrs. I, Gimo Yang, Helen Sheng, Andy Fan, Mory Tsai, Johnny Shen, Joe Wei

479

ROYAL
AIR FORCE
U-2 PILOTS

ROYAL AIR FORCE
U-2 PILOTS

Through agreement between the United States and the United Kingdom, the following pilots were trained in the U-2 aircraft.

Martin Bee
Michael G. Bradley
Richard Cloke
Basil Dodd
David E. Dowling
Harry Drew
John W. McArthur
Nigel Mills
Robert T. Robinson
Charles Taylor
Christopher Walker
Ivan B. Webster

MARTIN BEE
Royal Air Force
Crydon, England

Wife: Lilleba

My RAF training began at the RAF College Cranwell (similar to the US Air Force Academy) in 1955-1958. My first solo was on the tail wheel Piston Provost and then the Vampire jet. After receiving my pilot wings, I flew fighters, Hawker Hunters, Gloster Meteors and English Electric Lightnings. In 1960 we were the first Mach 2 squadron in the RAF.

My selection for the U-2 came out of the blue. One day my Station Commander, Group Captain Bird-Wilson instructed me to go to London for an interview. At the Ministry of Defense some senior officers talked in circles about going to the US, but they never told me the full story until a few days before I boarded the Cunard liner for New York. My guess was that the selection criteria included tail-wheel and high performance experience. I had certainly had no recce (reconnaissance) experience.

My period of service on "secondment" to the CIA began in 1964. (Secondment meant I was loaned to the CIA.) I traveled to New York by Cunard passenger liner with Squadron Leader Basil Dodd. Our flight planner/navigator, Alistair Sutherland and our doctor, Squadron Leader Nigel Mills, joined us a month or two later.

In the 1960s the RAF had about 100 personnel serving on "exchange" duty with several US air operations and, in turn, the Americans served on reciprocal "exchange" duty in the UK. The RAF personnel serving on the U-2 program had rather different orders than the other exchange personnel. We were never part of the regular 100 exchange personnel and were forbidden to meet up with them. Our initial month of training was with the USAF at Davis Monthan AFB. Gerald McIlmoyle was among the many I met through my instructor, George Bull.

We made six flights in the U-2A at Davis Monthan and then moved to Edwards AFB where we flew the much more powerful U-2C, U-2G, U-2F and U-2H which were owned and operated by the CIA from 1964 to 1968. We were still considered part of the RAF there but we seldom wore our uniforms.

Like our USAF counterparts, we traveled several times for pressure suit fittings to the David Clark Company in Worcester, Massachusetts. I was told the Clark Company manufactured women's undergarments prior to getting into the pressure suit business. As a gift on departure, we each were given a 1960 bra, which they also made in profusion.

One morning our Commander, Lt. Col. Miles Doyle called me to his office. He told me the following day we expected the Senate Armed Services Committee and some RAF VIP visitors arriving at Edwards to be briefed on our operation. I was selected to fly a demonstration for them to show the high performance of the U-2 and finish with some Field Carrier Landing Practice (FCLP) -- touch and go landings.

I flew a U-2G, a modified U-2C fitted with a slightly beefed up landing gear, a flap setting increased from 35 to 50 degrees and a tail hook. With a standard training fuel load of 400 US gallons, the aircraft would weigh a little under 16,000 pounds and have a thrust available of 17,000 pounds at full throttle. However, full throttle could not be used at takeoff because it was far too much "oomph" for a fragile aircraft and airspeed and "G" limits could be exceeded in seconds.

For the Senate and RAF VIP demonstration I made a normal "gated" reduced power takeoff, lifting off at about 90 knots and accelerating quickly. I rotated the aircraft to about an 80 degree climb angle, and selected gust control. I added full power slowly, and activated the fuel dump producing an air-show style twin contrail of fuel vapour from the mid-wing fuel dump points. I held the airspeed at 170 knots, going nearly vertical in a corkscrew climb. It took only one minute to reach 10,000 feet. Without the vapour trail, the aircraft would have been barely visible to the onlookers at the runway edge.

I had to get the aircraft back to the airfield before the VIPs lost interest. I made a quick stall check at 10,000 feet to ensure that both wings stalled symmetrically and that wing tank fuel was balanced evenly. Back in gust control with landing gear down and airbrakes out for maximum drag, I brought the bird down at 220 knots indicated airspeed. I made checks for a FCLP touch and go using the USN deck landing mirror system set up on our runway.

On finals at 90 knots with flaps at 50 degrees, the mirror "meatball" was picked up and held as a glide path reference. I slowly reduced airspeed to 82 knots as I approached the runway threshold. At about 20 feet the USN Landing Safety Officer (LSO) called "Cut One" at which point I retarded the throttle to idle. Moments later the LSO called "Cut Two" and I activated the spoilers. I eased back on the yoke a little further and the bird stalled at about a foot above the runway. Simultaneously the aircraft settled onto the twin main gear wheels and the solid rubber tail wheels. Now the fun started! I had to keep the wings level for the touch and go without the aid of the pogos by using deft aileron movements. With speed brakes retracted, flaps raised to take off position and elevator trim reset, the throttle was opened slowly to

485

takeoff power. This time in a sedate fashion, I turned downwind for a final full stop landing.

I made the final landing again from a standard mirror approach with the LSO calling height above the runway from the mobile chase vehicle. Instead of using the speed brakes this time, I deployed the tail parachute at a foot or so above the runway. The U-2 immediately slowed and settled on to the runway. Thanks to a light headwind, I rolled quickly to a stop, wings level and tips off the ground. The ground crew refitted the pogos, and with one man sitting on each wing to keep the wings bent down slightly to ensure that the pogos made contact with the runway, I taxied the U-2 back to the ramp.

In the climb, the view ahead is nonexistent. Pitch attitude is obtained from peripheral vision with much time spent looking at the airspeed, RPMs and the turbine gas temperature (TGT). Watching the TGT was critical to limit the increased hot temperature allowed at that particular high power setting and avoiding damage to the engine. The controls felt decidedly slack as the U-2 sat in a close vertical attitude on 17,000 pounds of thrust. The aircraft went up quickly, but came down slowly. It was like a glider, and had little drag. Landings required full attention to detail as the undercarriage track is less than a metre. The U-2 requires a two-point "tail dragger" style attitude at touchdown to avoid porpoising back into the air. Popping the drag chute just above the runway at one foot set up a perfect landing attitude.

As I reflected on my U-2 experience some 40 years later, I am extremely happy I was a young pilot in my 20s at the time these demos were flown. Very few had the opportunity to experience the overwhelming feeling of sheer power, spectacle and fun, unlikely to be permitted these days.

Martin Bee in the harness. Parachute training at Lake Meade, Nevada 1964.

Martin Bee in full pressure suit at Lake Meade for Parachute training 1964.

L to R: Lilleba Bee, Al Rand, CIA U-2 pilot,
and Martin Bee in the UK 1967.

Martin Bee at RAF Duxford Imperial War Museum
Standing by the U-2 in 1995.

RICHARD (DICK) CLOKE
Royal Air Force
King's Lynn, Norfolk, England

Wife: Gillyan

I joined the Weather Reconnaissance Squadron (Provisional) 4 at Edwards North Base towards the end of 1967 and I started flying the U-2 early in 1968. I think I was the first Brit not to check out at Davis Monthan. My conversion was all conducted on North Base's 6,000-foot runway.

Now for some highlights (and the lows).

On an early transition flight with full fuel, I flew our older C model known to buffet at altitude. Sure enough it happened to me and instinctively, I throttled back far enough to cause a flameout, the only one I ever had.

On another C model flight while at altitude, I punched in the next heading and started to complete the green card. As I wrote, the autopilot tripped out. When I looked up, I had about 120 degrees of bank. I recovered without too much difficulty. After landing, the camera boys were surprised to see the unusual view of the sun in the tracker camera.

During "tropical" tests on the new R model at McCoy AFB, we had a lot of problems with the liquid oxygen system. I believe it was because the system was taken from the SR-71. We didn't have the skin heating factor, only the false gauge reading. There's nothing like the oxygen showing zero to make 70,000 feet seem a very long way up. Returning from one of these tests, I let down, dumped fuel and ran into a wave of thunderstorms. I had difficulty finding McCoy in the heavy rain (Florida does not look anything like the Mojave!) and finally landed with only 15 gallons of fuel remaining. That was close.

In October 1969 I flew an R model from North Base to Kinloss, Scotland. About half way into the 12-hour flight, I turned my head to the left and my helmet locked in that position. I later learned a ball bearing had broken and jammed. The next few hours were very interesting, especially when it came to landing in typical Scottish weather of heavy rain and wind. It was a bit inconvenient with one's head stuck half left!

Later two of us Brits ferried U-2s from Upper Heyford, UK direct to North Base. My flight lasted 13 hours 55 minutes. With pre-breathing time added, plus a 30-minute hold on the runway waiting for the weather to clear for takeoff, we spent well over 16 hours in our pressure suits, half again as long as usual.

One special highlight was the carrier qualification. We had T2 training at Pensacola Naval Air Station, and mirror landing practice at North Base. We carried out our qualification aboard the aircraft carrier, USS *America*, a day after the Lockheed test pilot qualified the R model. The training must have been spot on because the carrier work was really straight forward.

* * * * *

In December 1968 I was climbing out of Edwards North Base for a high level sortie when there was a loud bang and the canopy disappeared. To cut a long story short, I dumped fuel and landed on the lake bed because the aircraft had developed an unusual heavy wing. At touchdown the yoke was at 90 degrees to the normal position. Subsequent investigation determined that when I dumped fuel, one transfer pump stuck in the "On" position, continually transferring fuel until only the collector tank fuel remained. What I should have done was to dump all my wing fuel until only the collector tank fuel remained. At the time, I wondered whether the canopy had caused any airframe damage. An airborne check did not reveal that whether attempting to dump more fuel would have accentuated the imbalance for a while.

The subsequent inquiry concluded that the canopy was not locked correctly at takeoff, though my Mobile Officer and I were absolutely certain that it was.

I had retired from the RAF over 30 years and was working for British Aerospace. In April 1999 I received a phone call out of the blue from a USAF major in Korea. He was conducting an inquiry into the loss of a U-2 canopy in flight, and had somehow learned of my experience. It happened that my loss of a U-2 canopy in flight was the first such loss, and over the years there had been several similar incidents, as well as incidents during pressurization checks on the ground. Modifications were recommended as a result, but exoneration was 30 years late as far as I was concerned! Ah well...

Left to Right, Andy Cumming-Flight Surgeon, Harry Drew-Pilot, Dick Cloke-Pilot and Detachment Commander and Rod Booth-Flight Planner

Dick Cloke in the cockpit of the U-2R at Edwards
North Base, approximately 1969

REMEMBER...

494

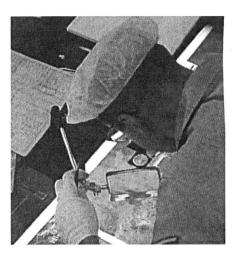

496

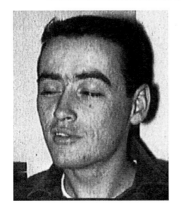

499

THE AUTHORS

Brig. Gen. (Ret.) Gerald R. McIlmoyle

Gerald McIlmoyle enlisted in the USAF in 1951 and completed aviation cadet training in December 1952. He was commissioned a Second Lieutenant and awarded his pilot wings. In August 1957 McIlmoyle reported to the 4080th Strategic Reconnaissance Wing as a U-2 pilot. In 1962 he earned a "spot promotion" to Major and piloted the U-2 over various parts of the world including the North and South Poles, Alaska, Argentina, Australia, Guam, and South Vietnam. McIlmoyle was one of the original group of pilots selected to fly reconnaissance missions over Cuba during the crisis in October 1962. He is a commend pilot with 4,376 hours flying time, including 47 hours of combat time. Military decorations include the Distinguished Service Commendation Medal, Air Force Commendation Medal, and Air Force Outstanding Unit Award. McIlmoyle currently resides in Venice, Florida with his wife, Patricia, where he is active in community and church activities.

LINDA RIOS BROMLEY

Linda Rios Bromley retired from Federal Civil Service after 33 years employment in such locations as Laughlin AFB, Texas, Charleston Naval Base, South Carolina, USAF Headquarters Europe, Wiesbaden, Germany, NASA and Internal Revenue Service, Houston, Texas. The publication of her first non-fiction book, *FREEDOM FLIGHT, A True Story*, chronicled the early life, entry into the Republic of China Air Force and U-2 flight training of Major Chang-di (Robin) Yeh. Linda was invited to a reunion of the 4080th Strategic Reconnaissance Wing veterans in 2005. At that event, she met USAF and Republic of China veterans and was inspired to tell the awesome experiences of the men who flew and supported the U-2 spy plane. She has been elected to the Board of Directors of the Laughlin Heritage Foundation Museum, in Del Rio.